MAKE 'EM WRITE!

The No-Mess Way to Extract a Dissertation from a Grad Student's Brain

MAKE'EM WRITE!

The No-Mess Way to Extract a Dissertation from a Grad Student's Brain

GENEVIÈVE BELLEVILLE
PHILIP L. JACKSON

Illustrated by CONSTANCE HARVEY

Presses de
l'Université Laval

Financé par le gouvernement du Canada
Funded by the Government of Canada | Canada

Nous remercions le Conseil des arts du Canada de son soutien.
We acknowledge the support of the Canada Council for the Arts.

Conseil des arts du Canada | Canada Council for the Arts

Each year, Presses de l'Université Laval receives financial support from the Société de développement des entreprises culturelles du Québec for their publishing programs.

SODEC
Québec

Bibliothèque et Archives nationales du Québec and Library and Archives Canada Cataloguing in Publication

Title: Make'em write! : the no-mess way to extract a dissertation from a grad student's brain / Philip L. Jackson, Geneviève Belleville; illustrated by Constance Harvey.
Other titles: Extraire une thèse d'un cerveau étudiant sans gâchis. English
Names: Belleville, Geneviève, author. | Jackson, Philip L. (Neuroscientist), author.
Description: Translation of: Extraire une thèse d'un cerveau étudiant sans gâchis : favoriser la rédaction et la persévérance aux cycles supérieurs. | Includes bibliographical references.
Identifiers: Canadiana (print) 20240029631 | Canadiana (ebook) 20240029658 | ISBN 9782763759555 | ISBN 9782763759562 (PDF) | ISBN 9782763759579 (EPUB)
Subjects: LCSH: Graduate students—Supervision of. | LCSH: Dissertations, Academic. | LCSH: Teacher-student relationships—Psychological aspects.

Print in Canada
Legal deposit 1st quarter 2025

ISBN: 978-2-7637-5955-5
ISBN PDF: 9782763759562
ISBN ePub: 9782763759579

Les Presses de l'Université Laval
www.pulaval.com

Z

A thousand thanks

We would like to thank all the people who contributed to making this book what it is, from our parents who shared their genes and passions to the volunteers who gave us bananas after the many races that kept us in shape during all those years.

Thank you to Josée and Marie-Christine for agreeing to serve as our first sounding boards on such a short notice. Now we know that at least four people like the book.

Thank you to the editors and reviewers who reminded us how we too can feel like students when receiving a marked-up manuscript. Thank you for believing in us. Learning is what we do best.

We are lucky to have many colleagues who, like us, aspire to get better at supervising students. Thank you for listening, and for the many hallway discussions about all the subjects which we are not formally taught.

Thank you to everyone who participated in the different workshops and research projects about graduate student supervision, for helping us develop our thinking.

To the many artists who produced the many, many songs that provided a Cure to our writing sessions, XCX, it's Closing Time.

We cannot emphasize enough how this book would be irrelevant without the students who inspire us every day at work. You are the reason we chose this career. Thank you for joining our teams.

Thank you to Marie-Christine et Marie-Josée who remind us that a wonderful world exists outside the university. Thank you to—in order of appearance—Émilie, Elliot, Jules and Clémence for filling it with so much joy; you represent our most significant contributions.

Table des matières

List of boxes

List of figures

List of tables

CHAPTER 1
This might sting a bit...

Of all the requirements for obtaining a Ph.D., writing the dissertation is the hardest, and unfortunately the most painful one. Having reached the highest level of academia, most doctoral students can sail through coursework, exams, training programs and tutorials without major stumbling blocks. What slows them down, and even traps them in perpetual studenthood, is writing their dissertation, a process that can become bogged down for good and not so good reasons. The legitimate reason that has to be acknowledged is that the task of writing a dissertation is fundamentally complicated and *hard*. It's the crowning labour of a research endeavour that itself grew out of trial and error, experimentation, analyses run and re-run, texts written and rewritten. Writing a dissertation is like sitting down to a fiendishly difficult jigsaw puzzle with 10,000 pieces and no picture on the box, one that doesn't just have pieces missing, but extra pieces that don't belong. We try sorting by shape or colour, and we curse our luck when we realize the two pieces we forced together don't match. Sometimes, pieces seem to fly together almost without our help, while other times we spend hours classifying our pieces without placing a single one.

In short, the process itself is difficult and chaos-ridden, even without taking into account the many complications of methodology, motivation and emotion that make the task still harder. Gaps in organizational skills and identifying and solving problems, dealing with competition and the pressure to produce output, procrastination, anxiety and perfectionism (remember, we're talking about students!) can all sap the momentum and plunge them into despair. Fortunately, someone is waiting in the wings to help... the advisor.

COME JOIN MY TEAM, I HAVE NO CLUE WHAT I'M DOING!

There's no doubt that being a university professor is the best job in the world, and out of the many thousands of responsibilities, advising Ph.D. students is right at the top. But as we take on this job, many of us find ourselves setting out blindly through uncharted waters. Given how important supervising students is for our job, and how critical our role is for the student's experience and ultimate success, it's flabbergasting to consider how little knowledge and preparation we have before jumping into this adventure. The success or failure of the student's writing process lies within our power, yet there is no formal training for guiding a student through their dissertation. University professors aren't even expected to have classroom training dedicated to teaching when they're hired, still less be trained to supervise graduate students! The usual method is to learn on the job, drawing on our experiences with our own advisors. We follow their example of what was helpful, but above all we strive to avoid those behaviours that made our own lives miserable as graduate students. Our prior knowledge shapes—and limits—the guidance we offer our students, which is generally modelled on what we ourselves received. Thus we leap head-first into the task of supervising new graduate students, with the best of intentions but, if we're being honest, very little framework.

A LITTLE BACKGROUND

The main source of inspiration for this book came from students. Having published *Assieds-toi et écris ta thèse* (in English, *Sit Down and Write Your Dissertation*) in 2014, Geneviève gave several talks and workshops, addressed to students, about the organizational skills and motivation needed to writing a dissertation. After these talks, many students asked tough questions about their advisors' rigid demands and unrealistic expectations that were adding to the difficulty of writing their dissertation. For example, when Geneviève suggested to students that they could force themselves to be more efficient by setting limits on their writing time, students would burst out, "You should tell my advisor that!" Some students even went as far as to suggest she should write a new version of her book, but this time address it directly to advisors. It's thanks to these students that this book became reality. Though the end product might not be exactly what they had in mind, that's probably for the best. While Geneviève considered simply rewriting her first book, she was seized by a nagging doubt: after giving more than 60 talks in Canada, France and Belgium, she felt she had a pretty good knowledge of graduate students, but she knew far less about advisors ... especially the ones the students were complaining about most! She needed another perspective, from a co-author who was familiar with the vagaries of research, and had experience in a wide range of disciplines at different research centers. Philip seemed the ideal candidate: not because of a high number of student complaints (at least, not that we know of!), but because of his impressive background, with 12 years as a research-track faculty member at three different research centers. An elected member of The College of New Scholars, Artists and Scientists of the Royal Society of Canada, he had served on the scientific and governing boards of numerous provincial organizations, as well as the juries for different grants and scholarships. He also had co-founded and co-directed a research group on neuroscience, mental health, and imaging. But what really caught Geneviève's attention was the endless hours they'd spent together, scrupulously revising admission criteria for a Ph.D. program in Psychology. Geneviève noticed that in addition his research skills and experience, he was full of thoughtful insights about selecting and guiding graduate students—not to mention, he had a wicked sense of humour.

The two of them were taking a train back from a conference when Geneviève mustered the courage to present her seat companion with the idea for this book and, more confidently, a gin and tonic. Philip accepted both without hesitation. Over many years, the interest and effort he'd devoted to training graduate students had led him to some pointed questions about the student–advisor relationship. Genevieve's idea presented an opportunity to put these thoughts into concrete form—without considering, in the first flush of enthusiasm, how difficult this task would prove. This moment was a turning point in our vision of the book. The thing was, all our discussions brought us to one brutal conclusion: we had no idea what we were doing. What we'd initially conceived as a book full of tips and best practices turned into an assemblage of thoughts, revelations, wonderment and often amusement, on the different facets of supervising graduate students.

In the end, we wrote this book for the sheer fun of putting our jobs as professors under the microscope and laughing at what we saw. It was fun to put down in black and white the unspoken rules of supervising graduate studies, this oh so crucial aspect of our jobs that we, ironically, were never trained to do. There was even fun in venting about the unending setbacks and complications (never the advisor's fault, of course!) that students seem to discover daily. If Charles Dickens wrote about supervising graduate students, he might say, "it is the best of jobs, it is the worst of jobs, the students are brilliant, the students are useless."

THIS IS NOT A COOKBOOK

During the many, many years that it took us to write this little book, we continued to ask ourselves questions. Though we can suggest some "ingredients" that will determine the success or failure of the final product (that is to say, the student successfully defending their dissertation), there are no step-by-step instructions on how to fulfill your supervising duties. Certainly there are no rules for you to follow that will make students write. What you'll find instead are some thoughts about our role as dissertation advisors, and all the implications that go along with it.

What makes us qualified to offer such opinions? We are just two professors with an interest in the subject, but who've had many occasions for reflection in the course of our roles advising graduate students (both the ones who graduated, and the few who, despite jumping ship, nevertheless taught us a lot!), as well as serving as directors of a Ph.D. program in Clinical Psychology, with enrolments of close to 100 students at any given time. More precisely, at the time of writing, we have ushered more than 50 clinical and research doctoral students across the graduation threshold, while losing six more along the way who left us to change labs or career paths.

We have a message to deliver about what we consider good advising practices, but this message doesn't originate with us. Far from revolutionizing the field, we've often struggled ourselves to practice what we preach! This book steers a course between hard facts and lived experience. We don't want to either over-generalize from our experiences, or create some set of rules that claim to be absolute. Rather, our hope is these pages will encourage you to join us in pondering this tricky question.

DEFINING ADVISING AND ADVISORS

Throughout the writing process of this book, we had to find words to describe the actions of the person who guides the graduate student, ensures they hit key milestones, and provides feedback as they write their dissertation. These actions are key, since the word we use for this person should reflect their role. Does the person direct, supervise, advise, or mentor? Are they therefore a director, supervisor, advisor or mentor? You might notice we've been inconsistent about using one term over another depending on the chapter (or even our mood). It might depend on whether the person is providing personal support or comments on a text, or on how much autonomy we assume the student has. Indeed, guidelines about this role might change based on the student's level of study (e.g., Master's thesis or Ph.D. dissertation), the discipline (e.g., humanities, health sciences, engineering or business administration), the institution, or even the country.[1]

1. Prégent, R. (2001). *L'encadrement des travaux de mémoire et de thèse: conseils pédagogiques aux directeurs de recherche*. Montréal: Presses internationales Polytechnique.

In 1990, Aimée Leduc[2] wrote that supervising graduate student research is the most complex and subtle form of teaching, with aspects that are personal (offering supportive encouragement), professional (teaching, giving feedback, advising, providing access to resources), and administrative. In short, we must start by acknowledging the complex, fluid nature of the role, and buckle in for a lengthy discussion!

We might not be able to define what an advisor's role is with respect to a student's dissertation, but we sure know what it *isn't*: to squeeze maximum productivity from the student in order to burnish the advisor's own C.V. Instead, the objective is to nurture the student's autonomy and help them develop their own writing skills. We can model the skills we want them to develop and help them toward their goals (in their research and career) while we keep our own house (our research projects, our lab, our careers) in good order. We'll say it again: this book is meant to help you help your students write, for their own benefit and not for your C.V. If that disappoints you, or you feel like we've wasted your time, feel free to write to us with your own ideas about exploiting your students, and we will gladly refund you (and be sure to acknowledge you in our next book, *How NOT to Supervise Graduate Student Writing*!).

This brings us to the next question: what should we call ourselves? Director, supervisor, mentor, advisor? How do we refer to the person who guides the student in writing their dissertation? French speakers in the Province of Quebec, Canada, use the term *directeur* or if feminine, *directrice de thèse,* which we might translate as "research supervisor," or "research advisor." In English, a "director" in the context of graduate studies is more likely to refer to the person in charge of a program or a department. The term "supervisor" (like the French *directeur*) captures the sense of leading and guiding students in their research, but the connotations of superiority run counter to our philosophy that the student should take ownership for their own dissertation. The term "mentor" evokes the sharing of knowledge and hard-won experience, and seems an apt description for the noble act that is our aim, to demonstrate the correct way of doing things to our wide-eyed, admiring pupils who, by soaking up our example will become knowledgeable enough to take flight on their own (leaving us with their eternal gratitude). But this rosy picture fails to acknowledge the responsibility the supervisor has towards their student, nor does it tell us what to do if the pupil is not so admiring, or resists our teaching. The romantic model of master/pupil (one might say Jedi/Padawan), in which the supervisor is the

2. Leduc, A. (1990). *La direction des mémoires et des thèses*. Brossard: Behaviora.

powerful master watching over a pupil who is talented, motivated, free from external demands, enthusiastic, and obedient, and transmitting their knowledge through unspecified yet challenging field exercises (while ideally "restoring balance to the Force"), doesn't really describe what we end up doing with most of our students.

In addition to giving guidance and advice, the supervisor is also responsible for knowing the rules and expectations of the graduate program in which the student is enrolled. Beyond being a good role model, they must consider other imperatives such as the expected duration of a program, and the support, financial or otherwise, available to help the student succeed. Indeed, they must *supervise*. But the tasks of a supervisor in a workplace, such as leading a team, overseeing their work, and making sure the rules are followed, are only part of our job. We must also support students in developing their own autonomy. This is why some people (us!) prefer the term "advisor," which emphasizes this coaching role, and is closer to, without being exactly, a mentor. In fact, we changed the term from supervisor to mentor to advisor so many times across multiple drafts of this book that you will likely still find traces of our early uncertainty. The process was further complicated by the bilingual writing process we'd committed to. For example, among the many tasks of the advisor is to give advice, something that in French would make them a *conseiller* (which is not the same as counselor, another hat we've often worn as psychologists—though not, of course, with our students!). Unfortunately, *conseiller* in French doesn't do a good job of capturing the serious responsibilities of a research advisor. Some people in French-speaking European countries use the term *encadrant* (from *cadre*, frame) which gives a nice sense of providing limits or guideposts, but it should not be confused with *encadreur*, the person who frames paintings. When we say that supervising graduate students is an art-form, that's not quite what we mean! Regardless of the word we choose for ourselves, we need to remember that we have (at least!) two roles: to give advice (thus fostering autonomy), and to supervise (making sure students follow the rules).

A PSYCHOLOGIST'S APPROACH

This book emphasizes not only the organizational aspects of advising graduate students, but also the emotional challenges associated with the task. For instance, when we discuss intellectual property, we aren't aiming to give legal advice so much as to describe the reactions, often intense, that can flare up during conflicts around these issues, and to offer strategies that can prevent or mitigate these conflicts from stalling a dissertation's progress.

As we catalogue the many problems that can arise during the writing process, we admit to feeling perplexed, if not annoyed. Are students worse now than when we started our careers? Are we stuck with a spoiled generation, incapable of writing, who resent all our efforts? How can we be expected to persevere with these precious snowflakes who give up at the least snag? But our research shows that these challenges are not new, even if past generations of advisors might have used different words. Rest assured that our own advisors had the same uncharitable thoughts about us! Aimée Leduc[3] writes that as far back as 1960, advisors were complaining that students couldn't write in the clear, precise and succinct style required for scientific writing. The topic seems evergreen. Throughout history, university professors have asked themselves how to make their students write. Why does the answer still elude us? Perhaps it is professors who are becoming worse at supervising dissertations! Or else, having suffered so much during our own graduate studies, perhaps we've decided, at least subconsciously, to make our students suffer too. Perhaps our obsession with efficiency and high output have closed our minds to other points of view. Or perhaps, having finally obtained the coveted role of professor, our egos are still too fragile for our new authority, such that basic communication skills desert us when we relate to our student subordinates?

While both the authors of this book are professors of Psychology, we bring different expertise, the result following different career paths. As a man and a woman, we have differences in perspective that should not be minimized, which we address fully in chapters 10 and 11. That said, our two perspectives stem from similar cultural and professional backgrounds, and we acknowledge that some of the principles championed here might not hold in different contexts, disciplines, universities or countries. When we were considering what writing style to use for this book (should it be personal or formal, first-person plural or a distant third-person?), we finally settled on a mix of styles and pronouns that reflected our ambivalence. In the end, we want to address our colleagues, you, with the same ease as if we're talking to each other. We've talked endlessly—more, in fact, than we've written, yet we rarely found answers, still less ones we could agree on. But it is exactly this process of asking questions about the best way to supervise graduate students that we want to share in this book, even more than the handful of answers we came up with.

This book was written by two people, to such an extent that neither of us could revise a section without hearing the critical voice of the other

3. *Ibid.*

person in our head. We argued about author order, especially when writing the chapter on intellectual property. We came up with the idea to write our names in a circle to avoid there being a first author (good luck to anyone indexing this book!). In fact, our contributions were equal. If Geneviève had the first idea and wrote the first book for students, Philip was responsible for many of the ideas that followed. If Geneviève wrote more words, perhaps it was because Philip is better at summarizing—and because she was writing in French, which can use up to 20% more words to say the same thing, while Philip was mostly writing in English. Perhaps the youngest should go first (though the first author isn't as young as she was when this project started!), or we should use alphabetical order? Ladies first? Certainly not in 2025, when chivalry is quite deservedly dead!

The writing of this book was also influenced by our experiences as program directors, which exposed us to some more difficult situations that we hope remain rare and not representative of most student–advisor relationships. Our secret goal with this book was to call to account those advisors who fail to treat their students well (write 100 times, "I will not exploit my graduate students"!). With the intent of having fun writing this book, and sharing this fun with you, our reader, we chose a lighthearted tone which may sometimes appear over the top, and an illustrator whose work reflects this buoyant tone. But it's not our intent to mock anyone, nor to pass judgement. We've taken utmost care to remove information that could identify any person specifically. We've changed details and combined stories, mixing our experiences with those of others, while avoiding giving information that could harm anyone. If you think you recognize yourself or a student, it's likely a coincidence resulting from the common experiences of professors and students across universities and research domains. We wish still less to trivialize or stigmatize the struggles of people who are having interpersonal difficulties with graduate students, or who are on the verge of burnout. Despite the lighthearted tone, we know that relationships with graduate students can be difficult, and that the pressure of academia takes its toll in terms of mental health. It's important to reach out to our colleagues, our bosses, or an Employee Assistance Program before our batteries run out. We must admit the irony that while we were having fun cataloguing the different issues related to supervising a dissertation, we often discovered the gaps and weaknesses in our own practices. Ultimately, while we may not be model advisors, we are passionate and dedicated to improving how we supervise students. Indeed, writing this book has changed our own supervising practices, and we are still learning as we go. We hope you'll join us in this fantastic journey!

CHAPTER 2
Through suffering, towards excellence

People in academia are motivated by the quest for knowledge and the simple yet noble act of learning. When we learn, we gather new information, master new skills, and what's more, we quantify things—an activity which leads us inevitably to compare. Such comparisons form the basis of competition, with all the challenges and benefits that come with it. The prestige and glory some people ascribe to metrics of excellence often shine brighter than the underlying quality being measured. Every day we are called to balance the quantity of work we produce with its quality. While these trade-offs seem to pose an impossible dilemma, acknowledging the difficulty is the first step towards not only finding our own balance, but also helping our students find an optimal flow during the long hours required to complete a dissertation. We are confident that in coming years the prevailing academic model of achievement at any cost will be replaced by more diverse and inclusive ways of recognizing success. But given that such fundamental changes can take a while, it behooves us to take the first steps, acting out the changes we want to see in ourselves and our students.

Academia is a competitive environment. A professor's performance is assessed on a regular basis via course evaluations ("Yes, I know I repeat the same material across classes, but then again, you don't seem to learn it the first time!"), grant reviews (a.k.a. the shredder), manuscript revisions ("Oh thank you so much for the 'constructive' comment, Reviewer #3!"), tenure review (pass or fail; "Congratulations, here's your raise or find a new job") and so forth. If we assume that in one year, a professor might teach two courses (one undergrad course of 50 students, one grad seminar of 15 students), submit two grant proposals and five manuscripts, and be evaluated for promotion, then we can conservatively estimate the number of individuals who comment on the quality of the professor's work at over one hundred. One hundred people who, often under the cover of anonymity, tell us frankly what they think our work is worth (and sometimes, unfortunately, let slip how they feel about it). Thus, we've been coached—or is that coerced?—into accepting criticism. Bitter though we may find it, this constant feedback enables us to improve our work, and toughens us against adversity (you can't please them all—and they won't let you forget it either!).

A student's merit is also assessed via comparative methods, whether that's grades, number of presentations, papers published, awards, or the number of years to complete a degree. Students, like professors, are driven toward constant improvement. However, they haven't yet built up a hard shell to protect themselves from this sustained pressure. While the system has the benefit of providing motivation (the donkey always straining toward the delicious carrot) the pressure can be too much, resulting in the fatalist doctrine of Publish or Perish (see *The Slow Professor*[1] for a fuller discussion). Rather than reject the drive for excellence, we should remind ourselves, and our students, that excellence is not the goal but a means to pursue our goals. These goals vary from one professor to another, as well from one student to another. Knowing that we don't all follow the same path, and reminding ourselves that, in the wise words of Jedi Knight Qui-Gon Jinn, "There is always a bigger fish," can help us and our students take deep breath and a few steps back and see competition in perspective with our own progress and achievements. If we compare ourselves to others, we can always find some group that outshines us—so instead, let's compare ourselves with ourselves. This is the difference between striving to be the best, and striving to get better.

THE GOOD SIDE OF COMPETITION (THE CARROT)

Competition is an endless source of motivation. To grow in a competitive environment means we try to improve ourselves, to get better, to succeed and surpass. Though the prize might not be an Olympic medal, competition offers rewards that keep us pushing forward. A student's exact source of motivation can vary. Some are driven by curiosity and the pursuit of knowledge, some by a specific professional goal, some by prestige, or fear of disappointing a demanding family. Whatever motivates these top students, all of them will have to finish writing their dissertation. Another advantage of competition, for both professors and students, is the way this infinite drive towards excellence can instill the same passion in others. Being in a competitive environment shouldn't necessarily mean competing against one another. We can all benefit from the success of other members of our lab or research group, and feel pride and motivation kindled by

1. Berg, M., & Seeber, B.K. (2017). *The Slow Professor: Challenging the Culture of Speed in the Academy*. Toronto: University of Toronto Press.

other people's accomplishments (see Box 10.3). We look better in the reflected glow of excellent people surrounding us, but more importantly, we *become* better.

A judicious dose of competition and adversity is also a good promoter of creativity. The competitive environment makes people try different methods to stand out and distinguish themselves from the regular pack, who adhere to the same old rules. Competition thus drives innovation, an essential aspect of a dissertation, its original contribution. Anyone who sets out to write a dissertation must find some way or another of innovating. In this sense, competition is qualitative rather than quantitative. The goal is not to come up with more ideas, but ideas that are different from those of your peers. If this makes competition sound easy, it isn't. Originality is hard work. In order to know that your idea is new and original, you must explore what else is out there, including looking over your competitors. The result of this competition is a better dissertation.

Show me yours, I'll show you mine

When we speak about competition and evaluation in academia, we can't avoid mentioning the peer-review process. The idea that our work undergoes constant, repeated and "objective" assessment by other people is generally a good thing. But those quotation marks around "objective" remind us that the review process is not a mathematical equation, but a process conducted by humans, and humans are subject to all sorts of biases (not that machines can't be biased too, especially if they base their decisions on human data). Asking other experts to review our work improves the odds of it becoming the best version possible, because their feedback forces us to think beyond our perspective. Whether or not this process leads to significant changes in a manuscript, it is at least valuable to the extent that it increases the level of scrutiny on the work.[2] It is quite different from the evaluation processes students experience during their undergraduate studies, where their work receives a mark, or perhaps a ranking. The comments they get may be useful for writing their next term paper, but it's rare that students can use them to revise the actual paper being evaluated. Taking a not-so-great paper and making it better is a luxury that comes with graduate studies. This ~~shredder~~ iterative process that dissertations pass through is part of the scientific rigour in writing that helps us polish our work and reach high standards. By initiating students into this review

2. We would like to take this opportunity to thank our two friends who reviewed this book and told us it was good; we hope they enjoyed the wine.

process early in their training, we can help reduce early disappointment (like getting three desk rejections on their first paper) and develop their ability to anticipate criticism and produce high quality work. In our own labs, we often ask that students *not* show their work to us first, whether it's an abstract, a scholarship proposal, or the draft of a manuscript. We ask students to review drafts amongst themselves, even when they aren't one of the co-authors. This can have the advantage that the version of the draft that reaches us is already better, but it also has the benefit of exposing students to criticism from peers. A big part of learning to write is learning to accept other people's points of view and analysis.[3] This training towards openness and humility complements the student's developing writing skills. Creativity feeds upon alternate perspectives, and the way to get these perspectives is by interacting with peers during the writing process. However, if competitive environments are to be beneficial, then the advisor must constantly to do their part to guide students away from the traps, the "dark side" of competition, whose dire consequences on health and productivity far outweigh any benefits.

THE BAD AND THE UGLY SIDES OF COMPETITION (WHEN PEER PRESSURE BECOMES SELF-FLAGELLATION)

Competition implies a drive to be better, always better. Working more, working faster, in order to produce more. Such a drive towards "the top," especially in the absence of clear objectives (see Chapter 5), will crash sooner or later against the barrier of human limitations. And in the case of intense competition, when immense efforts have been poured out, failing to reach the top (to be the best, to win the gold medal, to beat our best time at a 10 km race, etc.) is often misinterpreted as failure. In academia, we are usually our most demanding audience and our own severest critics. We excel at pushing ourselves, but we are less good at celebrating ourselves, at appreciating improvement, regardless of our ultimate aims, at valuing perseverance (running a 10 km race is a feat in itself) and considering extenuating circumstances (your time may not be as good because there were hills and heavy sun). Not being first isn't the same as losing. It's okay to feel bad about not achieving high goals as long as this feeling is temporary and transforms into positive drive toward learning new approaches and

3. This culture of sharing requires that the notions of plagiarism, contributions, and intellectual property (Chapter 6) have already been explained to students, and that professors are able to ascertain that students aren't making others do their work for them.

continuing to improve. The danger lies in interpreting one setback as a catastrophe. Transforming negative feedback or a negative outcome into positive energy requires the perspective that can only come with experience (see Box 2.1).

BOX 2.1—IT'S THE END OF YOUR GRANT, NOT YOUR CAREER, BUDDY

As a young graduate student, I witnessed a research supervisor's stupor upon hearing that one of his colleagues did not have his grant renewed. This supervisor spent what seemed like hours telling his poor student how cruel the research world was, and how outrageous this situation was. The very important grant of this supervisor's good friend, a very successful researcher, had not been renewed! It was all over, his career was evidently finished. As a graduate student, I didn't understand what the huge fuss was about, and I couldn't believe that a researcher who was so passionate and well-known could see their career evaporate just like that. Was my supervisor overreacting? Was he afraid that, in this competitive world of research, he would meet the same fate? I can't say, but I know that this episode stayed in the back of my mind for a long time. It didn't deter me from embarking upon this academic adventure, but it lurked there somewhere, waiting to resurface and teach me a lesson. This lesson came almost 20 years later. Fuelled by the energy of a productive Ph.D. and two post-docs, I had built my own team and launched a successful research career. A good part of this energy was directed to grant writing, and I quickly adopted a fire-at-will strategy by applying to quite a wide range of grant programs. I am not sure about my actual success rate because some competitions smashed my numbers (for example, applying 8 times before getting a grant from the Canadian Institutes of Health Research [CIHR]), but I managed to obtain several grants, and I quickly built a team of 20+ people. This pace lasted for almost 15 years until I hit a wall. I was exhausted, sick of it, wondering what all the effort was about (sounds like burnout, right?). I decided (or was more or less forced) to focus on one specific part of my research program. That meant I stopped applying for grants in different areas to focus on this one. It also meant I gradually had to reduce the number of research associates and graduate students on my team. This sounded like a very reasonable plan: quality over quantity, right? As grants expired and my team was naturally shrinking to what I thought was a more decent size, the unimaginable happened. I failed to renew my only remaining grant! I was instantly thrown back 20 years to my supervisor's office where I could hear my supervisor telling me what a catastrophe this was—but this time the respected colleague was me! I had failed. I had let him down, I had let myself down, I had lost everything. In trying to slow down, I'd been brought to a brutal stop. At the exact moment I received the news (thanks to my damned "smart" watch), I was in conversation with the co-author of this book. At least we weren't discussing the current chapter—that would have been too great a coincidence. Overwhelmed by this devastating news, I told her I needed to take a break and reflect about my career for the remainder of the afternoon (thinking I would need the rest of the semester at least!). During the next two hours, I engaged in mindless tasks such as sorting emails and cleaning my desktop. I even started drafting some emails about how I needed to step away from some tasks to focus on my research career (really!?). I felt I had failed completely. I'd decided to slow down, and fate had decided to put an end to my research career. What had happened?

As it turns out, someone at our Faculty Research Office had misread the funding agency's results. Two hours after the fatal email announcing I hadn't renewed my grant, the vice-dean of research emailed me to apologize for the mistake and told me that I'd renewed my grant for 5 years with flying colours, almost doubling my previous annual amount. So what message to take from all this? In the first few seconds, I thought of an episode of *The Big Bang Theory*, "The Tangible Affection Proof," in which one of the main characters has just made a speech to a group a single people on Valentine's Day about the importance of being there for one other, when they get invited out for coffee by a romantic interest and exclaim "*Later losers!*" I got that powerful and addictive feeling of victory: "I think I'm good, and I am, and those who don't know it are completely mistaken!" I also thought that the next time I would ask the research counsellor to triple-check when I failed to get a grant (since the double-check that my self-confidence drove me to ask for this time had proven insufficient). But in fact, this anecdote shows how our quest for excellence can blind us. We bet everything on the final result. I've thought back to this moment a number of times, and come up with a few conclusions that I share with students from time to time: (1) we are always vulnerable to falling into the trap of competition; (2) it is always possible not to renew a grant (or obtain a scholarship, or have a paper accepted); success is never guaranteed; (3) we are often so focused on final goals that we forget to take a deep breath and a few steps back; (4) we are worth more than the results of a competition, the value of our grants, the number of papers in our C.V., and all the other quantitative indexes we use to compare ourselves to others; (5) I really should have opened up to my co-author instead of fleeing her office.

This chapter is not about how to train your students to become more competitive (nor to make you more competitive yourself) but about how to balance the lurking pressure to perform that can have a corrosive effect on the quality of our work and the pleasure we get from writing. Working towards our goals should be fun, learning should be fun, learning to write should be fun. Thus, by knowing more about potential costs of striving for excellence, students can recognize the warning signs before they get caught in this maelstrom. Surfing a maelstrom might look exciting as you peer over the edge, but as you get closer and closer to the center, your speed increases, and it gets harder and harder to keep your balance without falling into the bottomless pit at the centre. Wouldn't it be just as enjoyable to try surfing plain old waves instead? Some of us also enjoy paddleboarding.

Our pressure is not their pressure

As university professors, we're surrounded by people who like competition and who have chosen this path and have learned to deal with all its aspects, good, bad, and ugly. Students have less experience with such levels of competition, and we can support them while they gain their own experience. We aren't here to shield them from competition, nor to make them fear it. The best way to help them is to be present and remain available while they face their own challenges. And since they will face their share of challenges, we also need to avoid dumping our own on them. Boundaries, boundaries! Do we have a deadline to put together our file for a promotion and we want very much to include one of the articles from our student's dissertation ? Don't confuse the deadline for our promotion with the deadline for their dissertation. Are we giving a talk in a few weeks and want to present some of the results from our student's latest experiment? No problem. We ask the student which results are available, which analyses will be completed in time for our own talk, and whether they agree for us to present them. What we shouldn't do is ask the student to prioritize doing new analyses just for our talk, especially if these new analyses aren't a priority for the student's dissertation. Students are not employees; they are not working to advance our careers. On the contrary, our careers include the task of guiding students during their studies, while always respecting their own pace, which will differ from one student to another, and also differs from our own.

FROM A QUANTITATIVE TO A BINARY WORLD

How many students have asked us, very early on in the writing process, how long a dissertation should be? How many pages should my dissertation have?[4] How many papers should it include? How long does it take to complete a Ph.D.? Are we there yet? This last comment reflects the obsession we have with finality that started from the back seat of a car during loooong road trips. Granted, the dissertation does have to be finished at some point, but getting there isn't only dependent on its quantitative aspects; what is written also matters.

The obsession with quantifying, and the need to generate rapid quantifications of our work, transforms our method of assessing performance from a scale to binary decisions: A+ students versus not-A+ students, above 25 H-index versus below 25, 100k dollars/year funds versus no funds, > 50 papers versus < 50 papers, > 100 citations versus < 100 citations… Some departments require professors to publish in journals with an impact factor of 3 and above, thus reducing the concept of impact factors (for those who like them) to yet another dichotomy of more or less than 3. There are many other examples where numbers have created such pass or fail criteria. Many of these metrics were intended to provide rapid, useful information; this is the advantage of numbers and metrics. But to focus exclusively on the metric until we forget where the numbers come from or what their frame of reference is, is a trap ("It's a trap!" as Admiral Ackbar famously exclaimed). Comparing numbers might sometimes be necessary, but as the following example shows, it's important to choose carefully what we compare them to. A former student of our department once said to one of us: "You know, during my undergrad, I worked really hard and I knew that I was among the best of my cohort. This allowed me to be selected in a very competitive graduate studies program. I was at the extreme end of the normal curve back then. When I started graduate school, I didn't understand why many people around me seemed to be doing better, working faster, and publishing more than me." She said that at first it felt as if she was failing, until she realized that a new normal curve could be drawn in her graduate school cohort, and that while she'd been in the top 10% in her undergraduate cohort, she was perhaps in the 50th percentile now. She realized that she was not in the top of her graduate program, but also that it didn't matter anymore. We think the student was harsh on herself. By measuring success in a limited number of ways, for instance by counting the number of submitted manuscripts, she missed the other qualities she had which

4. See some interesting research about the mean number of pages sorted by field of study: Beckmw (2014). *Average Dissertation and Thesis Length, Take Two.* <https://beckmw.wordpress.com/2014/07/15/average-dissertation-and-thesis-length-take-two/>; Roy, J.-H. (2016). Combien de pages pour une maîtrise ou un doctorat? *ACFAS Magazine.* <https://www.acfas.ca/index.php/publications/decouvrir/2016/11/combien-pages-maitrise-doctorat>

outshone many other students, humility being one of them. Quantity is always relative to context, and there are numerous ways to complete a valuable Ph.D. (or a valuable career, see Box 2.2). As our colleague likes to repeat, everybody's cup gets full at some point, but some people drink tiny espressos while others prefer extra tall americanos (see Figure 2.1). We admit tweaking the quote a bit here, as the reference is often used to cast shade on people who get "swamped" by workloads that seem to include relatively few tasks. This new version of the quote opens the door to considering the quality of the tasks as well as their quantity—and as defenders of strong concentrated espressos who like to drink less good stuff than more not-so-good-stuff, and because many espressos did indeed fuel the writing of this book, we think we should consider what is in the cup as well as the cup itself.

BOX 2.2—DIARY OF A 9 TO 5 PROF

I've always completed my duties as a professor by maintaining a steady factory schedule: arrive at 8 and leave at 4, Monday to Friday. Except under rare circumstances, I don't work in the evening or on weekends. Because of my background, my character and my values, my aspiration was not to stay within academia at any cost; it was only if I could stay within the limits of what I have to offer. It was a personal choice, I adhered to it voluntarily, and without trying to convince anyone that I'd found the right way to go at it. At first, I even tried to hide it from colleagues, fearing that I would be told that I wasn't working hard enough. But I had a Plan B in my back pocket. I was ready to jump ship for new job opportunities if what I had to offer in academia wasn't enough for a career. Years have gone by, and I'm still sticking to my schedule. I fulfilled all my duties as a professor, I got promoted and even made great achievements by working between 35 and 40 hours per week. The only difference today is that I don't hide it anymore. I'm still not trying to convince anyone that this is the right way. I'm not always convinced myself that it is, but now I feel the need to say (and to write) that this model exists, works, and can be successful. I've harboured many doubts, certain that one day I would be kicked out... but this never happened. Still, when people "congratulate" me for not working evenings and weekends it makes me uncomfortable, because this isn't an aptitude, it's a choice. When people ask me how I implement such a schedule, I don't dare saying anything, because people expect a magic formula. But just this once, I'm ready to give you the secret... if you really want to try. Here goes: at 4 p.m. I shut down my computer, then I leave. I repeat the same thing the next day. I skip weekends. That's it.

FIGURE 2.1 To each their own cup

BOOSTING PERFORMANCE IS OUT, OPTIMIZING PERFORMANCE IS IN

We work in an environment that encourages the drive towards excellence, and we feed on this motivational force. We want to lead students toward excellence, not shove them willy-nilly. But just as we do for ourselves (or should we say, unlike what we do for ourselves!), we need to take into account the students' capacity, their level of ambition, and their specific situation, all of which could be in flux, and involve a number of different challenges. The ultimate goal of graduate studies is a completed dissertation, but to get there, students will most likely need to improve their writing skills. There are little geniuses out there who write well, even very well, right out of the gate, but don't expect to come across many of them during your career. Steven Pinker[5] and others who have written books on academic writing insist that a person is not born a good writer, but becomes one, through practice. You'll have occasion to interact with many students with varied skill levels who will remind you what Darwin and others have said: "speaking comes naturally, not writing." As further elaborated by French

5. Pinker, S. (2014). *The Sense of Style: The Thinking Person's Guide to Writing in the 21st Century*. New York: Penguin Books.

neurologist Lionel Nacache,[6] writing and reading are new skills in term of human evolution, and particularly human brain evolution. The same can be said developmentally speaking; children typically learn to speak naturally through social interactions, while reading and writing need more formal teaching and take more time. Learning to write takes time, and learning to write well takes even more time. Yet not all students will become great writers. Umberto Eco put it simply when he said that we must tell students: "Do the thesis that you are able to do!"[7] So, each person should aim towards excellence, but also respect their own limits. As advisors, we clearly understand our role in the former, but we can also make a difference in the latter. Just as we have learned to seek excellence and to teach students to do the same, we can also learn how to help them do it in a balanced and realistic way. Remember, learning is what we do best!

6. Le Monde (2018). Les secrets du cerveau dévoilés par Lionel Naccache, neurologue. *Le Monde.* August 28. <https://www.lemonde.fr/medecine/video/2018/08/28/les-secrets-du-cerveau-devoiles-par-lionel-naccache-neurologue_5347039_1650718.html>

7. Eco, U. (2015). *How to Write a Thesis.* Cambridge: The MIT Press [Original text: Eco, U. (1977). *Come Si Fa Una Tesi Di Laurea,* Milano, Bompiani].

CHAPTER 3
Deal or no deal

When we accept the role of a graduate student advisor, we start a relationship that will last many years, and we agree to take part in a saga that will span many volumes and contain many challenges. We might not be the main character, but we are far from a mere background actor. The student is undertaking a path filled with doubts, questions, difficult hurdles, all-too-fleeting success, and disillusionment. Supporting students along this adventure is no easy task. That's why it's important to build the relationship on clear and solid foundations. Graduate studies are already so filled with uncertainties that research advisors need not add to them through their expectations and supervising methods.

GETTING ALONG IMPLIES UNDERSTANDING EACH OTHER

One way to head off problems with writing a dissertation is to be sure the research advisor and student are aligned in their vision of the final product and the various tasks required to reach it. Most of the time, students are ill-prepared for their new decision-making role with respect to their dissertation. Moreover, we all have different views on what makes a "good student" in terms of time spent in the lab, participation in activities, productivity (often measured as manuscript output), communication skills, frequency and topic of discussions with us, level of independence, and so forth. How we rate a student's competence will depend a lot on whether they are matching our expectations. For instance, they might make a decision in a situation where we would have preferred to be consulted first, or on the contrary, they might wait for instructions when we want them to be more proactive. It's a basic principle that precise, clearly stated expectations will make the supervising relationship easier. Yet a lack of alignment between the parties' expectations is at the root of most conflicts that hold back a dissertation's progress.

The best way to ensure that students will fail to meet our expectations is to remain vague about them. For some aspects, we might find it easy to explicitly express the rules we want to see followed, while for others we might not even be aware of what our own expectations of students are. For these aspects, it may be the case that every student who has joined our lab simply adhered to the rules implicitly. But the day will come when one student will seem to do everything wrong, and it's only at that moment that we'll realize we do have specific expectations after all. Students are generally relying on professors to define the different tasks they should carry out to complete their dissertation. We don't have to wait for student to fail to meet our expectations in order to make them more explicit.

We can start by clarifying our expectations for our own benefit. Ingrid Moses (1985)[1] created a Role Perception Scale that offers an interesting way to clarify expectations between a professor and a graduate student (see Box 3.1). Filing out this scale helps us know ourselves better as advisors by making explicit some of our expectations that may have been unconscious. Moses's work has appeared in published papers and online tools[2] which describe between 12 and 27 situations for which the person must identify where the responsibility falls, using a numbered scale ranging from "completely the professor's" to "completely the student's." Who sets deadlines, who decides the dissertation topic, who determines the frequency of meetings, who secures funding for the research, or for the student, who must learn the type of statistical analyses required by the project? Bégin (2018)[3] suggests using such scales mostly for ourselves, as professors, in order to help us become aware of our expectations, which will then be easier to transmit explicitly to students. This exercise should come with a warning: making our expectations more explicit should not lead to imposing them on students without room for discussion. On the contrary, a better understanding of our expectations should help us challenge them

1. Moses, I. (1985). *Supervising Postgraduates*. HERDSA Green Guide No 3, Kensington: Higher Education Research & Development Society of Australasia; Moses, I. (1992). Supervision: Expectations and standards. In Zuber-Skerritt, O. (ed.). *Manual for Conducting Workshops on Postgraduate Supervision*. Tertiary Education Institute: University of Queensland.
2. Aspland, T., Edwards, H., O'Leary, J., & Ryan, J. (1999). Tracking new directions in the evaluation of postgraduate supervision. *Innovative Higher Education, 24*(2), 127–147; Bégin, C. (2018). *Encadrer aux cycles supérieurs. Étapes, problèmes et interventions*. Québec: Presses de l'Université du Québec; Stappenbelt, B., & Basu, A. (2019). Student-supervisor-university expectation alignment in the undergraduate engineering thesis. *Journal of Technology and Science Education*. 9(2): 199–216 <https://doi.org/10.3926/jotse.482>
3. Bégin, C. (2018). *Encadrer aux cycles supérieurs. Étapes, problèmes et interventions*. Québec: Presses de l'Université du Québec.

if needed (why does this one feel so important to me?), and ease the process of adapting them to the contexts and needs of the student. Our aim in making our expectations more explicit should be to remain flexible, not to calcify our methods further.

BOX 3.1—ROLE PERCEPTION SCALE (MOSES, 1992)[4]

Read each pair of statements listed on this page. Each expresses a possible standpoint of the supervisor. You may not agree fully with either statement, in which case please estimate your position, and mark it on the scale. For example, if you believe very strongly that supervisors should select the research topic, you'd circle (1) for item 1.

Topic/Course of study

1.	It is the supervisor's responsibility to select a promising topic	1 2 3 4 5	It is the student's responsibility to select a promising topic
2.	In the end, it is up to the supervisor to decide which theoretical frame of reference is most appropriate	1 2 3 4 5	Students have a right to choose their own theoretical standpoint even if it conflicts with the supervisor's
3.	The supervisor should direct the student in the development of an appropriate programme of research and study	1 2 3 4 5	The supervisor should act mainly as a sounding board for the student's ideas and give advice

4. Moses, I. (1992). Supervision: Expectations and standards. In Zuber-Skerritt, O. (ed.). *Manual for Conducting Workshops on Postgraduate Supervision.* Tertiary Education Institute: University of Queensland.

Contact/Involvement

4.	Staff-student relationships are purely professional and personal matters should not intrude	1 2 3 4 5	Close personal relationships are essential for successful supervision
5.	The supervisor should initiate frequent meetings with the student	1 2 3 4 5	It is up to the student to decide when s/he wants meetings with the supervisor
6.	The supervisor should know at all times at which problems the student is working	1 2 3 4 5	Students should have the opportunity to find their own way without having to account for how they spend their time
7.	The supervisor should terminate supervision if s/he thinks the project is beyond the student	1 2 3 4 5	The supervisor should support the student right through until the thesis has been submitted, regardless of his/her opinion of the work

The thesis

8.	The supervisor should ensure that the thesis is finished not much later than the minimum period	1 2 3 4 5	As long as the student works steadily s/he can take as long as s/he needs to finish the work
9.	The supervisor has direct responsibility for the standard of the thesis	1 2 3 4 5	The supervisor advises only and leaves all decisions concerning content, format and standards to the student
10.	The supervisor should insist on seeing drafts of every section of the thesis in order to review them	1 2 3 4 5	It is up to the student to ask for constructive criticism from the supervisor
11.	The supervisor should assist in the actual writing of the thesis if the student has difficulties	1 2 3 4 5	The supervisor should be very wary of contributing too much to the thesis

Some of the items proposed by Moses might not seem complete opposites. For instance, for item 11 we might intend to help the student write while also remaining cautious to avoid writing their dissertation for them. In fact, we might be tempted simply to attribute the responsibility to both parties by selecting "3" for all items instead of sweating over whether to give more weight to the professor or the student. Based on this tool, we propose a similar exercise but using a visual analogue scale with less specific topics and a greater range of responses. We grouped different elements from the previous scale that seemed most likely to provoke differing opinions, and we propose, with a dash of humour, the CLUELESS scale (Clever and Legendary Universal Extended List of Expectations for Students and Supervisors; see Box 3.2). To fill it out, we suggest that for each topic, you indicate which person, the student or the professor, has the greater responsibility for making decisions, knowing that for most topics this responsibility is often shared (within the limits of each university's rules and regulations). You can even add topics that we have missed! But knowing our own expectations isn't everything—those of our students also matter. That's why we think that this exercise should be taken a step further from simply clarifying our own expectations, to inquiring about those of the student as well. It's important to leave room for the student's perceptions, and to acknowledge that they also have something to say about different aspects of how their dissertation is progressing. The idea behind this exercise is to uncover, as early as possible, any differences in perception about who is responsible for different decisions. Get your students to fill out the CLUELESS scale, or part of it; pay attention to any discrepancies in how you see things. Is this instrument valid and reliable? Who knows, as it has not yet been submitted to rigorous psychometric analysis! But try to put the student's sheet over yours in order to compare both answers by looking through the paper. What are the topics where you are furthest apart? Are there ones for which responsibility is more clearly assigned to one or the other? Discuss these topics in an open and transparent way. It may emerge that you have interpreted them differently. Good! This isn't meant to be a precise instrument but rather a tool to facilitate discussion. This exercise could even be repeated at different moments throughout a student's studies, especially considering that some topics might be more relevant at specific stages of the dissertation's progress (e.g., deciding whether it's of sufficient quality to be submitted for external evaluation). The point of all of this is for students and professors to have open discussions, in the interests of preserving a harmonious and long-lasting relationship.

BOX 3.2 THE CLUELESS (CLEVER AND LEGENDARY UNIVERSAL EXTENDED LIST OF EXPECTATIONS FOR STUDENTS AND SUPERVISORS) SCALE

Who's in charge? Who decides? Who settles the disagreements?

Mark an X at the place that represents your perception of who holds what share of responsibility for each topic.

Research topic

Strictly supervisor — Strictly student

Theoretical framework

Strictly supervisor — Strictly student

Methodology

Strictly supervisor — Strictly student

Resources and equipment

Strictly supervisor — Strictly student

Research funding

Strictly supervisor — Strictly student

Student stipend

Strictly supervisor — Strictly student

Ownership of data

Strictly supervisor — Strictly student

Dissertation content

Strictly supervisor — Strictly student

Dissertation structure (articles, chapters)

Strictly supervisor — Strictly student

Timeline

Strictly supervisor — Strictly student

Feedback — turnaround time, nature, and frequency

Strictly supervisor — Strictly student

Meetings — frequency and format

Strictly supervisor — Strictly student

Relationship boundaries

Strictly supervisor — Strictly student

Use of external resources in case of difficulties

Strictly supervisor — Strictly student

Writing style and quality

Strictly supervisor — Strictly student

Dissertation submission

Strictly supervisor — Strictly student

____

Strictly supervisor — Strictly student

____

Strictly supervisor — Strictly student

____

Strictly supervisor — Strictly student

Once you've identified your expectations, you can have a discussion to get on the same page. Ideally, this should happen over several conversations, to let the other person's ideas sink in. It is a double task: to state our expectations clearly and precisely, and to identify the student's needs, whether expressed or implied. Also, because there is often a discrepancy between what we say and what we actually do, it may help to prompt students to talk to other students of the lab or the program. This will help them clarify their own expectations, make sense of what they think the expectations of the research supervisor are, and get the big picture of how the lab or team operates.

Once expectations are well-aligned, it's time to write all of the conclusions that emerged from this collaborative endeavour. Whether we call it a contract, an agreement or a plan for collaboration, does not matter much. What's important is that its contents reflect what both parties have agreed upon. This agreement can address multiple subjects such as the research topic, roles and responsibilities, the co-supervisor's role, if any, the framework for supervision and modes of communication, funding (of the student and of the project), available resources, conference participation, agreements about authorship, extra-curricular activities the student should attend to develop specific skills, deadlines for various milestones, etc. At Université Laval, this document is called the Collaborative Agreement (*Plan de collaboration*), and is defined as "an essential instrument ensuring progress according to specified time limits"[5] set for graduate research training. This Collaborative Agreement is mandatory according to regulations, which state, "the supervision of a student enrolled in a graduate program must provide for the use of the collaborative agreement to ensure their progress".[6] This needs to include: "(a) the name of the research advisor, and, if applicable, the co-advisor or members of the master's or doctoral committee; (b) the research topic and an abstract of the project; (c) a timetable with the different milestones (courses, ethics review, research activities); (d) thesis or dissertation requirements; (e) supervisory framework".[7] This last point, supervisory framework, appears suspiciously brief and simple. Such a framework can encompass many different aspects of the relationship between student and professor, including frequency of meetings, frequency and format of giving feedback, participation in lab life, how to communicate with the professor and other team members,

5. Université Laval (2024). *Règlement des études*. Québec : Université Laval. <https://www.ulaval.ca/sites/default/files/notre-universite/direction-gouv/Documents_officiels/Reglements/Reglement_des_etudes.pdf>
6. *Ibid.*
7. *Ibid.*

what is covered by formal versus informal discussions, and so on. In our experience, this framework is where implicit and ill-defined expectations often lurk, providing fertile ground for conflict.

Throughout this process we must be aware that we, as professors, hold a greater share of power in the relationship with students. Unequal power in the supervision relationship is addressed in more detail in Chapters 7, 8, and 10. For now, let's simply remind ourselves that students may agree with whatever we say, especially at the beginning, because they want to please us, because they're afraid of displeasing us, or simply because they don't realize they're also allowed a say in their own supervision. For instance, one of us supervised a student who told them something like, "I will be like clay for you to shape," a sentiment that, while it was probably amplified by cultural differences, clearly indicated that they didn't think they would have any input into the tasks, decision-making, and setting of roles in the supervision relationship. Encouraging students to talk to more experienced team members or students from other groups is a good way for them to learn more about expectations from both student's and professor's perspectives.

Finally, it's important to proceed transparently. We should not have any reservations about other professors or students seeing our agreements: perhaps they'll get inspired, or offer useful criticisms. It's possible to be assertive and clear about our expectations, while also being open to revising them. As the captain of our ship (lab, team), it's okay to have a clear itinerary and to make the major decisions about how to get there. This shouldn't prevent us from listening to suggestions and making a few detours. Who knows, these might turn out to be short-cuts, or paths to unexplored regions!

AGREEMENT TO AVOID DISAGREEMENTS

Collaborative agreements favour clear communication. They define the nature and the framework of the different actions to be taken. They also ensure that the student's needs and the requirements of the study program will be met. From an ethical standpoint, they favour transparency, competency, and compliance with the rules of the organization that guide both the professor and student along their respective journeys. These agreements are also a teaching tool that allows professors and students to define work objectives and support their learning, supervision, and evaluation. They help to organize our ideas, and ensure that the students' research experience will be generally smooth by providing opportunities to plan major research activities and how they will be accomplished. Agreements can set out how to handle common challenges, such as the prolonged absence of a research advisor, and thus serve to prevent problems or to solve them more easily, establishing a framework that parties can refer to in case of disagreement. Lastly, agreements promote the development of a good working alliance between students and professors, based on transparency, trust, and openness.

Writing the agreement helps define the implicit expectations and assumptions of the different people and organizations involved. These unwritten rules can lead us to blame a person for failing to do something they never explicitly agreed to do. For instance, Suzan, Mary's research advisor, expects students to stay in the lab until a specific time. Mary, on the other hand, expects to be allowed to manage her own schedule, and leaves the lab earlier. Suzan interprets Mary's early departures as a lack of commitment and questions her motivation. Mary is upset because she believes she is completing all the tasks related to her graduate studies in the time she's allotted herself, and she thinks Suzan should grant her more independence. Suzan and Mary both expect the other to follow the rules of an implicit contract, and they're both frustrated with the other's behavior. Writing a clear agreement early on, and taking the time to modify it periodically, since not all developments can be foreseen, will reduce the conflicts arising from such implicit contracts. This is especially important when we supervise people from other disciplines, other universities, other countries, etc. It has the added advantage of avoiding unwritten rules that may be discriminatory (e.g., having expectations about lab hours that are not compatible with having a family with young children).

DON'T DELAY, AGREE TODAY

Evacuation plans are created before a fire can break out. However, when it comes to using a collaborative agreement, people are usually quick to say the process is unnecessary since everything is going fine and they've never had those kinds of problems. Sure, things usually go well... until they don't. The collaborative agreement is not a fire extinguisher, it is the whole evacuation plan. When everything is going smoothly and we have good collaboration, that's precisely the time we need to address thorny issues like who decides, who pays, and who owns the data.

An initial draft of a collaborative agreement can be drawn up in the first few weeks of graduate studies. It's possible at this point that the student hasn't yet pinpointed their needs and expectations, but the professor can show them standard examples from other agreements. This will at least lay the groundwork for discussion. It's likely that during this "honeymoon" phase of the supervision relationship, both parties will be eager to agree on things. We should also remember that students are usually ecstatic at the idea of starting their graduate studies in a prestigious and fantastic environment like our lab, and will thus tend to accept whatever we say, without grasping the magnitude of what we're asking of them (such as including three published articles in their dissertation). Over time, students will want to revisit a few elements of the agreement. Not only should we not be surprised by this, we should encourage it. The agreement should never be seen as fixed: it should evolve according to the context of the student, the professor, the lab, and outside partnerships, including financial resources, etc.

Regular revision of the agreement is indispensable. We might suggest once per year, as prescribed by the rules and regulations of our university, but ideally it should become a reflex to pull out the agreement whenever some element of it becomes pertinent to a student's trajectory. For instance, we can start by laying out a few broad criteria to determine author order in a paper that will be part of the student's dissertation, but for each specific paper it will be important to have another discussion about the elements related to its production: who does what, who is an author, what will be the language of publication, which journal will it be submitted to, etc. Another example is prolonged absences. Some are predictable (e.g., planned trips), others less so (e.g., parental leave), others not at all (e.g., sick leave). Prolonged absences on the part of either the professor or the student will require the collaborative agreement to be revisited.

Hence, the takeaway for this and all subsequent chapters is a sentence that we could simply copy and paste over and over: "this issue should be discussed right from the start." Most problems can be prevented or resolved through an open, honest, and caring discussion between the student and the professor. And, since we all know that the spoken word is transitory and the written word remains, we believe it best to make a regular practice of collaboratively adding the output of such discussion to the written agreement.

You might even wish to discuss some elements of the agreement before the professor agrees to supervise a student, or before the students decides to join the professor's team. Professors and potential new student should discuss issues like their supervision style, the decision-making process, available funds, and expectations of schedules and tasks, so a student can make an informed decision whether to pursue graduate studies with one professor or not. It's our responsibility to temper the early enthusiasm—of the student, eager to work with such an amazing professor, and of ourselves, pleased to attract such a high-quality student—and to be transparent about how things will work. There should be no skeletons in the closet as we enter into this complex long-term relationship.

The collaborative agreement is one of the tools that will help us build a solid working relationship and create the best conditions for student productivity as they pursue their goals. It isn't something to be completed hastily and without thought; it may take several meetings. This isn't just another piece of paperwork to clutter up our (administratively overburdened) jobs.

GETTING UNSTUCK AND GETTING HELP

We're convinced that the simple act of discussing, sharing, and attuning expectations between professors and students can prevent countless problems. When disagreements occur, we can fall back on the agreement and adapt it as needed to prevent the conflict from escalating. Discussing the collaborative agreement also prepares us to handle unforeseen scenarios. Both the professor and the student can build on the positive experience of reconciling their potentially different expectations should the time come for more serious disagreements.

Yet despite our best intentions, conflicts can arise that exceed the ability of both parties to resolve. As professors, we should foresee that there will be some conflicts that we'll be unable to settle by ourselves. Maybe these will truly be the exception, but we shouldn't see them as an anomaly, nor a sign of incompetence. On the contrary, when a professor reaches out for external help to solve complex issues with a student, they are displaying a high level of professionalism. It takes a lot of self-reflection and humility to recognize and accept that we need a third party to help untangle issues in our supervising relationship. We should think ahead about whom we could consult in these cases: a colleague, the director of the department, the dean of the faculty, or a professional at our institution whose job is to accompany professors and students. To go back to the fire analogy, our evacuation plan should also include a phone number to call the firefighters. We don't build evacuation plans because we want a fire to start, nor because we have a pessimistic attitude (nor because we are pyromaniacs). We build it because, if there is a fire, we want everyone to be safe.

It's wise to recognize that we might not always be the best person to accompany a given student who is experiencing problems. Our collaborative agreement can thus include a section about where to direct an external appeal. We're already used to seeing this kind of neutral third party identified on course outlines and research consent forms. Though we often skim rapidly past these sections about "participant concerns," it would be useful to have an open discussion with students about the possibility that for some issues the student may need to consult an external resource. We can state that in case of disagreement, we expect students to first talk to us openly, since openness from both parties is the basis of a good relationship. But we should also identify options if conflicts (overt or hidden) should arise; we need to be humble and understand that some students, in some cases, might not feel comfortable talking to us directly. If we want to help students reach their research goals (to finish writing their dissertation!), it might be necessary at such points to guide them towards someone else.

EXTENDED EDITION – THE SPECIAL CASE OF CO-SUPERVISORS

Now that we've talked about expectations and agreements, it seems like a good time to talk about co-supervision. Co-supervision carries a number of advantages, such as bringing together complementary expertise, addressing topics from interdisciplinary or transdisciplinary perspectives, and gaining access to equipment, resources, study populations, and networks. Co-supervision implies that supervision is shared between two or more professors. The more the merrier? Not necessarily.

Co-supervision should be approached realistically. One more person in the relationship implies another set of expectations and potentially new ways of doing things that must be reconciled. In our experience, there are a lot of myths out there about co-supervision, the most common of which is that it saves time and resources for the professors who share the supervisory tasks. Nothing could be farther from the truth. Co-supervision is not 50% of the work required for supervision. In fact, everyone involved, from the main supervisor to the co-supervisor and student, most probably will have more work than they would in a simple one-to-one supervision. In the best case scenario, each professor will invest the same amount of energy in a co-supervised student as they would as a solo supervisor. In the worst case scenario, each professor will have to adapt their methods and expectations to the other. For the student, this can double their workload. It could mean joining two labs, learning two techniques, adapting to two sets of rules, receiving two sets of comments on each draft (while praying they won't contradict each other), and more. It will be much easier if the professors already collaborate and their supervision methods are similar, but it will always remain more work than one-to-one supervision. In fact, if the two professors get along well and have similar expectations, it could put the student at a further disadvantage in the case of conflict (one student against two professors, in what's already an unequal relationship). It's therefore important to plainly disclose whatever professional or personal connections exist between two or more professors before embarking upon co-supervision. Students should know from the beginning about any pre-existing situation that could affect them, and be able to explicitly discuss any issues related to co-supervision. We don't mean to paint co-supervision as something bad to be avoided at all costs: there are multiple advantages in terms of increased breadth of expertise, potential collaborations, and career opportunities. However, it's important to realize that it adds several challenges that will require a greater commitment from the student, who cannot be expected foresee the emotional and labour costs of receiving twice the number of comments on the twenty-eighth version of the first chapter of their dissertation. Such challenges tend to be minimized or even ignored in the excitement of a fascinating, ground-breaking and unique opportunity for co-supervision.

Co-supervision also entails risks for professors. Sometimes we rely on the other professor for a specific component of the project (e.g., particular expertise, access to a study population or environment). If one professor doesn't fulfill their part of the agreement (for all sorts of reasons, under their control or not), then it falls on the other to compensate for the first one's lack of involvement in the student's project. We've also witnessed some co-supervision situations where one professor expects (explicitly or not) to share their expertise in a general fashion while the other (usually less advanced in their career) takes care of the day-to-day management and troubleshooting. This is not a fair division of tasks, where one person ponders the great ideas while the other has to think and worry about how to implement them. In co-supervision, the act of bringing expectations into tune implies a discussion involving both supervisors, otherwise students might find themselves between a rock and a hard place having to manage disagreement, or even outright conflict, between co-supervisors.

Some students will try to convince a very busy professor to become their co-supervisor with the reasoning that the task will be easier for them. Others will ask a professor to be their co-director to fill a gap in the expertise of the other professor related to a specific domain or research method. We suspect that it will be difficult to create harmony between the schedules and work methods of two busy professors when the only thing that links them is a student's project, and when the only grounds for collaboration is to make up for each other's shortcomings in time or expertise. Graduate students need to be aware of the risks of blindly pairing two people who don't know each other. It could work very well, or it could lead to drama. Are students ready to gamble their graduation or their mental health?

Collaboration between researchers is usually gradual and spans many years: the responsibility shouldn't fall to a student, especially not a new student. Of course, we've witnessed and been involved in several highly successful co-supervision relationships where the two professors barely collaborated outside the student's project. But even in these cases, the student shouldn't have sole responsibility for communication between all parties. While a student's project can give rise to new collaborations, the student should not be the only conduit of communication between the professors.

AVOIDING BAD SURPRISES

To sum up, developing a collaborative agreement doesn't just lay the foundations for a relationship based on openness and trust, it's also like an evacuation plan, making us think ahead about solutions to possible problems or conflicts down the road—before our house catches fire. To optimize this process, it can be useful to think about our expectations of students, whether these are explicit or unspoken, and what elements of our supervision methods are truly essential (and thus non-negotiable) or open to more flexibility. This makes it easier to explore the students' expectations, and to work together to bring the two sides into alignment. These expectations and work methods need to be articulated early in the development of the supervision relationship, and revised on a regular basis, at fixed intervals (e.g., at the start of each school year) and whenever it becomes relevant (e.g., at the start of writing a paper). The written agreement that grows out of these discussions is a flexible tool that facilitates good supervision practices, whose elements can evolve over time without becoming fixed. If, despite the agreement, differences of opinion, conflicts, or discomfort should arise at any moment during the supervision, we shouldn't hesitate to reach out to a third party to help preserve the relationship. Ideally, we should identify these people in advance and talk to students about the types of situations that could lead to calling them in. Finally, in the case of co-supervision, it becomes more complex to reconcile the expectations of each person involved, and thus even more important than for one-to-one supervision. Openly discussing the joys, challenges, and pains of the supervision relationship, whether it involves two, three or ten people (no comment), will give each person the opportunity to provide their informed consent.

CHAPTER 4
One pen to rule them all

One pen to rule them all
One pen to find them,
One pen to bring them all,
And in a thesis bind them

This nod to J.R.R. Tolkien's *Lord of the Rings* is a reminder that a dissertation is the work of one person, the student, who is the sole author of his or her dissertation, and rules over the words it contains, finding the right phrases and bringing them together, binding them into one original contribution. The advisor's role is not to wield the pen, however persistent the temptation may be. Their role is to help the student learn how to wield it themselves, how to use it. And if you read the title of this chapter and thought you were the one who was going to "rule them all," i.e., all the students, then the following chapter is particularly for you!

One of the greatest challenges of supervising graduate students is maintaining boundaries. This applies not only to writing but to many areas of the supervision relationship which will be discussed in Chapter 7; but here, the boundaries we're talking about are the ones that delimit the thoughts and ideas of the advisor from those of the student. Distinguishing what we as professors would write from what the students should write is often very difficult. Commenting, questioning, and challenging within a teaching context are quite different from editing, re-writing, censoring, or even showering with praise.

The kind and quantity of comments we provide can be influenced by a number of factors including: (1) our own experiences receiving comments; (2) the academic level of the student (undergrad, master's, etc.) and where they sit on the normal distribution curve in terms of writing skills; (3) the advisor's experience with different writing styles, and where they sit on the curve in terms of supervising abilities; (4) the availability of the advisor; and (5) how the comments are communicated. We'll discuss each of these factors in the following paragraphs, not with the intent of dictating rules and guidelines, but rather as a means of raising awareness about these forces that shape our supervision skills. When we become professors, we've been in school for much longer than most people. Some of our friends think that we were very slow to graduate, but of course we defend ourselves by citing our passion for learning and our goal of standing "on the other side of the desk." But learning in an academic context never ends. Advising students on their dissertation and other writing assignments is a part of our learning experience, one in which we should get better with time. It helps to remember that the student isn't the only one learning.

ROLE MODELS VERSUS CLONE MODELS

As former students, we remember what we went through to complete our dissertation. Some had more fun than others (and to the students who dare read this book, know that your advisor likely found it hard, no matter what they say!). We also had at least one advisor, and many had more than one. Some think they had great advisors: "They must have been, they steered us through, we couldn't have done it without them!" Some think theirs wasn't so great: "We did it! ... *despite* our advisor's indifference, micro-managing, selfishness, etc." Some of us recall our advisor commenting on (or disputing) every single word of our dissertation, while some of us suspect our advisor barely read what we wrote yet managed to propose three alternate titles.

How different are we from our advisors? Do we strive to be like them, or do we try to be different at any cost? Not all of us will be influenced in the same way by their past experiences with advisors, but reflecting upon them might help us realize that sometimes we're too focused on either following or avoiding their example. We have numerous colleagues who wanted to tell their students, or at least hint at what the little voice in our head is saying, "I had it tough, so toughen up!" Reflecting on our past experiences as students, but from the new perspective of an advisor, can help to reframe some of our expectations and also to distinguish bad habits from the annoying, but in retrospect highly relevant, suggestions we received from our own advisors. Ideally, we hope that what we want is the same thing our own advisors wanted—to transmit what is the best of ourselves.

No matter how hard we try to replicate, or avoid replicating, the supervision skills of our advisors, the abilities we have now were at least partly developed, for better or worse, out of those past interactions. Each relationship between student and advisor is unique. The same graduate project, the same dissertation conducted by different students or supervised by different advisors can lead to countless outcomes. Our supervision "technique" can change from student to student and be adapted to their individual needs. Moreover, our skills will be honed by each interaction we have with students and colleagues. Given that our own skill levels are potentially not constant, the challenge becomes how to treat our students equitably, over time and depending on their varying levels of skills.

SHOW ME YOUR CV AND I'LL PREDICT YOUR WRITING ABILITY?

Since practice makes perfect in writing as in other skills, the level of writing the student has already produced can provide one clue as to their future writing potential. Some of us might believe that writing skills are good selection criteria when choosing students. On the other hand, because acquiring a skill usually takes time, a student's output before starting grad school may not fully reflect their capabilities. Some students might rapidly acquire a lot of publication experience simply by being in the right place at the right time—but the right place to enhance their C.V. isn't necessarily the right place to learn. Often the actual contribution of the student is difficult to distinguish from that of other authors (e.g., group work, final reports for scholarship projects that were part of a researcher's grant, being the 11th author on a 15-author paper, etc.). One way to test a student's writing skills is to have them read a few pages of an article or a long abstract and ask them to write a summary and/or a plan for a follow-up study. This kind of "live" test can provide a more objective idea of the student's capabilities, but one concern is that factors like stress and pressure could result in lower quality work from a student who, in other contexts, might have very good writing skills. Sure, you can evaluate their ability to work rapidly under stress, but writing a dissertation is generally more about long-term endurance than short bursts. Since the point of graduate studies is, by definition, to learn, one can expect that a student's writing skills will improve. Assessing them early should be seen more as a way to identify strengths and weaknesses and to guide supervision. Rather than using a student's early performance as a predictive tool to gage how much work the advisor will have to put into them during their studies, such timely assessment can serve as a map to identify where the student will need more guidance, and what skills they should practice. It serves as a baseline from which to measure and document progress. Ongoing assessment (i.e., reading several drafts and versions of each document) is even more important for determining the student's progress, which will be driven more by our input than by the student's initial skill level.

Ultimately, although there are minimal standards that students must meet to complete a dissertation, we need to remember that not all students will be excellent writers. Some will never measure up to our own level (whatever we think that is), while others will be endowed with exceptional skills, stirring in us a subtle but pernicious feeling of jealousy toward their precioussss... that is, their pen. Our role is to support both the exceptionally good and the exceptionally awful by reminding them to write, write, write, no matter their current skill level. Some might require more effort from us than others, but there is no such thing as a student who requires none.

HOW MANY DISSERTATIONS HAS THE ADVISOR SUPERVISED?

The evaluation report of a thesis defense often provides a fascinating snapshot of how a professor's style changes, for better or worse, over the course of their career. We observe that an Assistant Professor's report can be 10 pages long, including 2 pages of grammar and stylistic corrections. Comments tend to be short, and to the point. A Full Professor's comments are typically broader, even generic, and the whole report only fills half a page. Note that in a manuscript revision process, the reviewers' comments tend to follow the same pattern—the less experienced the reviewer, the more numerous, detailed (and sometimes picky) the comments are. In fact, we dug into our own archives and randomly selected a few evaluation reports to confirm that they contained about 3,700 words in the first two years of our careers, 2,000 words after five years, and 1,100 words after 10 years. If we extrapolate this trend toward the end of our careers, our last reports might contain three words, either "Wonderful, congratulations doctor!" or "Fail, game over." This evolution reflects how at the beginning of our careers we focus on the specific, and invest a lot of time reviewing a dissertation, while later in our careers we tend to view the broader picture (sometimes by reframing questions around our own interests), and the time we have (or are willing to give) for each task has shrunk. The corollary is that, as our skills evolve over the course of our career, it's likely that the way we provide feedback to our students does as well. We learn to become a good advisor in a complex, informal way, by giving and receiving advice. Occasionally, it's possible to get an outside perspective (some might call it "objective"...) by discussing such issues with our colleagues, or by serving in a position such as program director, human resources, or even ombudsperson, but we very rarely learn this skill formally. Some universities offer a half-day workshop on this subject, often on a voluntary basis. Others will impose such training only *after* things have gone sour with a student. But in general, most of us receive no training whatsoever to teach what many of us (including the authors of this book) consider to be the most important task of our job. But whatever advantages formal training might have, it could never replace informal experience, mentorship, and sharing amongst colleagues (including writing fun books like this one).

Learning to be a good advisor is achieved mostly by advising. Although university professors have the best job in the world (*authors' note: the neutrality of this statement may be disputed*), freedom of thought does come at the price of constant evaluation. Our teaching is evaluated (formally, informally, and unrelentingly), our grant proposals get shredded, our manuscripts get kicked around before (maybe) getting accepted, our C.V.s get scrutinized for promotion, and so forth. More often than not, the substance of such evaluations is not what stings most, but the manner in which they are delivered. Some complain that we have it tough, but if we can look past the not always gentle delivery, these evaluations give us many opportunities to learn. Undoubtedly, we've been trained to take harsh criticism on the chin, and we would like our students to develop the same toughness. However, when providing comments on our students' drafts, the words we choose can make a big difference in how they are received. Once again, we observe that less experienced advisors tend to be harsher. More experienced advisors might soften their choice of words, which the students likely appreciate, but this should not be done at the expense of substance, or lead them into complacency.

THE ADVISOR'S AVAILABILITY: OPEN DOOR VERSUS REVOLVING DOOR

One of the most important qualities that graduate students are looking for in potential advisors is that they make themselves available. This has been corroborated by a qualitative analysis of interviews with graduate students, who were asked specifically about their expectations regarding the advisor relationship. Availability even seems to surpass the advisor's perceived expertise in his or her field of research.[1] Paradoxically, what is the top quality we look for in a graduate student? For many of us, our minds leap to independence. Of course, leading the student to independence is

1. Belleville, G., Foldes-Busque, G., Guay, F., & Jackson, P. (2021). *Déterminants des trajectoires d'anxiété, de perfectionnisme et de procrastination menant à l'abandon des études chez les doctorants.* Fonds de recherche du Québec - Société et culture (FRQSC). <https://frq.gouv.qc.ca/histoire-et-rapport/determinants-des-trajectoires-danxiete-de-perfectionnisme-et-de-procrastination-menant-a-labandon-des-etudes-chez-les-doctorants/>

the ultimate goal, but how much value should we place on it early in their studies? Independent students demand less time because they already know what they're doing, or are efficient at finding answers by themselves. But are these answers and actions they take on their own always the best possible ones? Perhaps the advisor still has something to contribute. This apparent contradiction between advisor and student expectations stems from the perception that availability is measured strictly quantitatively. Being available does not imply that the student can reach you instantaneously and at any moment they desire. If you are receiving and responding to text messages at 11 p.m. at night, you might have strayed off course. On the other hand, repeatedly ignoring emails or not showing up to scheduled meetings isn't reasonable either. This brings us back to the basic principle of discussing expectations very early on, and ideally before the official start of the trainee–advisor relationship. These should be revisited periodically, since situations do change for both the student and the advisor. From a student's perspective, it can be helpful to understand that the advisor has many other responsibilities, while we remind the advisor that following up on our students' progress is part of our job and we must find (and safeguard!) a space for this task in our busy schedules.

Setting aside time to interact with students is the first challenge, but the next important one is determining a preferred mode of communication. Thanks to technology, we now have many alternatives to the traditional face to face meetings and written communication. Some offer clear advantages, but be aware that some only provide the illusion of availability. Beyond the frequency of contacts and feedback, we should consider their authenticity. By that, we mean that the interaction is meaningful, involves careful preparation in terms of agenda and sharing documents beforehand, and that both parties are engaged with the interaction ("Leave that cellphone on mute!"). Some digital forms of communication can create a gap in authenticity. Imagine never meeting a student and never being able to discuss the content of their dissertation in direct conversation. Would you be able to confirm that the dissertation was theirs? More than avoiding the obvious pitfalls of plagiarism, meeting students regularly ensures that you're tracking their progress and preparing the student to defend their ideas. Writing a dissertation is hard. Defending it should be easy for a student who's had good support, but ill-prepared students will find that producing the dissertation was a breeze compared to standing alone up there at the defense.

The bottom line regarding availability—which applies to the student's availability as well—is that, whether you meet in person or online, for short or long meetings, every week or every month, these decisions should be agreed upon by mutual consent and with full information (and of course, flexibility, since schedule can also change). These choices might depend on the student's level of independence, but be prepared to look below the surface, since even seemingly independent students may still need you.

THE SHAPE-SHIFTING COMMENT

Regardless of the quality of the student's draft, it is up to the advisor to decide how to comment on it. Here are some examples, including two that were the preferred methods of our respective graduate advisors (try to guess which ones): throwing the draft in the garbage can in front of the sobbing student, crossing out whole pages with red ink, writing a single word in the margin ("Revise"), rewriting sentences completely (with or without track changes), or rewriting whole paragraphs.

The tone used to comment on student's work is important and should be carefully considered, as it will have an impact on how the comments are received. Re-reading our own comments before sending them to students provides a quick check that can weed out reactive comments that are unhelpful and can even cause the student to disregard what would be relevant comments if they'd been phrased differently. Consider the same set of comments presented in Table 4.1 using either a reactive or an objective tone. They might have come from different advisors—or the same advisor prone to daily mood-swings!

We can also classify comments by their specificity. Varying the level of specificity can be a good way to balance feedback between generalities ("The intro needs to be reworked"), learning opportunities for the students ("Remember that an Introduction should be built like a funnel from the general to the specific"), and precise suggestions for improvement ("Have you considered presenting the fabulous work of Belleville and Jackson in your third paragraph ?"). Take another look at Table 4.1. Increasing specificity often increases the potential for learning, ranging from general comments to an explanation of the principles that underpin the comment. However, too much specificity (such rewriting whole paragraphs without explanation) represents a missed opportunity for learning. Seeking a balance between types of comments is important. Students need to know about their weaknesses, so they can learn both to correct them, and how to avoid them. Moreover, when commenting on a text that requires a lot of work, it's better to pick your battles and go through more iterative revisions, rather than trying to get it all right the first time. This makes the advisor's job easier, and the process is less overwhelming for the student. Finally, by reducing the amount of work, we can get our revisions back to the student more quickly. Indeed, good feedback should not only be clear, it needs to arrive at the right time.

TABLE 4.1—Some ways of offering the same comment with varying degrees of specificity and thoughtfulness

REACTIVE	THOUGHTFUL
Crap	Revise.
What?	Please revise
This is not good	Please consider revising
This is not clear	I do not understand this part
This part here is not clear	I do not understand the link between construct A and construct B here
This part is not clear because you have poor arguments	I do not understand the link between construct A and construct B here because you have not yet introduced construct B
This part is not clear because you have poor arguments and you did not do the ground work	I do not understand the link between construct A and construct B here because you should have introduced construct B in the previous paragraphs
This is not clear because you have poor arguments and you did not do the ground work as I told you to	This paragraph should read: "……" and you need to add this to the previous paragraph to introduce construct B: "……"

As advisors, we want to give our students the means to develop their full potential. We want to bring what's best in our students, not in ourselves. Yes, it takes more time to teach people to write what they want to say than it would simply to write the idea ourselves, but the former is our goal. As most of us have not received any training on how to train students, this part of our job is a learning experience. We must adapt. When one of the authors of this book was a new intern during hospital rounds, a supervisor asked them, "What are you good at"? And the terrorized (yet in retrospect, surprisingly humble) intern answered, "Learning"! The beauty of teaching is that it is a perpetual learning experience.

CHAPTER 5
To infinity and beyond

If we want to be worthy of our calling as advisors, we should spend at least some of our time advising, an activity which implies taking into account our students' goals and their ability to attain them. These goals can take different forms, all of which drive the motor of steady written output. Let's start by surveying this great variety—but rest assured that if you find yourself tempted to slam this book shut and curse us for the overwhelming number of goals, that this exhaustive list is not mandatory. The idea here is not to track every type of goal, with every student, at every meeting. Rather, this chapter can be seen as a guide to help identify problems that can occur with different kinds of goal-setting. Once such problems are recognized, that makes it easier to orient our discussions and tailor our solutions accordingly.

In order to provide structure to a work as long and complex as a dissertation, we'll consider four types of goals: long term goals, specific or weekly goals, time management goals, and project-related goals. Much like planning a long trip with a limited budget, one must plan the final destination, the pit stops, the means of transportation, and the general route to take. Of course, the plan can change along the road (as we start to regret that third coffee), but ideally such a decision is made by comparing the initial plan against the new plan, rather than following a spur of the moment decision. The consequences of changing objectives along the way, and the degree of pondering this decision requires will depend on the importance of the objective relative to the overarching goal, and the extent of the changes necessary. But the fact that a plan can be changed should not be taken as an excuse not to draw one up in the first place.

LONG-TERM GOALS: I HAVE ALL THE TIME IN THE WORLD

Long-term goals are the ultimate achievements, the marathon finish line. Students generally excel at setting long-term goals (whether these are realistic is another story!). Their objectives are often shaped by the university calendar, for instance, "I'll hand in a complete draft of my introduction just before Christmas"—with the result that that advisors often receive a large number of manuscripts just before their vacation. This might also explain why so many advisors have a hard time truly unplugging over their holidays.

Long-term goals involve longer time scales, whether in weeks or months, and represent some fixed destination, much like the mountain summit for a climber. When these goals are met, they increase our motivation level and sense of self-determination (and even altitude-induced euphoria, in the case of very high mountains!). They represent important milestones, and are thus good markers of progress. However, such fixed goals can also cast a sinister shadow over students who become discouraged as the distance between them and the summit never seems to diminish (see Figure 5.1).

FIGURE 5.1—Dreading the climb

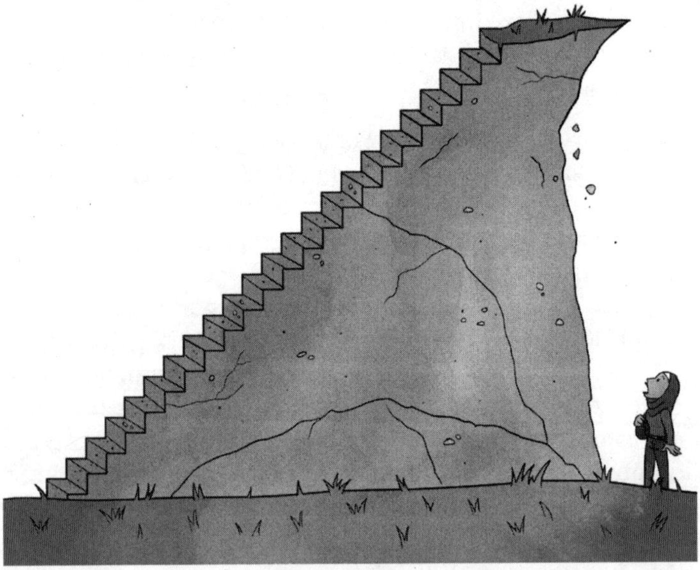

The tallest mountains cast the biggest shadows over the path of climbers. Setting goals that are too high can lead to discouragement if each step toward the summit seems to dwindle to insignificance. Moreover, it's hard for an advisor to give concrete, productive feedback on such lofty goals.

Advisor: *So, how goes the writing of your manuscript?*

Student: *It's going okay, I keep moving forward...*

Advisor: *Good job, keep up the good work and see you next time!*

By their nature, when we set long-term goals, we think we have all the time in the world to reach them, but as time passes we have to contend with the scary feeling that we'll never get there. While these goals are easy to set and do provide superficial motivation, on their own they won't be enough to encourage students to write on a regular basis, nor do they provide advisors with an accurate assessment of the student's progress.

SPECIFIC GOALS: REALITY CHECK

Long-term goals need to be broken down into small, precise, easily attainable short-term goals, whether these are weekly or from meeting to meeting—provided the latter are reasonably frequent! We want to guide students in elaborating intelligent, or SMART goals (see Box 5.1). This involves identifying key milestones necessary to attain a long-term goal. Usually, students should be in charge of this planning, but the advisor has the additional experience to help spot missing steps and adjust time estimates for each milestone. Note that many of us are still over-optimistic when judging the time required for a written task or assignment, but we trust that most of us have, through hard-fought academic experiences, acquired the skills necessary to estimate overall workload (at least, for other people!).

Defining specific objectives allows a necessary reality check. For instance, a student who wants to hand in a text before the end of the semester should be reminded that there are only eight weeks remaining to reach this goal. What needs to be done each week to achieve this target? If we chunk the workload into eight parts, what would the load be for each week? Is this realistic, considering the time the student actually dedicates to writing? If so, great! If not, two courses of action are possible: either the student puts more time and energy into this task, or the long-term objective needs to be revised. This reality check can be stressful for the student and tends to make us look harsh. But what's worse? Crushing the student's unrealistic "dreams" and recalibrating their goals? Or letting them think they can reach unrealistic goals, and then, when they fail, believing that they don't have what it takes, when the truth is the task was doomed from the start?

Setting realistic writing goals comes from experience. Thus, the task of the advisor may not be to set realistic goals for the student based on their strengths and ability level, but rather to reflect accurately, yet with kindness, the potential mismatch between goal setting and abilities. Advisors can question students about how they set goals, whether they usually reach them, and at what price. When they don't reach a goal, what was the cause? Was it because they were too hard or too lenient on themselves? The stance of the advisor will depend on how they see their own role. Do you want the student to finish the dissertation as soon as possible, or do you want them to learn all the skills necessary for writing a dissertation? Do you want to set realistic goals for them and make sure they can reach them, or do you rather let them learn by themselves how to set realistic, productive writing goals, accepting that this will take some trial and error? Remember that, in the end, the student is the sole author of the dissertation (for those who had forgotten, read Chapter 4 again).

We want students, especially those ones who keep promising and breaking their promises to send us work by a certain deadline, to develop the ability to set SMART goals that will help them maintain a regular output (Table 5.1). This will help build their confidence and encourage them to write at a steady pace, ideally by avoiding the hubris that comes from measuring productivity solely on the basis of form rather than content. A common pattern in students is to alternate between setting mega objectives that lead to a feeling of guilt when they aren't met, and putting off writing with the intention of working harder later, which leads to them setting even more unrealistic goals. Though it's possible for a bout of inspired, flow-state writing to produce large volumes of text—reinforcing bad habits with the occasional success—such binge writing during graduate studies sets the student up for anxious thoughts, cycles of procrastination and avoidance, unproductive doubts, and finally painful imposter syndrome (see Chapter 9).

TABLE 5.1—SMART goals

SMART	UNPRODUCTIVE GOALS	PRODUCTIVE GOALS
Specific	– Write dissertation – Finish theoretical background – Continue discussion	– Write Participants section of the Methods – Integrate results of Musquin & Preskovic, 1982 – Make detailed plan for Introduction of first manuscript
Measurable	– Finish literature review – Revise text	– Include a description of Skywalker, et al. 1977's model in the research question section
Achievable	– Work on my dissertation every night after my day job (*knowing that you are usually too tired in the evening to be productive*)	– Set aside three 2-hour periods dedicated solely to writing
Realistic	– Hand in a first version of my manuscript next week (*when it is barely started*)	– Make a detailed plan of each section of a manuscript, including the results, and discuss them with my advisor
Timely	– Finish writing my discussion this week – Write (*until passing out*)	– Write the theoretical implications section of the discussion this Thursday from 10 a.m. to noon

TIME MANAGEMENT GOALS: TO WRITE, YOU NEED TO DEDICATE TIME TO WRITING

Really. This is worth repeating: to write, you need to dedicate time to writing.

Many students will need to hear this often. To make progress on your dissertation, you must dedicate quality time to it, a lot of quality time. As advisors, we are often asked different versions of the same question which is essentially: "If I hold two jobs this summer, take part in a practicum, teach a class, undertake a humanitarian mission, and help my parents, siblings, or friends on a project that will take most of my free time, do you think I'll be able to finish writing my dissertation?" Early in our careers, we hesitated and tried to avoid crushing the student's hopes by commenting on their time management. Who were we to doubt the abilities of students who set ambitious objectives? We knew that we ourselves would never be able to accomplish this, yet we left the door open for the possibility that some students might have extraordinary abilities and capacities. Early in our career, we smiled, gave the somewhat vague answer that everything is possible with a good plan, and wished them good luck and safe travels. But at this point in our career, the answer is much simpler: no way!

It's simple because we know that if students do not dedicate time specifically for writing, the dissertation will not progress. In the midst of multiple tasks and responsibilities, priorities have to be set; either one accepts that the dissertation will not progress, or one cuts back or quits other jobs and commitments. Of course, in most cases, we wouldn't go so far as to demand that a student do nothing else but write their dissertation, since it can benefit the student's C.V. to take on other responsibilities during graduate studies (teaching, attending conferences, etc.), especially for those who set their sights on an academic career. Moreover, a change in focus is healthy for the brain (see Chapter 9). However, let's not forget that to write we need to dedicate, maintain, safeguard, and even aggressively defend some time specifically for writing. Our preference is short and regular intervals of quality time, daily if possible (see Box 5.1), when the student is alert and in a favourable state of mind. Writing at night for night owls, why not. Writing at night after a long day's work, after having put the children to bed and feeling really, really tired, maybe not. Writing a dissertation is not a hobby that one starts to work on after all the "real work" is done.

BOX 5.1—BUT, SERIOUSLY... (AND JUST BETWEEN US): MUST WE REALLY WRITE EVERY DAY?

Most writing advice suggests writing every day, or at least on a regular basis. But is this an absolute requirement? When we discussed these ideas, most people we talked to admit they don't follow this rule. Some are ashamed to admit it, and blame themselves for being disorganized, others are proud to show off how productive they are by concentrating their writing time over a few very productive days separated by long breaks. In fact, a large-scale survey conducted by Helen Sword revealed that only two out of one hundred "successful academic researchers" interviewed said they adhered to a strict daily writing routine.[1]

1. Sword, H. (2016) "Write every day!": A mantra dismantled. *International Journal for Academic Development, 21*, 4, 312–322. <https://doi.org/10.1080/1360144X.2016.1210153>

So where does this tyrannical idea of sticking to an ultra-strict daily writing routine come from? One potential source is the work of Robert Boice, Emeritus Professor of Psychology at the State University of New York, Stony Brook. In the 80's and 90's, Boice led a number of studies on the professor productivity.[2] One of the most striking findings was that professors who followed a rigid system of consequences, also called contingency management (in this case, sending a $15 cheque to an organization they hated every time they failed to adhere to their writing schedule) produced three times more than those who wrote spontaneously when they felt like it (3.2 pages per day compared to 0.9). In general, Boice's experiments showed that following a regular writing schedule combined with management of contingencies (i.e., rewarding or punishing yourself for precise behaviours) is more productive and leads you to generate more ideas than unstructured writing habits.

This impressive finding has often been reported by numerous people interested in academic writing, but as is often the case with second and third-hand (or hundredth-hand) sources, the information has lost part of its accuracy and context. What were essentially experimental findings have probably been transposed too hastily into broad-reaching recommendations.

Where does the truth lie? Is it that people who adhere to a strict writing regime feel more justified lecturing us with many rambling books about their miraculous methods? Maybe. The dictum "Write every day!" that stemmed from Boice's work has often led to a sense of guilt and failure in professors who were unable to stick to the strict schedules that they imposed on themselves (As Helen Sword put it, "Remorse and self-flagellation invariably followed"[3]). Our aim here is certainly not to add to the anguish of professors who never feel as if they're doing enough. They are already hearing this pernicious message in almost all aspects of academic life.

2. Boice, R. (1990). *Professors as Writers: A Self-Help Guide to Productive Writing.* Stillwater: New Forums Press Inc.; Boice, R. (1983). Experimental and clinical treatments of writing blocks. *Journal of Consulting and Clinical Psychology, 51*(2), 183–191. <https://doi.org/10.1037/0022-006X.51.2.183>; Boice, R. (1983). Contingency management in writing and the appearance of creative ideas: Implications for the treatment of writing blocks. *Behaviour Research and Therapy, 21*(5), 537–543. <https://doi.org/10.1016/0005-7967(83)90045-1>

3. H. Sword (2016). « Write every day ! » : A mantra dismantled. *International Journal for Academic Development, 21*(4), p. 313. <https://doi.org/10.1080/1360144X.2016.1210153>

> Indeed, Helen Sword challenged the absolute need to write every day. A professor of comparative literature who specializes in writing, including academic writing, she adopts a more flexible approach that highlights the diversity of writing methods. While acknowledging that there is a correlation between the frequency of writing sessions and productivity, she points out that this link is weak. The take-home message is that writing every day is probably neither necessary nor feasible for most university professors. Still, the fact remains that writing on a regular basis, whether that's every day or just recurrent blocks of protected time, has many advantages. It demystifies the writing process, keeps ideas in the forefront of your mind, stimulates creativity, and wards off the blank page syndrome. It was, after all, the strict scheduling, but not so strict following, of writing periods dedicated to this book that made it possible.

We aren't going to preach to you about the need to write every day, or even on a regular basis. Such a sermon would be hypocritical coming from two people whose writing habits are almost at the opposite ends of the spectrum when it comes to regularity. But it's important to remember that students are not used to scientific writing; they are still at the stage where they're learning how to improve these skills through practice. And for many students, the practice itself (i.e., the writing) is a source of anxiety. Too often, they respond to this anxiety by avoid its source, finding numerous excuses for why they can't start, some seeming legitimate (e.g., very long literature reviews, re-starting their statistical analyses over and over) and others flagrant procrastination (e.g., internet shopping). We'll discuss this further in Chapter 9. Encouraging students to adhere to a structure as they write, including blocking out regular dedicated writing time, will help them advance, and also help us to track their progress by revealing their strengths and pinpointing their weaknesses.

Ultimately, writing is a prerequisite for students to master their field of research, and not the other way around. A writing practice makes us focus our ideas and promotes learning. It implies thinking, extracting ideas from one's brain, shaping them, putting them into words, assessing which ones will stand up to scrutiny, and expressing them in a clear and precise manner. Transposing our reasoning into written words also helps us identify gaps, which become avenues of future readings. The dissertation itself is not the only outcome of doctoral studies. The scientific writing that goes into a dissertation is not a product *per se* but rather a skill, an ability that develops during studies and beyond.

THE PROJECT'S OBJECTIVES: WHY AM I DOING THIS?

Students get stuck and don't know what to write. But have they asked themselves why they are writing? And do you, as their advisor, know?

Writing is much easier when the objective of a text, an article, or a dissertation, and of each of its sub-components, is well thought out in advance. The objectives guide the writing of each section. In the introduction, the text is structured by choosing arguments that support the objectives—which means that yes, those great sections that were so fun to write but do not support the objectives will need to be cut out. As Stephen King[4] said, borrowing a phrase from others and making it his own: "Kill your darlings, kill your darlings, even when it breaks your egocentric little scribbler's heart, kill your darlings" (p. 222). Again, in the Methods, the objectives guide the writing, as we explain how these objectives were addressed. They give structure to the Results, since this is the section where the questions we asked get their answers. And they shape the Discussion, which, subject to a few differences depending on the research domain, usually begins with a reminder of the objectives, a summary of the findings addressing each one, how these findings fit into the existing literature, potential theoretical, practical, methodological or other implications of our interpretation, and future perspectives that will help formulate new objectives.

To guide students through this process, a first step is for them to write their objectives down. Of course, as the student progresses through their work, the initial objectives can (and should) be revised (many times!). This process of identifying and writing clear objectives from the start, and revisiting them on a regular basis, will provide a useful compass to guide the student and their advisor.

NO GOALS, NO DISSERTATION

In conclusion, keeping track of different goals is an important part of mentoring graduate students. As we've stated earlier, it isn't something that needs to be done rigidly, or should dominate every meeting with every student. Procrastinators might need more reminders of their time management goals, dreamers might need to be reminded to make their goals more specific, and some lost sheep might need to be nudged toward the core objectives of their project. But as a rule, a goal is more likely to be met if the advisor follows up about it on a regular basis.

4. King, S. (2000). *On Writing: A Memoir of the Craft.* New York: Scribner.

That's why, regardless of the advisor's supervising style or methods, it's essential to establish, re-visit, and discuss the student's progress with respect to their goals. Failing to meet goals can make students question their own abilities when in fact their goals were simply not realistic. It's the advisor's job to help students refine them, which can mean setting long-term goals, but also identifying the necessary steps to reach them, protecting their dedicated writing time, and understanding and integrating the objectives of the dissertation they are trying so desperately to write. Encouraging students to write on a regular basis, following specific and realistic objectives, will help them understand that writing is a skill that develops with practice, and will help them face the many challenges that writing brings.

CHAPTER 6
The propriety and improprieties of intellectual property

The capstone of graduate studies is the production of a thesis or dissertation, which is usually accompanied by an oral defense. This process results in a title being awarded to one person, and the author of the dissertation itself is usually one single author. By definition, a Ph.D. or doctorate is awarded in recognition of a unique contribution, be it a discovery, a novel interpretation or an original creation, by the awardee. In fact, the cover page of a dissertation usually bears a copyright symbol. So far, most of us would agree on these clear facts—but the path that leads to this magnum opus can wind through many grey areas in terms of intellectual property and copyright, since many people may have contributed directly or indirectly to the work over the (sometimes interminable) number of years involved. In some cases, the role of the graduate advisor can be particularly difficult to disentangle from that of the student. The student's dissertation is an achievement that marks their contribution and demonstrates their expertise; it also paves the way to future career opportunities. Let's examine this central principle, which should guide our actions in the increasingly collaborative world of research.

The authorship of a "traditional" dissertation, which consists of a series of chapters written solely by the student, none of which are published independently of the dissertation, is probably the simplest case and doesn't present many problems. This traditional model is more common in the arts and humanities, social sciences, and law, where there is less of a trend toward multiple authors contributing to one work. In fact, in these fields, the dissertation often leads to a book whose single author is the recently graduated student. Where things get murkier is when the dissertation is composed of a series of research articles, which have been published or submitted for publication independently and entail the participation and co-authorship of the advisor, other students, collaborators, and third parties with or without commercial interests. Such dissertations-by-articles are more frequent in natural sciences and engineering, or medical and health sciences, and can lead to tricky conflicts and sometimes questionable practices. The more authors there are on a publication, the more difficult it becomes to apportion their contributions fairly.

As well as the humans involved, external factors can also influence authorship. For instance, funding agencies or industries that support the work may have specific expectations, such as the professor or researcher who was awarded the funds being first author. If this is the case, it should be discussed in advance to avoid compromising the progress of the student's work, and to clearly define their involvement. Doing the equivalent of a first author's work only to be denied recognition is not only unfair, it can create roadblocks to the dissertation's progress.

Most universities and departments have clear rules governing how a dissertation is written, but major discrepancies exist across faculties and disciplines. A few years back, our Faculty of Graduate Studies revised their rules, surprising us and many of our colleagues in the process, as we discovered how publication culture differed across disciplines. The new—or perhaps, newly articulated—rule states that for dissertations-by-article that include submitted or published manuscripts, the manuscripts need to be written by the student, and they must be first author on all of them. This seemed obvious to many of us, but apparently this practice was not universal across departments (and still isn't across universities). Some faculties had been accepting dissertations containing manuscripts whose first author was the student's advisor, or another student, and for some, the order of authors for a manuscript was determined alphabetically. One of us has served on the jury for a dissertation that included an article in which the student was the 4th author. As a result of these variable practices, the question of "who does what" in a dissertation often remains murky. For authorship to be attributed fairly, issues around authorship should be discussed early on, and revisited periodically in light of what work was actually done.

SUPERVISING WRITING VERSUS REWRITING

How does one reconcile the role of advisor with the role of co-author? Some might wonder if professors who don't co-sign any work with their graduate students are really teaching them about research; however, it's possible that professors who don't co-sign work with their students are actually in a better position to teach them about writing and the research process in general because they aren't as directly involved with the end product (they remain supervisors but not co-authors). This distance is more natural when the subject of the dissertation doesn't overlap completely with the professor's expertise. As Umberto Eco[1] elegantly put it, supervising students on topics distinct from our own research is more honest and more generous. It ensures that expertise differs between master and pupil, a distance which also provides an opportunity for the professor to broaden their base of knowledge. The supervision is thus more likely to focus on the process, while making it less likely that the professor's suggestions will steer the manuscript towards something that reads like what they themselves would write. Authorship issues are also much easier to resolve.

When students work directly in the same specialized field as the professor, it may be more difficult to assess the overall quality of the student's work. If a professor rewrites every manuscript, how can they distinguish the best possible manuscript a student can write from the best manuscript they can write themselves? How can the professor evaluate the student's work (aside from thinking how marvellous it is—*But of course, I rewrote the whole thing!*)? Would such heavy involvement on the part of the mentor compromise the student's leadership (i.e., first-authorship) role? How can we train students to write without writing or rewriting each sentence ourselves? There is immense temptation to break this commandment (*Thou shalt not rewrite!*). Some of it is driven by the pressure of external considerations that range from a hoped-for promotion to an important grant, to the simplest one, lack of time. It takes less time for an experienced mentor to rewrite the faulty sentences than to identify what's wrong with a paragraph, return it to the student with suggestions how to improve it, let the student write it again, and review it a second (or third, or fourth) time. Publishing multiple articles with co-authors during a Ph.D. does provide important opportunities for collaborative training, but when the work depends on the professor's grants, and the results of the student's work will affect the advancement of the professor's career, it's understandable that many advisors face strong motivation and temptation to contribute more than their share to the student's dissertation. We need to remind ourselves that after graduation students should become experts in their own niche, and that their specialty should be at least partly distinct from ours. If we remember this objective, the distinction between our student's contribution and our own should be clearer.

1. Eco, U. (2018). *Comment écrire sa thèse.* Paris: Flammarion. [Original text: Eco, U. (1977). *Come Si Fa Una Tesi Di Laurea*, Milano, Bompiani].

AUTHORSHIP OF MANUSCRIPTS INCLUDED IN A DISSERTATION

Manuscripts with multiple authors are increasingly being included in dissertations. Having clarified which person should write the dissertation, how do we determine the role of other people who contributed to the work? How do we decide the order of authors in a multi-author manuscript? In some research domains, they are listed in order of decreasing contribution, while others ascribe great importance to the first and last authors. Some fields follow an unwritten convention that the Principal Investigator who supervised the student and whose funding made the work possible goes last, while co-advisors are second to last, etc. Others simply proceed by alphabetic order (e.g., Mathematics[2]). Incidentally, alphabetical order was the means by which one of the authors of this book got her first undergraduate poster as first author. This was also before the current trend to share first authorship between several people. And no, the alphabet is not how authorship order for this book was determined!

Some fields offer guidelines and definitions of who may be considered an author or contributor. For instance, the International Committee of Medical Journal Editors (ICMJE[3]) recommends four criteria, also called the Vancouver Criteria. These are: contributing to "the conception or design of the work, or the acquisition, analysis or interpretation of data," participating in drafting or revising the manuscript, approving the final version, and—perhaps often neglected—accepting accountability for the entire work. Such guidelines are important to standardize the contributions of authors of manuscripts, and similar guidelines should be enforced consistently across journals and research domains. However, they underline the need to carefully assess the insertion of articles in a dissertation, as articles with multiple authors are by definition the product of many people's combined effort. This raises the problem discussed above, that the work presented in a dissertation can stem from the efforts of many people, including many students. Determining an equitable author order in such cases becomes crucial. For instance, when students are first author of manuscripts that come out of their doctoral work, it is a clear indicator that they led the work and that these manuscripts can be considered part of their dissertation.

As the average number of authors per article has more than tripled in less than 50 years from fewer than two to almost six according to

---

2. American Mathematical Society (2015). *The Culture of Research and Scholarship in Mathematics: Joint Research and its Publication.* <https://www.ams.org/profession/leaders/culture/JointResearchandItsPublicationfinal.pdf>
3. The Website: <www.icmje.org>

MEDLINE/PubMed,[4] such considerations become increasingly important (though not according to everyone; see an argument against the value of author's position in collaborative work[5]). This collaborative tendency also leads to situations that highlight the limits of current authorship practices, such as a paper with 5,154 authors.[6] The value of an individual's "contribution" should, in theory, decrease as the overall number of authors increases, and it becomes difficult to weigh the relative value of an author's position unless they are among first few, or the very last. Perhaps this is the point of collaborative work, and in such cases reverting to alphabetical order would make sense.

Another phenomenon that appeared in recent years, likely related to the increase in number of contributors as well as the pressure to "publish or perish," is sharing first authorship between two or more people. While this can be indicated with an asterisk and relevant explanation (ideally, something more informative than "these authors contributed equally to this publication"), it poses yet another problem for including an article with multiple first authors in a dissertation. If there are multiple student first authors, in whose dissertation does the article belong? Should a manuscript with three people sharing first authorship be included in the dissertation of all three? What if there are four, or nine (yes, it's possible to have more than nine first authors)? If work is shared between more than one dissertation, will we end up seeing collaborative dissertations in the near future? This trend towards collaborative work in science plainly comes with a problem of blurring the boundaries between each author's contribution (but see[7] about "team-ness"). The push towards open science and collaborative work is noble, but as long as there is a need to attribute work to specific people (such as for a dissertation), we need a way to measure contributions. A not so fun fact, which anticipates the theme of Chapter 10:

---

4. National Library of Medicine. (2023). Number of authors per MEDLINE®/PubMed® citation. *PubMed.gov*. <https://www.nlm.nih.gov/bsd/authors1.html>
5. Kiser, G.L. (2018). No more first authors, no more last authors. *Nature, 561*(435). <https://doi.org/10.1038/d41586-018-06779-2>
6. Castelvecchi, D. (2015). Physics paper sets record with more than 5,000 authors. *Nature*. <https://doi.org/10.1038/nature.2015.17567>; Aad, G., et al. (ATLAS Collaboration, CMS Collaboration). (2015). Combined measurement of the Higgs boson mass in *pp* collisions at $\sqrt{s} = 7$ and 8 TeV with the ATLAS and CMS Experiments. *Physical Review Letters, 114*(19), 191803. <https://doi.org/10.1103/PhysRevLett.114.191803>.
7. Kiser, G.L. (2018). No more first authors, no more last authors. *Nature, 561*(435). <https://doi.org/10.1038/d41586-018-06779-2>; Sauermann, H., & Haeussler, C. (2017). Authorship and contribution disclosures. *Science Advances, 3*, e1700404. <https://www.science.org/doi/10.1126/sciadv.1700404>

some studies have shown that when a woman and a man share first authorship, the man's name is more frequently put first.[8]

BEYOND THE DISSERTATION

The dissertation isn't the only document during graduate studies in which writing skills are developed and put to good use. We want students to engage in different opportunities. For instance, professors often receive invitations for book chapters and review articles, and they can invite students to collaborate. Professors can also cultivate collaborations with other teams that lead to publications. These examples, which can fall outside the "protected zone" of the student dissertation, also need to be discussed early and explicitly (e.g., through the collaborative agreement), and revisited frequently. Such extra work should benefit the student, and should generally not compromise progress on the dissertation. The involvement of other people, other research teams or third parties such as industry or non-profit and government entities that have their own relationship to the professor can create additional challenges for graduate students. These third parties may have specific expectations that range from wanting to publish very rapidly at the expense of thoroughness, to putting embargoes on publication to avoid competition in developing products or methods. The involvement of a third party also implies another set of expectations in terms of legal considerations that can further delay publication. Any intellectual property contracts must consider the needs of the students involved in such projects in terms of their productivity. Note that conditions such as embargoes are becoming more and more untenable in projects that receive funding from government agencies, which have an increasing number of rules about access to data, and publication within a reasonable time after completion of a study.

Rather than trying to give in-depth coverage of every possible case of problematic authorship, we've chosen a few examples inspired by our own experiences and those of our colleagues, to illustrate how such issues can be addressed and sometimes resolved for the better.

---

8. Tscharntke, T., Hochberg, M.E., Rand, T.A., Resh, V.H., & Krauss, J. (2007). Author sequence and credit for contributions in multiauthored publications. *PLoS Biology, 5*(1): e18; Fishman, M., Williams 2nd, W. A., Goodman, D.M., & Ross, L.F. (2017). Gender differences in the authorship of original research in pediatric journals, 2001-2016. *The Journal of Pediatrics, 191*, 244–249. <https://doi.org/10.1016/j.jpeds.2017.08.044>

CASE 1: WHEN YOUR STUDENTS ARE GO-GETTERS

Can a student write a paper with other researchers that does not include their advisor(s)? We have experienced several variations on this situation that differed in terms of how the event was perceived and felt. One important factor influencing how the event was looked at was the stage of the professor's career. The confidence one gains as one advances, the success of achieving tenure, and to put it bluntly, a person's maturity, all impact how we perceive and interpret the fact that one of "our" students is writing with someone else. Reactions can range from betrayal to pride.

Early in their career, one advisor was asked by two ambitious students if the advisor could give them feedback on a manuscript they'd written together and were about to submit. The advisor's first reaction was, "Uh, WHAT? A paper from my lab without me?!" They soon realized that the students had written a review paper for a section of a journal dedicated to students. So, all was well, the advisor gave them feedback, including praise for their initiative and hard work, the manuscript was submitted, and eventually published. Would the advisor's reaction be different if the students had written a review to submit to the standard track of a journal? Possibly. An experimental paper that used the resources and expertise of the lab? Almost certainly. Thinking about that experience made us realize the challenges trainees face building their self-confidence as they steer a course between establishing some level of independence and continuing to ask for mentorship. As mentors, we need to move past our preoccupations and doubts about our career progression and dedicate time to helping students build their confidence as well. In this case, the students' publication was generally a positive experience for everyone, except perhaps for that two minutes of shock ("My students have betrayed me!"), which could have been avoided if the ambitious students had openly discussed their project from the start. But then again, we suspect that developing autonomy, including their own ideas and initiative, was part of their goal, and they wanted to surprise their advisor with what they considered a near final version of the manuscript.

CASE 2: ONE STUDENT TWO PROFESSORS: THE STORY OF A CO-SUPERVISION

Co-supervision of graduate students offers many advantages but also brings extra challenges. Double the expertise, double the feedback for graduate students, but double the intricacies of determining authorship.

This is the story of one advisor who agreed to co-supervise a bright student with a colleague from another department. The dissertation topic fell exactly where the expertise of the two advisors intersected. However, the co-advisor from the other department was also supervising a productive post-doc at the same time. The post-doc involved the student in many projects, to the point where the grad student ended up as the lead on a paper that was outside their main focus. The line of research was relevant to the student's training, but it wasn't part of the dissertation, so the main advisor wasn't involved. Naively, or as a mark of trust, the grad student asked this advisor to give feedback on the manuscript. This situation raised several questions. The first one was, should this advisor have also been co-author on this work? ("Hello, I'm here, I know this stuff!"). Perhaps not at the stage where the advisor found out about it, because simple revision of a manuscript does not necessarily (and indeed, rarely does) justify authorship. But then, shouldn't the advisor have been informed? Were they right to feel upset when they heard about the existence of this work? Perhaps if they'd known earlier, it would have helped explain why the student wasn't always fully dedicated to their dissertation, or perhaps it would have allowed the advisor to contribute more from the start?

Fortunately, things were progressing smoothly with the student's dissertation, and since the relationship with the co-advisor was excellent, the situation ended on a positive note (for the student, the publication of a paper without their advisor even helped demonstrate their independence). But questions remain, and one can easily imagine how things could have turned sour under other circumstances. What if the dissertation hadn't been progressing well? What if the advisor hadn't heard about this work until after the paper was published? Thanks to the student's productivity and brilliance, the same situation occurred in reverse a few years later. The student led a project with other students from the main advisor's group, yielding another publication outside of the student's dissertation. Was the co-advisor included as author of this publication? No. Should they have been? Perhaps. Here too, the co-advisor could have been involved from the start, but since the previous publication had unfolded without any snags, this one simply followed the same path with the roles reversed, as part of a well-balanced shared supervision from two competitive and productive professors. Nevertheless, we see more clearly in retrospect how such situations lead to conflict, and we encourage students to be open and transparent about work outside their dissertation. Of course we'll support it... provided we're included as co-authors!

Just kidding. The correct response is, provided the dissertation is progressing well.

CASE 3: THE GRAD STUDENT WHO BECAME A POST-DOC WHO BECAME A COMPETITOR

The transition from graduate studies to post-doctoral status seems to change some rules around collaborative work. Practices vary across research domains, but generally post-docs acquire more independence and can benefit from many new opportunities after graduation. The level of interaction between a post-doctoral fellow and their former doctoral supervisor is varied, and it can even be severed entirely by one or the other party. The arrival on the scene of a new supervisor (the post-doc supervisor) can also add complications and grey areas in terms of collaboration. When the student's research focus changes between the dissertation and the post-doc, the situation is usually easier, and post-docs have no trouble separating themselves from their advisor's field in the expected way. This was the case for both of us as graduate students. This transition allowed us to finish the work we started during the dissertation independently from the work we started as a post-doc, and each supervisor's involvement could be limited to their respective area. We consider it a good idea to instill this leadership very early on by encouraging students to develop their own expertise, a process which they can pursue after graduation. There are exceptions to this, when students work on projects from a grant proposal that pre-dates their arrival in the lab, and is central to the lab's long-term work over many years. A dissertation based on such a grant can still turn out very well if the students can make the topic their own and even push the work further than was originally envisaged. Some students in this situation have pursued careers in research management, while others join labs that focus on a population different from the original lab's main research interest. A happy ending for everyone. But then the publication of a single article can shatter this happy picture...

A former student of one of our colleagues had written a theoretical paper that the advisor wished they had written themselves. Worse, the student wrote this article with people from their new lab and other collaborators, on the topic of their former advisor's lab (which was different from the focus of their post-doc). The former advisor (the one who supervised the Ph.D.) could tell that some of their current students were perplexed by this situation. One student saw this paper first, and brought it up at in a meeting, probably waiting to see the advisor's reaction. The advisor was truly happy to see their former student making their way and being successful, but they were perhaps slightly disappointed (actually, they were quite upset) that the former student had chosen not to mention that they were writing a paper on a topic that not only interested the advisor, but was related the grant that had supported the student's Ph.D. work. This silence from the former student may have suggested that they weren't sure how to broach the subject, and were worried about the advisor's reaction, or that their current post-doc advisor had told them not to include the former advisor. Alternatively, the student might have decided not to include them as a statement of their independence. All's well that ends well, and in this specific case, it didn't lead to a major problem, nor did it cause a breach between the student and their former advisor, mainly because the latter, with their well-established lab, didn't let themselves feel threatened by this potential sign of competition. Had the advisor been earlier in their career, they might have felt differently. It can be a humbling experience to remind ourselves that students can and will outgrow us, and that their doing so was the goal of our work.

CASE 4: GIVING A TALK ABOUT A STUDENT'S WORK

Let's switch perspectives now. During our graduate studies, how did we feel when our advisor presented the findings of our graduate work at conferences? The first few times, we were incredulous at being noticed, proud perhaps to have generated something worth presenting, then grateful to have the opportunity to work with someone who offered visibility to our research; but with time we grew perplexed as to why we couldn't present the work ourselves, and finally angry that our advisor was taking all the credit. We've all heard (and possibly given) talks where the presenter uses photos of their students to identify who did the actual work. Many people do this, but not all. Reminding ourselves of each person's contribution to research is essential to be able to assign proper credit and, in the case of graduate students, it is the mentor's responsibility to see that proper credit is given. Better yet, the mentor has a responsibility to discuss these issues with students and to provide opportunities for them to take an active role in going out and presenting their own work.

One of our colleagues had an experience as a student where a situation regarding authorship became tense. So tense, in fact, that it led to an unusually heated argument with the director of a research centre. Here's what happened in a nutshell. One day, this student was looking for their co-advisor at the research centre and was told by staff that they were giving a talk to clinicians in the same building. The talk was on the topic of the student's dissertation. Actually, their topic wasn't 100% of the talk, but it included themes and data from the student's work. The student flipped out right there on the spot, thinking their work was being presented without their knowledge at an informal internal meeting. The student quickly sought the opinion of their main advisor, who immediately supported their interpretation that an injustice was underway. The student then stormed into the office of the director of the research centre to complain, and a heated discussion ensued. Heated because the student was already worked up, and because the director of the centre was firmly defending the co-advisor's perspective. The student's big mistake was in not having talked to the co-advisor first. By talking, they would have had the opportunity to learn that the talk included other subjects than the student's work, and could have calmly expressed that they themselves were available and eager to present their work whenever possible. They could have received assurance that their work and contribution were indeed acknowledged during the talk. On the co-advisor's side of things, discussing the talk with the student beforehand could have opened up a conversation about contributions and the grey areas between the two lab research programs and how the student contributed to each. But the frustration of being available, in the same building even, and yet not asked to present their own work! Here again the co-advisor could have helped them understand that giving a talk to non-researchers is a different skill involving the ability to adapt the level of language and explain results differently, something grad students don't necessarily possess early in their studies. In this case, inviting the student's participation would have provided an opportunity for them to learn such skills. In the end, a simple conversation (ideally before, but even after the presentation) would have defused most of the tension and allowed the student and co-advisor to gain a better understanding of each other's expectations.

We would be surprised (to put it mildly) to learn that a student had presented the findings of their research at an international conference without telling us, and without acknowledging our contribution. Most of us would deem such behaviour unacceptable. But all of us share the responsibility for discussing varied levels of contribution. As advisors with greater experience, we have the greater responsibility for guiding discussions around these issues and reaching consensus between everyone involved.

CASE 5: A STUDENT'S QUESTION THAT STILL RESONATES

One day, a student asked their advisor the following simple question: "What is *your* project?" The student knew that the advisor was involved in the projects of all the students in the lab, but what they meant was, "What do you work on that isn't a student project?" The advisor's initial response was that they were very busy and satisfied with the supervision of student projects, that they spent most of their time securing grants for these projects and the lab as a whole and overseeing the different steps of such projects. Their research program was essentially the sum of their students' projects, and there were no "secret projects" that students were unaware of. At that time, the advisor looked on their students' projects as being their own and they couldn't imagine conducting their own studies without involving students or post-docs. The normal progression was that once a project was begun, their trainees would gradually acquire enough experience to assume a leadership role. The advisor never pursued projects that involved data collection and experiments on their own behalf. Indeed, one reason the advisor didn't undertake such projects was that they felt that students might perceive a disparity between the priority the advisor set on their own projects versus the students' (a sentiment that we've noticed among students from other labs, and even felt ourselves as graduate students). Also, at that time, the advisor had no exciting parallel projects (like writing a book with a friend!). This simple and valid question from a first-year graduate student still echoes in the author's head as they ponder how to the balance their level of involvement in student projects. Again, quite recently, when they were preparing a calendar for a weekly journal club, one student asked, "Can you schedule one period for yourself? We all want to hear what you're working on." That made the author smile, and brought back the memory of the first student's question. It also made the author realize the importance of pursuing individual projects—without, of course, neglecting those of our students! As we encourage our students to take ownership of their projects and become increasingly independent, we risk feeling that when students graduate, they are taking part of our expertise away with them. The truth should be that they leave with their own expertise, that we helped them develop.

THEIR DISSERTATION, THEIR CONTRIBUTION, THEIR PRECIOUS

This chapter, with its different cases studies, illustrates the importance of differentiating between the advisor's expertise and that of the student. If the student is a clone of their advisor, such that one can easily substitute for the other, not only does this lead to thorny, complex situations, but it fails to achieve the "prime directive" of doctoral studies, which is the original contribution. If the student gradually becomes an expert in their field, then opportunities to give talks, review papers, organize symposiums, etc., will also gradually come, and the advisor should accompany the student in this process, not compete with them. Competition will come soon enough, and bring with it the emotionally-charged issues of authorship and contributions. As a supervisor, you will be called on to tackle these challenging issues, so test your understanding of them in Box 6.1! Better be prepared when these delicate situations arise, and remember: discuss early, discuss often.

BOX 6.1—CONTRIBUTION QUIZ

Q1: How do we measure a research contribution ?

a) A contribution is measured in terms of time

b) A contribution is measured in terms of money

c) A contribution is measured in terms of intellectual content

d) A contribution cannot be measured, so why bother

Q2: True or false: The advisor's name must appear on all scientific output of a student for as long as the student remains in the advisor's lab.

a) True. We pay for everything

b) True. We have all the great ideas

c) True. We're the boss, and we say so

d) False

Q3: True or false: Someone who collected all the data of a study will necessarily be co-author of the paper.

a) True. Do you know how many hours it took to train those rats?!

b) False, if the person was paid (no double dipping!)

c) True. No data, no paper

d) False, if the contribution was limited to the data collection part

Q4: When should we discuss authorship order?

a) Before writing starts

b) Before the study starts

c) No discussion needed, the first author decides

d) No discussion needed, the Principal Investigator decides

e) Before submitting a manuscript for review

f) Before submitting the proofs

Q5: To which students should we dedicate more time?

a) We should dedicate an equal amount of time to each student

b) Those who have the best skills

c) Those who show more potential

d) Those who follow in our footsteps

e) Those who are struggling the most

f) Those who show the most independence

g) Those who listen, watch and learn

Responses to the quiz

Q1: (c) A contribution is measured in terms of intellectual content. Which does raise the question, "What is an intellectual content?" Which makes response (d) tempting, but we should not give in to the dark side…

Q2: (d) False. The advisor must contribute to the work in order to be co-author. Students may produce work that is not directly related to their dissertation nor the focus of their supervisor's research. But we do encourage all parties to talk about such projects *before* embarking on them.

Q3: (e) False, if the contribution is limited to the data collection part. According to the ICMJE, a contribution should also involve writing, approving the final version, and accountability.

Q4: (b) At the latest, and even before if necessary. This doesn't mean that authorship order will be fixed until publication; rather, it should be discussed periodically.

Q5: Although we can rule out some answers, such as (d), this question is one we are still trying to figure out…

CHAPTER 7
It takes two to tango

At the heart of every mentoring task that leads to a completed dissertation, lies a relationship between two people: the graduate advisor and the student. Unlike the students whom we teach for only one class per week, the relationship we develop with graduate students on our team is more sustained, unique, and important. It is significant, not only as teachers and students, but as human beings. Indeed, a strong relationship can contribute to reducing dropout rates, while a poor one can lead to all sorts of difficult situations that will impede the dissertation's progress. For now, let's examine the positive angle, and leave mentorship's "dark side of the Force" for the next chapter.

The self-determined motivation necessary to complete a dissertation depends on satisfying three psychological needs.[1] To stay motivated during writing, students must satisfy their needs for autonomy, competence, and relatedness. Autonomy comes out of a solid relationship with the advisor based on trust and collaboration; this relationship is made possible by the presence, openness, availability, and flexibility of the advisor. Autonomy does not imply leaving the student to their own devices. Instead, the role of the advisor is comparable to the role of a coach in a marathon. The coach cannot run for the athlete, but they can accompany them throughout the many necessary steps to prepare them to reach their goals (and when the athlete wins, it's thanks to their skills, but when they don't, we blame the coach, right?). In order to foster competence, the advisor can create a stimulating environment where students can interact regularly with the advisor and with each other, throughout the different stages of their training, and depending on their level of experience and ability. Finally, relatedness refers to the quality of the relationships, but also to the sense of belonging to a community, like a research team, a research centre,

1. Litalien, D., & Guay, F. (2015). Dropout intentions in PhD studies: A comprehensive model based on interpersonal relationships and motivational resources. *Contemporary Educational Psychology, 41*, 218-231. <http://hdl.handle.net/20.500.11794/13745>

a professional association, etc. The advisor is often the central element around which the members of a team revolve; through their words and behaviour, advisors can influence the quality and degree of connectedness between people.

The dissertation advisor obviously plays a key role in helping students navigate the many questions that arise during the writing of a dissertation, and they can strengthen, or sometimes unwittingly undermine, students' motivation to carry on their studies.[2] However, the relationship with the advisor can itself become a source of anxiety,[3] especially when students perceive ambiguous expectations from their advisor.[4] Interpersonal conflicts with the dissertation advisor are often cited as a factor that can increase stress and distress,[5] and are one reason why graduate students drop out.[6] Thus, it would not be possible to write a book about how to increase a graduate student's productivity without addressing this relationship, and the advisor's responsibility to ensure that it remains a good one.

NOT MY FAULT!

Before exploring this subject, we would like to make a somewhat obvious point about relationships: there are always at least two people involved. As any good couples therapist will tell you, interpersonal conflict always emerges from the interaction between two people. That means that even when one person is clearly out of line, no conflict exists until the other person responds. No interaction, no conflict. Note that a response need not be verbal: rolling eyes or a pointed silence is also a response. In fact, the absence of response can be the most telling, the kind that only intensifies

2. Fernando, D. M., & Hulse-Killacky, D. (2005). The relationship of supervisory styles to satisfaction with supervision and the perceived self-efficacy of master's-level counseling students. *Counselor Education and Supervision, 44*(4), 293-304.
3. Grady, R.K., La Touche, R., Oslawski-Lopez, J., Powers, A., & Simacek, K. (2013). Betwixt and between the social position and stress experiences of graduate students. *Teaching Sociology, 42*(1), 5-16. <doi:10.1177/0092055X13502182>
4. Golde, C.M. (2005). The role of the department and discipline in doctoral student attrition: Lessons from four departments. *The Journal of Higher Education, 76*(6), 669-700. <doi:10.1353/jhe.2005.0039>
5. Gunnarsson, R., Jonasson, G., & Billhult, A. (2013). The experience of disagreement between students and supervisors in PhD education: a qualitative study. *BMC Medical Education, 13,* 134. <doi:10.1186/1472-6920-13-134>
6. Golde, C.M. (2005). The role of the department and discipline in doctoral student attrition: Lessons from four departments. *The Journal of Higher Education, 76*(6), 669-700. <doi:10.1353/jhe.2005.0039>

the conflict (e.g., a professor who fails to respond to a student who asks to meet them).

Thus, as advisors we always play a role in initiating, prolonging, and resolving conflict in the mentoring relationship. Moreover, because we are in a position of authority in the relationship, the responsibility to initiate a resolution to the conflict is ours. This doesn't mean that the entire responsibility for resolving conflict falls on our shoulders, but that the advisor needs to take the first steps and remain open to different solutions. As our job is to make students learn, and because this learning process is facilitated by a positive relationship with the advisor, maintaining these good relations is part of our job description.

WORKING ALLIANCE: DON'T BE THE ADVISOR WHO TERRORIZES THEIR STUDENTS

Let's say first of all that in any long-term relationship, it's inevitable that some form of conflict will occur at some point. This isn't pessimism speaking: in such a long-term relationship, based around a task as complex as writing a dissertation, and between two human beings, we must expect some bumps along the way. Sometimes, a student's anxiety will impact their capacity to complete tasks or even talk to us. In other cases, interactions with students will be unpleasant because they are trying to test our limits. After all, we are the model that they're trying to improve upon, the authority figure that they measure themselves against: shouldn't the student try to surpass their master? But though we would like to see them try to best us in terms of actual academic performance (i.e., a student fired up and ready for action), we sometimes find they put their efforts into trying to prove that we're wrong, or at least not fully right, whether in our approach to research or to life (e.g., "I will succeed without making all those sacrifices!"). Sometimes we'll disagree on specific objectives and tasks, other times we'll get on each other's nerves on a day when nothing seems to go as planned.

The first lesson is thus to adopt an open attitude towards conflicts in general. Conflicts are not human rights violations that need to be addressed with anger and aggression, nor avoided like catastrophes, nor politely ignored like food stuck between the teeth of the person we're talking to. Just as being out in nature entails encountering some bugs, there is no use in getting mad about them, and they aren't usually dangerous. And depending on the situation and type of insects, ignoring them will not necessarily reduce the number of bug bites, nor the itching afterward. We are using "conflict" to refer to all types of tensions and misunderstandings, of various intensity and duration, that can compromise or even threaten the collaboration between a student and their advisor. Conflicts during graduate supervision can take many forms, from a simple disagreement to a recurring power struggle (i.e., from a single mosquito to a swarm of wasps). They grow out of misunderstandings, misreadings, awkwardness, and disagreements, and may or may not be either deliberate or conscious.

Some authors use the term "alliance ruptures" to identify these moments of tension and conflict in collaborations or during communication.[7] A working alliance, within the graduate supervision context, can be broken down into three parts: the agreement between the student and the advisor on the objectives, their agreement about the tasks that need to be undertaken to meet those objectives, and the positive bond between the student and the advisor.[8] The fit between the expectations and the objectives of the two people involved in this type of relationship are more important than what the individual expectations actually are (see Chapter 3). The greater the gap between expectations, the more effort will be necessary to build and repair the alliance.

A working alliance is a dynamic process founded on perpetual cycles of construction and repair. Active listening, empathy and positive regard are necessary to build and maintain a good working alliance. Active listening is harder than it seems. We hear a lot of sounds and words each day, but we aren't always listening (as our spouses like to remind us). Even when we deliberately put more effort into the act of listening, the level and quality of this listening varies. Sometimes, we're listening for what we want to hear, meaning we sift through the information until we hear what we're waiting for and then instantly seize this topic to wrench the conversation in our direction. Other times, we listen in order to assess, not for understanding but to judge the content of what's being said. We listen while scanning for moments when we can jump in and make a correction. We also judge whether the conversation is pleasant or not, accurate or not, etc. The most effective active listening, and that which requires the most effort, is when we deliberately put our own objectives and thoughts aside, and try to understand exactly, through verbal and non-verbal cues, what the other person is thinking and feeling. No, this is not easy. And yes, it takes time.

---

7. Safran, J.D., Muran, J.C., Stevens, C., & Rothman, M. (2008). A relational approach to supervision: Addressing ruptures in the alliance. In Falender, C.A., & Shafranske, E.P. (eds.), *Casebook for Clinical Supervision: A Competency-Based Approach* (pp. 137–157). Washington, DC: American Psychological Association.
8. Bordin, E.S. (1983). Supervision in counseling II. Contemporary models of supervision: A working alliance based model of supervision. *The Counseling Psychologist, 11*(1), 35–42. <https://doi.org/10.1177/0011000083111007>

But when facing threats to the alliance, it's only through such listening that it becomes possible to truly understand the student's situation and be in tune with them.

Sometimes, we need to let go of our own perspective to understand the other. This letting go of one's perspective to understand the other is an important part of empathy. It involves putting ourselves in the other person's shoes and trying to understand their situation and the impact our words and attitude can have on them, considering their context and how they see things in order to get a broader understanding of their experience. One way is to recall how we interacted with our own dissertation advisor, while keeping in mind that our current student probably differs from us in any number of ways, just as we almost certainly differ from our advisor. Still, our past experiences can point to key areas where a student and an advisor may be out of synch, in terms of generation, culture, and other aspects, that are easy to forget but can have an impact on the working alliance ("My child, in the good old days, we had no internet"; "Gramps, in the good old days, you acted as if you lived in a world without consequences").

Finally, a good working alliance cannot be built without positive regard towards the students. In other words, we need to like advising students, we need to like the students (though not too much, obviously, as we'll see in coming chapters). It seems likely that your student admires you or they wouldn't have chosen you as their advisor, but do you appreciate them? We need to like teaching, sharing knowledge, accompanying these students through their intellectual and personal development, even with their naivety and arrogance (after all, we were the same in our day!). We need to believe in their potential, find their strengths, nourish their talents, and improve their skills. We need to feed their motivation. Asking them to work hard and put in more effort is not enough, we also need to maintain their interest and fuel their passion. Our goal should be that they will leave each meeting more motivated than they were at the beginning.

Even with all these noble intentions, there will come a time when the alliance will fracture. These instances can be obvious, such as when voices are raised and tempers flare. But they can also be more subtle. The first alliance ruptures can seem as minor and insignificant as a brief puzzled look on a student's face, after which they appear more withdrawn and sullen. We can see that something has been left unsaid. Students aren't always comfortable voicing their frustrations and disagreement to their advisor, so signs that the collaboration is becoming less productive will often be conveyed non-verbally. We might feel that the atmosphere of a meeting suddenly changes, that it's more distant, less cordial. Or the student is less engaged with the task at hand. They might talk less, nod at everything even if we feel they don't agree. We find ourselves feeling suddenly tired, tense, and ill at ease. Our first reflex will often be to continue as if nothing was wrong and to wait for the moment to pass. In some cases, if everyone is just having a bad day, this might be the best course of action, giving everyone a break in order to start fresh the next day. However, many researchers tell us, and the data supports what many of us have experienced: when an alliance ruptures, ignoring it won't make it heal on its own. Pretending everything's okay or sweeping bad feelings under the rug will not lead to a happy ending. On the contrary, this perceived carelessness may brew other conflicts that, if they are also ignored, could spiral indefinitely. Much like rust, such problems tend to spread and have a corrosive[9] effect on the supervision relationship.

MAINTAINING THE PROPER DISTANCE

One of the greatest challenges of building and maintaining a good working alliance with students is to find the appropriate distance. The complexity of the task stems from the complexity of the relationship. Indeed, when it comes to the student's dissertation, the advisor is not their boss, but they do wield a lot of authority. The advisor is not a course instructor, but they do teach and evaluate. The advisor is not a counselor, but they support the personal and professional growth of the student. The advisor is not a friend, even though they may play a significant role in the student's social network. Depending on experience, values, and personality traits, some advisors will maintain more distance, while some will be more friendly than others. We would like to point out that we should not oversimplify and think that the friendlier the advisor the better. Some very friendly people make horrible research advisors, and some strict and distant people make excellent advisors.

To illustrate the nuances of an advisor's approach to maintaining a healthy distance with students, we can imagine a target that has two axes: one axis represents the degree of distance, the other axis represents the positive or negative character of the relationship (see Figure 7.1). Too much distance can make the relationship cold to the point of losing the bond necessary to maintain the working alliance. From their pedestal, the advisor who stubbornly maintains a strict and rigid boundary between work and personal life can appear inaccessible or insensitive. The moderate advisors

9. Watkins Jr, C.E., Reyna, S.H., Ramos, M.J., & Hook, J.N. (2015). The ruptured advisory alliance and its repair: On advisor apology as a reparative intervention. *The Clinical Advisor, 34*(1), 98-114. <https://doi.org/10.1080/07325223.2015.1015194>

will remain flexible even when they are focused on specific tasks, and they will be exacting without criticizing. On the opposite side of this axis (toward the top), when there is not appropriate distance, boundaries might blur between dissertation-related tasks and the personal life of students or advisors. This can lead advisors onto dangerous ground where some behaviour can be inappropriate (see Chapter 8). The same goes for the character of the relationship: some advisors are strict, others softer. For lack of better words, we used the terms "negative" and "positive" (see the x-axis) but what is more important is that on this axis, the middle part is the target to aim for. A too-close relationship should be avoided, as should an abusive one. There is a danger zone where attitudes and behaviours are not bad in themselves but can increase the risk of problems. Thus, an advisor who is too friendly can cause as much damage as one who is short-tempered. And just because you're not warm or affectionate doesn't make you a bad person: it's okay to be collegial and focused on the task. Inversely, keeping tight control of your anger does not make you soft: you can still be firm and rigorous. It's all a question of good judgment. But problems can arise if we find ourselves flipping back and forth along these axes when we interact with different students, particularly if our attitude towards them changes according to aspects such as age, gender or any other individual characteristic.

FIGURE 7.1—Aiming for the right distance

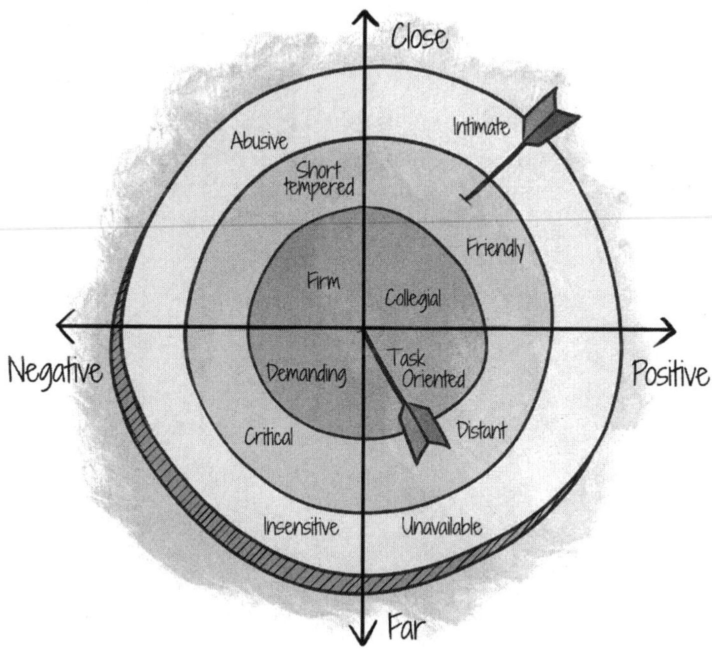

As too-close relationships are obviously off-limits, and since we put maternal and paternal relationships in this category, advisors who describe their labs as "one big family" scare us a bit. This may be because we sometimes have complex relationships with our own families (... but we'll discuss that in a future book, when we are through with our respective psychoanalysis). Comparing research teams with families is uncomfortable mostly because of the potential lack of professional boundaries that comes from thinking of ourselves as mother or father to our students. The uneasiness may also come from the gender roles associated with those labels (Dad decides everything, Mom forgives everything). We acknowledge that this family metaphor comes from the best intentions, from a desire to create strong positive bonds and a feeling of belonging among group members. However, neither of these extreme stereotypes (i.e., the authoritarian father figure and the overly indulgent mother figure) represent important or even desirable qualities in a research advisor. We have similar reservations towards labs that are built like a corporate hierarchy, with senior members supervising junior members, in which there are so many students that just meeting one's advisor becomes as daunting a task as getting an audience with the prime minister. These labs are often very productive and offer opportunities that are hard to find elsewhere (high impact publications; excellent networking), yet the distance between students (especially new students) and their advisor, and the rigid hierarchy, tends to colour all interactions with a flavour of "I had it tough, and so should you."

COMMUNICATION

The best tool to build and maintain a healthy student–advisor relationship is communication. Whether in written or oral form, communication is our means of defining the parameters of our relationship with students. Generally at work it's more professional and effective to have an assertive communication style. However, the very nature of the advisor's work will bring an extra layer of complexity, because we're often called on to give corrective feedback to students. Moreover, because the supervision relationship spans several years, there will be a need to discuss and adjust how we communicate with students, or they communicate with us. We might call this metacommunication.

The basics: being assertive

Mastering the basics of assertive communication gives us a tool that can prevent most conflicts. Basic elements of communication include expressing yourself clearly (i.e., conveying one message at a time), avoiding blame and offensive language, verifying that the other person has understood, listening carefully (i.e., paying attention to both verbal and non-verbal cues), and making sure you've understood by summarizing or reflecting the content of the message back to the other person. Assertive communication is the clear and authentic transmission of one's thoughts, and implies both self-respect and respect for the other. In their book *S'affirmer et communiquer* ("Asserting Yourself and Communicating"), Jean-Marie Boisvert and Madeleine Beaudry[10] distinguish assertive communication from passive, manipulative or aggressive behaviour. Communication is passive when we seemingly put aside our needs in favour of those of others. The putting aside of our needs is in appearance only; in fact, this form of communication is usually accompanied by complaints and passive-aggressive messages (e.g., the infamous "I'm not angry, I'm just disappointed"). Another form of non-assertive communication is manipulation, which seeks to exploit others and achieve one's ends by using false assertions, whether these are threats or flattery. Finally, too-assertive communication, where we put our own needs ahead of those of others, shades into aggression, which is the hostile expression of our needs in an attempt to subjugate another person.

Revisiting Boisvert and Beaudry's work with a view towards defining good communication skills in the advisor–student relationship calls to mind multiple examples of conflicts we have witnessed, directly or indirectly, that spiralled out of control in part because the advisor failed to use assertive communication. Like the advisor who left their student floating for a year and a half before complaining that the student wasn't meeting their expectations (passive communication), or the advisor who "forgot" to approve the final version of a dissertation until a specific task in the lab was completed (manipulative communication), or the advisor who yelled at a student and humiliated them in front of the rest of the team because of an ongoing disagreement (aggressive communication). Assertive communication in the context of graduate supervision balances the needs of the advisor and the student while taking into account the advisor's position of power within the relationship. Not all needs will be met; however, all needs can be voiced and acknowledged.

10. Boisvert, J.-M., & Beaudry, M. (2012). *S'affirmer et communiquer*. Montréal: Éditions de l'Homme.

Giving feedback

The specific context of the advisor–student relationship is supervision, implying that the advisor must give feedback to the student. They comment on the student's manuscripts (see Chapter 4), offer advice on their decisions, and guide their course of study and career choices. This adds another level to their communication. Most students both hope for and fear getting honest feedback from their advisors. Feedback should be given in such a way that students can make good use of it to improve their manuscripts, decisions, and trajectories. We need to pay attention not only to what feedback we give, but how we deliver it (see Box 7.1). To make matters even more complex, despite being masters in the art of feedback ourselves (obviously), not all students have developed the skill to receive and use feedback. This is therefore another skill that students sometimes need to be taught (see Box 7.2). It may be obvious to us that giving them feedback is part of our job, but it may not necessarily be obvious to them. Sometimes it can be helpful to articulate this clearly.

BOX 7.1—THE SANDWICH METHOD OF DELIVERING FEEDBACK

One technique for conveying more difficult comments is the sandwich method. This consists of placing a constructive comment between two positive ones. Positive feedback is important in its own right; too often we take it for granted and assume we don't need to talk about what's going well. However, students appreciate being told when they're doing something right. In addition, positive feedback helps to deliver more difficult messages. When giving feedback on written text, this can be as simple as giving overall positive impressions in an initial comment, marking the text itself with comments and suggestions (not too many, and chosen with sensitivity), and then ending with congratulations for all the work done. The sandwich method is also useful when you want to encourage a change in student's behaviour. In a conversation, it could sound like: "*I appreciate the time you spend in the lab helping others and sharing your experience. I would like you to find a way to set aside more time to write the general discussion of your dissertation; you seem to be pretty far behind. What do you think?* [...] *So, if we summarize, from now on, you will set aside two hours a day to work exclusively on your dissertation, and you'll be able to hand in something next week. That works for me. I'm glad we talked about this, and thank you for your openness.*" Here we illustrate how the advisor carefully validates the intention behind the behaviour they want to see be changed, and ensures the interaction ends on a positive note. However, the bulk of the discussion is still about the corrective feedback and the changes that need to be made.

BOX 7.2—TEACHING STUDENTS TO RECEIVE FEEDBACK

The transition to graduate studies involves a huge paradigm shift in terms of receiving feedback, and not all students find it easy to adjust to this change. Try to remember how it felt back in the classroom, when getting feedback—in the form of corrections and red ink on our assignments—was generally a bad sign. The more corrections there were in a text, the worse it was. On the contrary, work with almost no annotations was rewarded with an A. In graduate school, a complete U-turn takes place: from one day to the next, research projects, manuscript drafts, and sections of dissertations all come back dripping with red. On our computers, the Track Changes function means that revisions can be counted by the dozens, sometimes even the hundreds. This is normal for us who have been in this business for a long time; the peer review process always involves our manuscripts receiving suggestions, questions, and comments. Eventually, as an advisor or reviewer, having nothing to say starts to feel as if you're doing a bad job. But students entering grad school face a double shock; they are used to performing well in school, something that until now has manifested as very few corrections in their work, and they are highly sensitive to their advisor's good opinion. Feedback can thus provoke very negative knee-jerk reactions: my work is bad, my advisor hates me, I'm incompetent. Every student who moves on to higher education must learn to accept and use criticism to improve their work, without perceiving it as an attack on their self-worth. The speed of this learning, and how smoothly it goes, depends on the student. The advisor can play a role facilitating this learning process by explaining the peer review paradigm, by asking about the student's reactions to their comments, and by heading off at the pass reactions such as "my paper is bad," or "I'm terrible at this." A healthy discussion can make it explicit that the advisor's job is to give feedback, while recognizing that the student finds themselves in the bind of wanting and fearing feedback at the same time. The art of advising comes down to a balance between leaving room for the student to express their fears, and not giving in to them; we cannot stop giving feedback in order to minimize the student's discomfort. Instead, the advisor will want to help the student get used to their methods of giving feedback, interpret it accurately (e.g., pointing out a poorly written sentence doesn't mean the student has poor writing skills), and use their feedback in the most effective way possible to improve their skills and ultimately their self-sufficiency.

It is the students themselves who must develop the humility and self-reflection necessary to become independent researchers. While previous years of study may make graduate students experts at performing certain tasks, they are still beginners in terms of scientific thinking. They have new skills to acquire, and they must accept a certain level of discomfort inherent in the process of learning them. A good advisor can convey this message to the student without making them feel belittled or criticized. Humility is built on confidence, not on doubting our abilities.

If we consider how mentoring relationships evolve over time, tensions or conflicts related to feedback are almost inevitable. In the early stages of these relationships, students are very dependent on their advisors: they need their support to develop a working method, to guide them in the elaboration of their research topic, to transmit the knowledge and skills they will need to complete their dissertation, etc. By the end, however, students are expected to be independent, to defend their dissertation on their own, to make an innovative contribution to the field. To reach this point, it's natural that at some point between the beginning and the end they must detach themselves from their advisor. But this separation is not as neat as detaching the bottom part of a form where the dotted line is perforated. Rather, it is accomplished through trial and error, through sudden swerves between autonomy and dependence, and through both pride in demonstrating one's emerging competence, and frustration at displaying one's limitations. At some point, the student's desire for emancipation may outpace the skills they need to become independent. At other times, it may be the advisor who, consciously or unconsciously, resists being surpassed by the apprentice. We have sometimes observed that more experienced advisors tend to grant more independence to their students, to let them wander further from their own way of doing things, an attitude that seems less common earlier in a professor's career. There are several reasons this attitude might change: the experience of having supervised several different students, the relative importance of the student's contribution to one's own career path (e.g., promotion, publications, funding), and more. These dynamics will necessarily colour what feedback is given, and how, as well as the way the student receives and uses this feedback.

There are also personality differences, and we can readily understand that if two people aren't getting along well at the start, they will have still more difficulty down the road where one has to give feedback to the other. There is extensive literature in psychology on personality traits (e.g., extroverted, conscientious, open to new experiences), and in education on teaching and coaching styles (e.g., permissive, structured, Socratic). Personality types may indeed clash, but we believe that this is less important than putting effort into finding good ways to provide feedback, teaching students to receive feedback, and showing empathy toward the student. As long as the advisor is understanding, tries to minimize the negative impact of their comments, and can accept being questioned, the challenges caused by personality differences should not be harmful. On the contrary, they can enrich the relationship and the experience of both parties. Moreover, if adequate boundaries are maintained throughout the relationship, as discussed earlier in this chapter, personality differences should not have a major impact on the ability to carry out mentoring tasks. Indeed, if an advisor cares about their student's success, without letting this goal define their sense of self-worth or performance as a professor, and without expecting any personal gain from it, they will probably find it easier to tolerate and even take on board ways of perceiving, reacting and working that are different from their own.

The essence of an advisor's job is to give the best possible feedback to students. Many factors, such as how the principles of peer review are understood and implemented, the professional development stage of the student (and their advisor), the personality traits of both, and how this feedback is delivered, can add difficulty to this task and make it far from optimal. Not only is the inability to provide feedback very frustrating for both the advisor and the student, it is detrimental to the student's learning. When several attempts at giving feedback fail, the advisor may be tempted either to give up and let the chips fall where they may (thereby diminishing the quality of their teaching) or to assert their authority in a more uncompromising way (thereby jeopardising the quality of the relationship with the student). Both attitudes mean the student won't get the training they need. But before we reach that point, we suggest a tool for managing conflict in the advising relationship: metacommunication.

When you're stuck and everyone is frustrated, maybe it's time to get "meta"

Despite everyone's good will, there will be students with whom it is more difficult to communicate. And even when things generally go well with a given student, there will be the occasional rough patches.

As the quality of the mentoring relationship depends on the quality of communication, it can be useful to take some time to explore the ways in which we talk to each other. This is called metacommunication. In metacommunication, we put aside a particular topic (what we are talking about) in order to address the way the discussion is going (how we are talking about it). We initiate a metacommunication intervention to better understand each other and work together, never to police or dictate someone's (i.e., the student's) conduct, or to blame them. Thus, a good metacommunication intervention requires a voluntary effort to detach from one's own perspective and understand that of the student, in good faith and humility. Metacommunication can take a variety of forms, some of which are simply making explicit how you would like a conversation to go or soliciting the student's reaction to what you have just said.[11] Other metacommunication interventions have emerged from psychotherapy techniques[12] and have been adapted to the clinical supervision of psychology trainees.[13] Inspired by this process, we propose a sequence of steps for effectively implementing metacommunication in Table 7.1.

11. Baltzersen, R.K. (2013). The importance of metacommunication in supervision processes in higher education. *International Journal of Higher Education, 2*(2), 128-140.
12. Safran, J.D., & Muran, J.C. (2000). Resolving therapeutic alliance ruptures: Diversity and integration. *Journal of Clinical Psychology, 56*(2), 233-243. <https://doi.org/10.1002/(SICI)1097-4679(200002)56:2<233::AID-JCLP9>3.0.CO;2-3>
13. Safran, J.D., Muran, J.C., Stevens, C., & Rothman, M. (2008). A relational approach to supervision: Addressing ruptures in the alliance. In C.A.F.E.P. Shafranske (ed.), *Casebook for Clinical Supervision: A Competency-based Approach* (pp. 137-157). Washington, DC: American Psychological Association.

TABLE 7.1—Steps for metacommunication

IN "ONE" WORD	IN MANY WORDS	HOW TO SAY IT
1. Realising there is a problem	In order to initiate a metacommunication process, it is necessary to become aware that there is a problem. The first step is therefore to clearly identify the interaction or pattern of interactions that caused tension.	*I would like for us to go back to the interaction we had when we were discussing such and such a subject, is that OK with you?*
2. Disengaging from the problematic conversation and changing the subject	Metacommunication requires taking a step back, pausing the discussion in terms of content and clearly redirecting the discussion.	*I'm not happy with the way this conversation is going, and I get the impression that you're not either. What do you say we take a look together at what's going on? We can come back to the topic later.*
3. Acknowledging one's own contribution and exploring the student's perception	Obviously, such a break that highlights a problem could be worrisome or threatening to the student. To avoid a defensive reaction and keep the focus on solving the interpersonal communication problem, once the problem has been identified, it may be less threatening for the student to start by acknowledging one's own contribution and exploring the student's perception.	*I feel like I'm trying to convince you that I'm right, instead of helping you develop your own idea. Did you feel the same way?*
4. Remaining empathic	Showing empathy will also help to avoid taking a menacing, critical or moralistic stance. Remember that acknowledging and validating the student's perception and reactions is not the same as "being right". Regardless of who is "right", listening and striving to understand the other's perception helps to establish the collaboration and build the trust necessary to resolve the conflict and repair the alliance.	*Yes, I understand how frustrating it is that I am asking you to revise your text again. I can see how I might have given you the impression that I am slowing down your progress. How do you react in those instances?*

(following)

TABLE 7.1—Steps for metacommunication (*following*)

IN "ONE" WORD	IN MANY WORDS	HOW TO SAY IT
5. Helping students receive comments	Only by building on a positive relationship of trust and care can we really help students to interpret our comments differently and to see them more as learning opportunities rather than mere criticisms.	*What does it say about the way you react to these comments? Yes, of course it is frustrating to be corrected… But is it possible to perceive these comments differently?*
6. Finding a real motivation for the students' behaviour	Digging through our own experiences as students, we can often find good reasons to explain students' motivation for some behavior. Stating how we perceive this motivation can show our empathy for their situation while clarifying our intentions.	*When you commit to many activities other than your thesis, you want to develop your professional experience and build your C.V. I do not want to cut your momentum, on the contrary.*
7. Proposing change	After inquiring about the student's motivation, accepting their perception and their reactions, all with kindness and good will, it will be easier to directly address the behaviour that we would like them to change. Even then, suggestions formulated through Socratic questioning will be better received than affirmations.	*How much time have you actually spent on your thesis in the last month? If you continue at this pace, can you realistically meet your goals? What changes could you make? What obstacles could prevent you from making those changes?*
8. Remaining aware of students' avoidance	Let us remind ourselves that the ultimate objective is not only that the advisor is satisfied with the discussion. We want students to apply the feedback provided. To ensure this, we need to remain aware that students might try to avoid this type of discussion.	*I'm happy that you agree with me, but I can't stop thinking that you agree only to please me. Am I wrong? I would be even happier to know that you are at ease to express freely what you really think and that we can find a common ground.*

Let's examine how this recipe for metacommunication could help us untangle ineffective patterns in our relationships with our students. First, we present examples of typical problematic interactions in clinical supervision[14] which we've adapted to make them relevant to graduate supervision (Table 7.2). These relationship patterns are inspired by transactional analysis,[15] which postulates that in everyday communications there are verbal and non-verbal interactions that at first glance carry a legitimate purpose, but may also hide an ulterior motive of maximizing the gains and minimizing the losses of the person initiating the conversation. According to this theoretical framework, such interactions are called psychological games, where the overt message, called the social message, is different from the covert one, called the psychological message. For example, when we tear ourselves down in hope of attracting more praise from another person, or when we give our boss an exaggerated account of how tired and overworked we are in an effort to avoid receiving extra work, then consciously or not we are playing psychological games. Some games are quite benign (for instance, doing someone a favour in hopes that they will also help us out when we need it), others are more harmful (for instance, consciously manipulating someone to make them do what we want). Whether this theory applies to graduate supervision remains to be shown, but it's possible to recognize some of these stereotypical interactions between advisors and students, with either side as the instigator. Students may initiate such interactions with the aim of avoiding the advisor's criticism or reprimand (whether real or feared), or lowering the latter's expectations. Advisors may initiate such interactions in order to boost their feelings of importance, competence, and omnipotence, or to hide their incompetence (whether real or feared).

---

14. Kadushin, A. (1968). Games people play in supervision. *Social Work, 13*(3), 23-32; McIntosh, N., Dircks, A., Fitzpatrick, J., & Shuman, C. (2006). Games in clinical genetic counseling supervision. *Journal of Genetic Counseling, 15*(4), 225-243. <doi:10.1007/s10897-006-9029-4>
15. Berne, E. (1961). *Transactional Analysis in Psychotherapy: A Systematic Individual and Social Psychiatry.* New York: Grove Press.

TABLE 7.2—Some stereotypes of interactions in the supervision relationship

GAME NAME	GAME DESCRIPTION	MOTIVATORS	INTERVENTIONS BY THE INTERLOCUTOR THAT MAY PERPETUATE THE GAME
Student-initiated			
Poor little me!	Student offers poor self-assessment, downplays abilities, and promotes image of being less capable.	Decreases/avoids criticism and negative feedback, reduces workload/responsibilities, increases advisor support and encouragement.	Advisor reassures (*Of course not, I think you're good and competent!*) and postpones the more difficult feedback they had in mind.
I have a little list	Student begins an exhaustive self-assessment and list of questions, leaving no time for the advisor to give constructive criticism.	Controls the focus of feedback, presents themself as insightful and motivated.	Advisor answers all questions, becomes the first source of information consulted by the student, no longer takes the time to provide their own feedback.
I did like you told me	Student asks for specific prescriptions, which he applies superficially and robotically, without success.	Deviates the responsibility of the work to the advisor.	Advisor finds themself on the defensive, justifying their recommendations, giving even more details.
Evaluation is not for friends	Student makes efforts to develop a peer relationship with advisor.	Avoids negative feedback, reduces discomfort of being in an inferior position in the relationship.	Advisor follows into more personal territory and is uncomfortable coming back to the tasks at hand for fear of appearing cold and unsympathetic.
Be nice to me because I am nice to you	Student addresses advisor with deference and flattery.	Deflects the focus of the discussion, avoids negative feedback, reduces demands.	Advisor thanks the student, allows themself to discuss their own work.

My dog ate it	Student does not complete the agreed upon tasks, offers many excuses that put them in a favourable light to explain the situation.	Reduces risk of taking personal responsibility for unfinished work, avoids criticism.	By accepting the excuses, advisor avoids the unpleasant task of confronting the student, and is perceived as being understanding.
Advisor-initiated			
Pop quiz	Advisor interrogates and corrects student, gives them no time to research information before testing them on it.	Displays superiority, avoids having to answer the student's questions.	For fear of being caught out, student does not expand on answers, does not take chances, does not deepen their thinking.
Make this other little change	Advisor gives a lot of "picky" or unsubstantial feedback.	Exerts control over student, appears demanding and professional.	Student becomes more perfectionist and anxious when writing, begins to procrastinate more, and the quality of their work suffers.
One good question deserves another!	Advisor systematically responds to each question with another question, asking the student's opinion.	Facilitates the director's work, who hands over all responsibility for the accuracy of the answers to the student.	Student decreases the frequency of their questions, no longer dares to ask the advisor's opinion before making decisions.
I won't tell you what to do but I will say you're doing it wrong	Advisor gives vague instruction purposefully, offers no help when asked, and then negatively criticizes the student's effort	Maintains control/power over student, increases perception of superiority.	Student decreases the frequency of their questions, hides the parts of their work that they are not sure about.
Remember who's the boss	Advisor demands that the student do exactly what they say and does not tolerate questioning.	Maintains control over student, appears all-powerful, avoids criticism.	Student gives in to the advisor's will, does not develop autonomy.

Since it is important for the student–advisor relationship to be open, honest, authentic, and aim for the good of the other, these kinds of stereotypical interactions, which contain covert messages and motivations, are necessarily counter-productive. They not only sabotage the development and preservation of a transparent and collaborative relationship, they create discomfort and uneasiness in the best case scenarios, and unprofessionalism and ethical concerns in the worst. Such an interaction style usually intrudes subtly; rarely is the exchange obviously inappropriate. However, the advisor might feel a certain uneasiness, an impression that the conversation is artificial, that they are continuously being required to justify themselves. What distinguishes the examples in Table 7.2 from a series of ordinary questions, compliments, and legitimate excuses, is the presence of an undisclosed agenda. That being said, we shouldn't assume that a student's intentions are always malicious or manipulative. Isn't it natural to try present ourselves in the best light and to try to avoid criticism? Students have a legitimate and understandable underlying need to appear motivated and competent. The art of supervising lies in the advisor's ability to meet these needs while staying on target for tasks that need to be done and feedback that needs to be given, all while maintaining a relationship of trust, authenticity, and support. In the following example, we illustrate a spiral of stereotypical and artificial interactions that, once the advisor recognizes the discomfort and the student's hesitation to respond, can be resolved with a metacommunication intervention. Resolving this conflict will actually strengthen the working alliance.

Advisor: *Did you complete the analyses that we discussed last time?*

Student: *As a matter of fact, no. The statistician was unavailable.*

Advisor: [Surprised, as the excuse seemed superficial] *Oh? But I thought this was something you would be able to do by yourself? It seemed pretty straightforward to me.*

Student: *Actually, I didn't have any time to think about it this week. I had an exam and I had to run experiments in the lab.*

Advisor: [Accepting the student's excuse] *Okay, but when I gave you some feedback on the first version of the abstract, didn't we say that we needed these results to submit the abstract for the upcoming conference? The deadline is this Friday...*

Student: *Yes, but I thought that if it came to that, we could add them at the last minute.*

Advisor: [Impatient] *Okay, but neither I nor the co-authors would be able to review the final version before you submit.*

Student: [Ill at ease] *Er, no, that's true. I hadn't thought of that.* [Silence] *Would you rather I didn't submit the abstract?* [Proposing a drastic solution that puts the responsibility on the shoulders of the advisor].

Advisor: [Backing up, feeling guilty] *Of course not! I guess we can send the previous version of the abstract. If worse comes to worst, we'll have the new results for the presentation.*

Student: *I'm sorry, I know I left it to the last minute. I'm not as well organized as you are. I can manage to run the analyses this week. I could send you the abstract Thursday night?*

Advisor: *Hm, okay... I guess... let's see...* [Looking at their agenda, really wanting this abstract submitted but frustrated to be stuck with it at the last minute and trying not to add to the student's stress] *For this time it's okay, but usually I need a few days to be able to provide feedback.*

Student: [Feeling attacked, on the defensive] *Okay, but there's really nothing I could have done differently, plus you only mentioned the new analyses at our last meeting.*

Advisor: [Sharply] *It's your job to organize your time and I expect you to manage yourself.*

Here, the interaction starts in the "my dog ate it" mode, with the student formulating excuses to explain why their work hasn't progressed. The advisor responds by dismissing the excuses one by one with growing irritation. Such an interaction, with the student coming up with excuses that are systematically dismissed by the advisor, does nothing to help the student focus on the task. On the contrary, this interaction devolves into "poor little me" mode, where the student adopts a self-deprecating tone ("I won't be able to submit the abstract," "I'm too last-minute") and the advisor reacts impatiently while feeling guilty about hurting the student. This guilt does nothing to ameliorate the advisor's impatience, which, on the contrary, only increases. Consequently, the interaction veers towards the "But I did exactly what you told me!" mode, in which the frustrated student tries to shift the responsibility for the uncompleted task onto the advisor and their overly high expectations. Uncomfortable, annoyed, and eager to put an end to this unpleasant interaction, the advisor shuts down the conversation with a "remember who's the boss" tone. At the same time, we might notice that the advisor hasn't necessarily been crystal clear in their instructions (did the student know the new analyses were essential for submitting the abstract?), and that they might have some ulterior motivation for wanting it submitted (or else why forge ahead when the advisor isn't satisfied with its content?).

There is no melodrama in this interaction: no one was attacked, bullied, or exploited. Everything was expressed in a respectful and polite tone. There was no Machiavellian manipulation. However, the interaction was not transparent: neither person clearly expressed what they thought or felt. Each one tried to influence the other's behaviour through covert means. And, most importantly, the training objectives were not met. The conversation is at an impasse: if the advisor sticks to their agenda and forgets about their role as a mentor, they have turned towards the dark side. The abstract might be submitted, but no one would feel satisfied from this interaction, and most of all, no one would have learned from this experience. If the advisor lets their irritation and impatience influence how they perceive the student, if they attribute the situation to the student's lack of respect, motivation, or some other negative interpretation, it's easy to see how the situation could start to deteriorate. Our objective with this scenario is to show how day to day interactions can feed negative feelings, with a bad effect on future interactions and the student–advisor relationship. Nobody's perfect, of course, but conflict grows out of such repeated unpleasant interactions, gradually leading to the deterioration of the working alliance.

Let's see what the advisor could have said to save the day.

Advisor: *Let's take a pause here. We seem to have reached an impasse. Do you see it as well?*

Student: *Um... I don't know.* [Hesitating to say what they really feel, fearing the advisor's reaction]

Advisor: *I would like to take a few minutes to discuss it. Do you agree?*

Student: *Okay.*

Advisor: *I have a feeling that we aren't addressing the problem effectively. We seem to be trying to convince one another, instead of trying to solve the problem together. What do you think is going on?*

Student: *I really wanted to run those analyses but it seems like when I sat down to do it, nothing was working.*

Advisor: *I can understand this. Anxiety around statistics is common in university students. You suddenly doubted your abilities, and the feeling paralyzed you. You would have liked to consult with the statistician, but she wasn't available so you ended up putting everything off. Is that right?*

Student: *Yes, that's it. But I want you to know that I'm not slacking off.*

Advisor: *I know you're a hard-working student. But I feel as if, when you didn't reach the goal that we'd set together, you wanted to put the responsibility on my shoulders, to make me sweep in and save the day.*

Student: *Yes… once you put it like that, it's true. I wished that you could solve this problem for me, but I need to solve it myself.*

Advisor: *In fact, I'm here to help you find a path and look for solutions with you. This is my role and I'm happy to do it. I can't do the things you have to do yourself, but I do want you to feel at ease to come and talk to me when you're facing challenges. I enjoy working with you.*

Student: *Me too. But whenever you give me lots of comments, it feels like I've been sent back to square one.*

Advisor: *Yes, I know it can be frustrating. I remember feeling the same way with my own advisor's feedback. But, what's an alternate solution? Would you like me to refrain from commenting?*

Student: *Of course not.*

Advisor: *How could we work together to make our collaboration go more smoothly?*

Student: *From my end, I guess I could talk to you before problems get too big.*

Advisor: *Yes, that would be good. And if you want, I would like you to provide feedback on my own feedback. If there are ways I say or do things that are less useful for you, I would like to know about them. Providing feedback is the most important part of my job. I want to be sure to focus on whatever is most useful for your progress.*

Student: *That sounds good.*

Advisor: *Also, I overreacted a little earlier. Attending conferences is important to me; it's where I go to meet colleagues, so it's important that I show up. I might be overly invested in your project, and I admit I got impatient. I'm sorry.*

Student: *It's okay. I think I also need to be careful not to do things at the last minute.*

Advisor: *Excellent. Now, let's get back to those analyses, and what we can do for this abstract and the upcoming deadline.*

In this example, the advisor clearly pauses the discussion about the abstract to focus on the way the discussion is going. The advisor makes sure that the student agrees with this change and tries to articulate the problem in an unthreatening way by acknowledging how they have also contributed to the tension in the interaction ("We seem to be trying to convince one another"). The advisor acknowledges and normalizes the experience of the student ("Anxiety around statistics is common"). At the same time, while questioning the student's reaction and stating clearly why they're making an intervention, the advisor is teaching them how to receive feedback ("I can look for solutions with you, but I cannot do the work for you"). Finally, the advisor talks about their similar experiences as a student and adopts an open attitude to receiving the student's feedback to better align with the student's needs. This makes the interaction less confrontational for the student, but still puts part of the responsibility for an effective interaction back into the student's hands.

HUMILITY AND AUTHENTICITY

The previous example was designed to show an intervention where the advisor takes a firm position—the student did not run the analyses that were their responsibility—but openly discusses similar difficulties that they themselves have experienced. The advisor recognizes that they also contributed to the problematic interaction, and identifies and questions their own motivations which are related to their own performance (how they want to appear in the eyes of their collaborators) rather than the student's. The advisor asks the student for help to make their supervision more effective. Thus, openness, transparency, humility and authenticity represent essential attitudes in developing and maintaining an effective working alliance. These qualities can sometimes be wrongly perceived as weaknesses, false modesty or obstacles that undermine the advisor's authority over rebellious students (at the end of the day, they still have to run those bloody analyses!). Maintaining a humble attitude doesn't mean we can't be assertive, and it doesn't mean we deprecate ourselves. Being able to identify our own contribution to difficulties in communication, and being willing to adapt our behaviour in an effort to preserve the quality of the relationship is a measure of authenticity.

As illustrated by Watkins and collaborators,[16] the advisor's humility acts as a remedy for the tensions that can emerge from the hierarchical relationship and the unequal distribution of power. Openness towards conflict and the motivation to attend to the supervisory relationship can help resolve minor tensions that arise in a relationship where both parties are well-meaning, but where misunderstandings unavoidably occur. One study reports the views of twelve advisors, judged to be very competent by their peers, about resolving conflicts during supervision.[17] The element which they identified as the most important is an open attitude towards conflict, i.e., admitting that conflicts can be unpleasant at times, but knowing they are part of the supervising experience. Thus, the qualities of a good advisor shine out through their capacity to identify and manage conflicts with students with calm good will, and not through their ability to avoid them. Moreover, the use of metacommunication strategies doesn't imply enforcing tighter control over your students. Without authenticity, without good will, these strategies can indeed become manipulation. The goal is not to break students so they adhere to our own way of doing things. We want to improve our listening skills and better understand the impact of our feedback so it will be received and used as effectively as possible.

In short, while the dissertation is the work of one person, the student, getting there is a tango that definitely takes two. The pitfalls of graduate supervision will be easier to manage with a good working alliance between the student and the advisor. We should be careful not to confuse the working alliance with friendship, nor our good will with complacency. We should not take advantage of our authority to exploit or manipulate the student's

---

16. Watkins Jr., C.E., Reyna, S.H., Ramos, M.J., & Hook, J.N. (2015). The ruptured supervisory alliance and its repair: On supervisor apology as a reparative intervention. *The Clinical Supervisor, 34*(1), 98-114. <https://doi.org/10.1080/07325223.2015.1015194>; Watkins, C.E., Hook, J.N., Ramaeker, J., & Ramos, M.J. (2016). Repairing the ruptured supervisory alliance: Humility as a foundational virtue in clinical supervision. *The Clinical Supervisor, 35*(1), 22-41. <https://doi.org/10.1080/07325223.2015.1127190>
17. Nelson, M.L., Barnes, K.L., Evans, A.L., & Triggiano, P.J. (2008). Working with conflict in clinical supervision: Wise supervisors' perspectives. *Journal of Counseling Psychology, 55*(2), 172-184. <https://doi.org/10.1037/0022-0167.55.2.172>

work to further our own personal goals (not even a tiny a bit). Instead, we must find a good professional distance that fosters a positive relationship while leaving room to address difficult issues. We must communicate clearly and assertively, while always listening. When faced with misunderstandings, we must stay Zen. While an ounce of prevention is worth a pound of cure, we must remember that throughout the years of the mentoring relationship, conflicts are virtually unavoidable. We must acknowledge misunderstandings and tension with openness. Adding a dose of humility, and focusing more on the student's learning goals than on our C.V., will guarantee a magnificent tango.

CHAPTER 8
With great power comes great responsibilities

As discussed in the previous chapter, the different tasks involved in the supervision of graduate students are carried out within the context of a relationship. The stronger this relationship, the better the student's motivation and the feeling of competency. We even suggest that a good working relationship will help the dissertation advance, thereby implying that as graduate supervisors we should, from time to time, tear our attention away from our computer screens and show—at least some—interest in the human beings in front of us.

However, the supervising relationship is one where power is unequally distributed between the two members of the dyad. The students do have a role in ensuring the quality of their experience, but the supervisor's role confers greater power, and thus greater responsibility for setting and maintaining standards of supervision. Graduate supervisors who fail to acknowledge this inequality place themselves at risk of engaging in unethical and potentially abusive behaviours, whether on purpose or not, and regardless of their best intentions.

LAWS, REGULATIONS, ETHICS AND OTHER SCARY WORDS

It will be obvious throughout the next few paragraphs that we, the authors of this book, are not lawyers, jurists, or experts in ethics. Still, we'll share our—perhaps simplistic—understanding of these concepts as we zero in on the actual objective of this chapter. The law (legal system) is a set of rules adopted by a country, state, or province. It is applied the same for all people in that group and, as we often hear, *ignorantia juris non excusat*, ignorance of the law is no excuse. Through its legal system, a society incites people to follow its laws, and provides sanctions for those who break them. Thus, a dissertation director who steals money from a student's wallet is engaging in an obviously unethical behaviour, but also an illegal one. This type of behaviour isn't what we'll be discussing in this chapter.

In addition to laws, most institutions have regulations that apply to all their members. In this case, it's up to the institutions to make sure people follow their rules, and to apply sanctions to the offenders. In academia, you can find these rules in one or more documents, but we hope we aren't telling you anything new when we say that these rules don't apply only to students. They can cover numerous aspects of the learning environment and the people involved, for example defining the role of a graduate supervisor, specifying the tasks of a program director, describing the procedure to retake a failed exam, and so forth. Many of these rules are specifically directed at professors. Though we haven't read all the rules of all universities, we're pretty sure that a professor who doesn't provide adequate supervision to one of their graduate students is contravening some of their university regulations. This brings us closer to the topic of this chapter, but we are not quite there yet.

There are also codes of ethics that are specific to professions, and which are established and overseen by professional associations. Lawyers, engineers, physicians, notaries, pharmacists and other professional associations all have a code of ethics. For instance, article 14 of the *Code of Ethics for Psychologists* in the province of Québec states, "[t]he psychologist must respect the privacy of persons with whom they enter into a professional relationship, refraining from gathering information and exploring aspects of private life that have no relation with the professional services agreed on with the client."[1] Thus, it's not against the law to meddle in other people's personal business, but it can be unethical to do so (even for a psychologist!). While researching this chapter, it quickly became apparent that in general there aren't many such codes of ethics for university professors, in contrast with teachers at the elementary and high school levels.[2] Individual universities may have such a code, but we didn't find any that applied to a whole province like Québec or a country like Canada.

The main topic of this chapter revolves around ethics in the context of supervising graduate students. The limited availability of professional codes of ethics for professors makes this topic even more relevant. Ethics consist of reasoned reflection aimed at good conduct. It refers to our examination of the moral values and principles (where a principle can be based on more

1. From the *Code of Ethics of Psychologists*, Article #14. <https://www.legisquebec.gouv.qc.ca/en/document/cr/C-26,%20r.%20212>
2. Here is an example from the province of Ontario, Canada: <https://www.oct.ca/public/professional-standards/ethical-standards>.

than one value) that should guide our actions in different situations.[3] Discussing ethics in the context of graduate student supervision implies that we reflect on the best conduct to adopt as research advisors. The focus should go beyond what comprises a good or a bad action towards a student, and should help define the questions supervisors should ask themselves when they choose a course of action. Because different values may be in conflict with each other depending on the context (for instance, pushing a student to be more productive could be detrimental to their mental health), we find it useful to identify these values and how they underpin our reflection. Following the list of values proposed by the university where we currently work (Université Laval), we base our discussion of the ethical aspects of the supervising relationship on the values of responsibility, respect, courage, integrity, inclusiveness, and solidarity.[4]

Needless to say, our concept of what is ethical can vary from group to group, and even from one individual to the other. What seems bad to one person can seem good to another. Some people consider giving money to a person living on the street to be a good action, while others consider this action inequitable and prefer to give money to organizations. In the same way, some will find that sanctioning a student is justifiable, fair, or educational, while others find it insensitive, pointless, or cruel.

What emerges from all these definitions is that ethical dilemmas arise within a specific context in terms of environment, culture, and time period. Some, but not all unethical behaviours are also illegal. Some go against a university's rules, while others do not. Some behaviours would have been acceptable twenty years ago, but are considered unethical today. Just think of all those sexist, racist and homophobic jokes that used to be commonplace and would no longer be tolerated in most departmental meetings. In short, no single written document can encompass all of what is or isn't considered ethical at any given point in time.

We could offer a detailed list of student's rights and professors' responsibilities, but you can likely find many such policies, rules and regulations on your own university's website (Zzz). Save this fun reading material for your next trip to the beach! Or, you can learn piecemeal as we did, from the experiences of others as well as our own, passing through a surprising exhibition of What Not To Do. The important point to remember is that

3. Translated from Commission de l'éthique en science et technologie (s. d.). Quelle est la difference entre éthique et morale? <https://ethique.gouv.qc.ca/fr/ethique/qu-est-ce-que-l-ethique/quelle-est-la-difference-entre-ethique-et-morale/>.

4. Université Laval (2022). Mission, vision, and values. <https://www.ulaval.ca/en/about-us/mission-vision-and-values>

students have a right to quality training, a safe environment, and fair evaluation, and that it's up to professors to ensure this is the case.

FIRST AND FOREMOST, TO BE COMPETENT

In all professions, one of the basic principles of ethical conduct is to ensure that one has the necessary competency to perform one's professional tasks. A pediatrician cannot decide overnight to practice neurosurgery. A psychologist specializing in the treatment of anxiety disorders will not undertake to evaluate a criminal's level of dangerousness just because they feel like it. A dentist who is faced with a case that goes beyond their expertise will refer their client to a colleague such as an orthodontist (or at least, we hope they will!). Competency, and a concern with acting competently and maintaining our competency over time, is likely to prevent many potential mistakes or bad conduct. But what does it mean to be a competent research advisor? A professor's job offers countless and recurring "opportunities" for them to be evaluated (see Chapter 2), but these rarely relate to our ability to supervise students (the number we supervise, sure, but not the quality of supervision).

We can break competency down into two components. First, there is our discipline, the research domain in which we've developed our specialization, which is our field of expertise. It is usually easy to define our expertise, and we tend to accept supervision of students whose research projects fall within or near our domain. Professors vary in terms of where they perceive the limits of their field (some have sprawling, many-acre ranches, some have tiny city garden plots), but most will choose to supervise projects for which they have sufficient expertise, or will seek help to fill any gaps through a co-supervising arrangement.

The second component of competency relates to supervision itself, which is not so well circumscribed by guidelines and definitions. Just as competency in teaching is distinct from the subject matter of a course, competency in supervising transcends the topic of the student's research. Professors can know everything there is to know about a topic and still not possess the skills to teach it effectively (we all remember that one professor whose monotonous speeches went on for hours). Professors can be experts in a research topic but still fail at the task of supervising graduate students. We all have a sense of what makes a "good" or "bad" advisor, and we can even list the skills we think are essential to the task, but while there are some guiding principles out there (see for instance those of the Canadian Association for Graduate Studies in Box 8.1), operational definitions of supervising competency are few and far between.

BOX 8.1—GUIDING PRINCIPLES FOR GRADUATE STUDENT SUPERVISION ACCORDING TO THE CANADIAN ASSOCIATION OF GRADUATE STUDIES[5]

1. **A Supervisor should be identified in a timely fashion.**

2. **Supervisory committees or equivalents should be established early.**

3. **Expectations, roles and responsibilities of graduate students and supervisors should be made clear.**

4. **Supervisors should be readily accessible to their students, and regular monitoring and feedback should be ensured.**

5. **Student–supervisor relationships should be professional.**

6. **Intellectual debate and challenge should be encouraged and supported.**

7. **Supervisors should be mentors** in areas such as the development of appropriate professional skills, applications for funding, networking opportunities with colleagues in academia and beyond, assistance with publications, and career development.

8. **Issues of intellectual property and authorship should be made clear.**

9. **Conflicts should be resolved at the lowest level possible,** as close as possible to the source of the problem (i.e., at the lowest level of administration). If the student and supervisor cannot find a solution after discussing the problem, they should then involve the supervisory committee or equivalent. If the problem cannot be resolved at the student–supervisor level, it may be dealt with by the program. The University should ensure that appropriate resources (e.g. ombudsperson, equity office) are available to assist.

5. From Vessey, M.J.K., Davies, G., Driver, J.C., Lalande, F., & Smith, M.B. (2008). *Guiding Principles for Graduate Student Supervision.* Ottawa: Canadian Association of Graduate Studies. <https://cags.ca/documents/publications/working/Guiding%20Principles%20for%20Graduate%20Student%20Supervision%20in%20Canada%20-%20rvsn7.pdf> The twelve principles are reproduced literally but only part of some explanations are reproduced here.

10. **Continuity is important in graduate supervision**. As a consequence, a change in supervisor should be made only for strong and compelling reasons such as a mutually agreed major shift in academic direction of the research, major academic disagreements and/or irreconcilable interpersonal conflicts.

11. **Alternative supervision should be available**. This should cover situations beyond the control of the student (e.g., temporary or permanent absence of supervisor), situations that may arise from conflict of interest, and situations that result from personal relations between supervisor and student.

12. **Students have substantial responsibilities for managing their own graduate education**. The university, graduate department and supervisor are responsible for providing an appropriate environment for high-quality graduate education, but success is ultimately in the hands of the student. It is therefore essential that universities inform students of their responsibilities, and provide them with the information and support that they need to carry out their responsibilities.

Some may argue that professors are hired first and foremost based on their scientific expertise and research skills, and that if some professors have poor supervision and teaching skills, well, no one can excel at everything. They will likely find that representatives of student associations and the administrators of the Office of Academic Quality have a different opinion... In any case, this stance is not helpful if our goal is to assist students with their writing skills. Let's therefore pretend that most of us want to become "good" research advisors.

So, what makes a research advisor "good"? Once again, we can find some interesting parallels with clinical supervision in healthcare fields (psychology, medicine, nursing, etc.). That said, most descriptions of the qualities of a good clinical supervisor (for instance, open, authentic, flexible) are somewhat circular and can leave us wanting more. Aren't we all trying to be our best? We've never met a supervisor who aspired to become stubborn, obtuse, arrogant, or tyrannical. So, the question isn't what are the qualities of a good supervisor, but rather how and when these emerge in real-world situations. One study asked 128 current or recently graduated students in clinical psychology about the behaviours of clinical supervisors they perceived as "best" or "worst." The results showed that the best supervisors encouraged independence, strengthened the supervising relationship, were open to discussion, had positive personal and professional qualities (e.g., honesty, friendliness), demonstrated good clinical knowledge and skills, constructively challenged their trainees, offered feedback and reinforcement, and prioritized and engaged with their supervision.[6] The implication is that good supervisors are not only experts in their field but, according to these students, they are people who care about the quality of their relationships with students, and about their students' progress.

Another model of clinical supervision classifies the main competencies of supervisors as the capacity to collaborate with trainees, to nurture them emotionally, to enable the trainees in developing competency, and to instill them with a sense of professionalism.[7] This suggests that we should pay close attention to a professor's ability to initiate and maintain a good working alliance (see Chapter 7) as a fundamental competency of supervision. Too many professors act as if their supervision skills are secondary to their research skills. As we ourselves have documented by asking 29 doctoral students about their perceptions of a good graduate supervisor, students didn't only mention knowledge on a specific topic, but also identified qualities of the supervision itself (e.g., providing structure to their supervision, adapting supervision to their students' needs, providing constructive feedback), along with availability and relationship skills.[8] A surprisingly high number of students told us that they appreciated their supervisor's "humanity," as if this were not a basic trait of all professors...

In any case, while we ponder how best to retain our humanity, we can remind ourselves that self-reflection is the competency that usually helps regulate all other competencies. Some people use the term metacompetence to refer to our capacity to know what we know and what we don't know, to determine what competencies are required for a given task and, if necessary, to seek more information, more training or collaboration. There is no ultimate level of competence to be attained. Rather, a competent research advisor engages in a continual process of improvement. Adhering to these principles of self-reflection and career development, combined with the values of honesty, integrity, and commitment to personal responsibility, will help advisors provide an ethically competent supervision.

---

6. Ladany, N., Mori, Y., & Mehr, K.E. (2013). Effective and ineffective supervision. *The Counseling Psychologist, 41*(1), 28-47. <https://doi.org/10.1177/0011000012442648>
7. Pront, L., Gillham, D., & Schuwirth, L.W. (2016). Competencies to enable learning-focused clinical supervision: A thematic analysis of the literature. *Medical Education, 50*(4), 485-495. <https://doi.org/10.1111/medu.12854>
8. Belleville, G., Foldes-Busque, G., Guay, F., & Jackson, P. (2021). *Déterminants des trajectoires d'anxiété, de perfectionnisme et de procrastination menant à l'abandon des études chez les doctorants.* Fonds de recherche du Québec - Société et culture (FRQSC).

We seem to have wandered away from advice on helping graduate students to write their dissertations, haven't we? That's because we believe that practical writing strategies will never be enough to bring out a student's full productivity, and even less the highest quality of their learning experience. The latter depends on the competence of their research advisor. In fact, a competent supervisor might even recommend that a student slow down their writing (for instance, in cases where the student has mental or physical health problems, or is uncertain about their career path). Thus, competent supervision cannot be separated from the role of research advisor.

TRANSPARENCY INSPIRES TRUST: THE PRINCIPLE OF INFORMED CONSENT

In healthcare, a patient can consent or not to a treatment. In a research project, a participant can consent or not to taking part in a study. Such consent is valid only if it is informed and given freely. It is informed when it is given with full knowledge of the facts, and free when it is given voluntarily without pressure from someone else. Historically, the notion of informed consent has become necessary in contexts where previous traditional paternalistic models had dictated the relationship between people in authority and those in vulnerable situations. There is an obvious parallel to be drawn with the supervision of graduate students. Even if doctors, when they take the Hippocratic Oath, swear to respect the principle of "beneficience", this does not imply that they will always know exactly what is best for their patients. Similarly, research advisors who have a lot of experience and knowledge in a very specific discipline don't always know what is best for each student. There is no need at this point to review all the historical evidence in research or medicine about the abuse and exploitation of people from non-dominant cultures.[9] It's easy to imagine similar

9. Spigner, C. (2007). Medical apartheid: The dark history of medical experimentation on Black Americans from colonial times to the present. *Journal of the National Medical Association, 99*(9), 1074–1075. PMCID: PMC2575876; Scharff, D.P., Mathews, K.J., Jackson, P., Hoffsuemmer, J., Martin, E., & Edwards, D. (2010). More than Tuskegee: Understanding mistrust about research participation. *Journal of Health Care for the Poor and Underserved, 21*(3), 879–897. <https://doi.org/10.1353/hpu.0.0323>; Armitage, K.J., Schneiderman, L.J., & Bass, R.A. (1979). Response of physicians to medical complaints in men and women. *JAMA, 241*(20), 2186–2187. PMID: 155167.

horror stories that have unfolded in professor–student relationships. Don't believe it? See a few examples here.[10]

As well as keeping people safe, outcomes are better when we collaborate with the people we are studying or treating: research is more relevant and rigorous when it is governed in part by participants affected by the field of study, and treatments are more effective when patients are involved in medical decisions. We can bet that students who have the opportunity to develop within a relationship based on trust and respect will also write better.

Even if professors aren't required to obtain informed consent from the students they supervise, this seems like a good practice considering the length and the complexity of the task being undertaken (to write a dissertation), and the student's subordinate position in this context. We've already discussed the importance of the collaborative agreement as a tool for discussing the expectations of students and professors; this tool, sometimes seen as a "contract," helps describe from the start how the research group works and what is expected of each person (see Chapter 3). We've also discussed the importance of students and supervisors agreeing on goals and specific tasks to accomplish. This is at the heart of the working alliance, and is a key determinant of student productivity. It is also central to the satisfaction that both the students and the professors get from the relationship (see Chapter 7). Clearly and explicitly defining elements such as the frequency of meetings, the use of e-mail or other forms of communication, attendance at laboratory meetings, participation in team projects, publications, funding applications, and professional activities outside the laboratory, also enables students to give their free and informed consent to what will be expected of them during their studies.

Obtaining informed consent from students is a way of giving back some of the power and responsibility to the student in their choice of graduate supervisor. It also lays the groundwork for a transparent and honest professional relationship based on collaboration. Indeed, it would be a grave abuse to use this exercise to bend the student to our will (too bad, you

10. Scali, D. (2018). Ces directeurs qui rendent leurs étudiants fous. *Le Journal de Montréal*. April 3. <https://www.journaldemontreal.com/2018/04/03/ces-directeurs-qui-rendent-leurs-etudiants-fous>; Oransky, I. (2017). The Harvard lab head, the grad student, and the restraining order: An ongoing saga. *Retraction Watch*. <https://retractionwatch.com/2017/07/27/harvard-lab-head-grad-student-restraining-order-ongoing-saga/>; Young-Powell, A. (2018). When the relationship with your PhD supervisor turns toxic. *The Guardian*. January 22. <https://www.theguardian.com/education/2018/jan/22/when-the-relationship-with-your-phd-supervisor-turns-toxic>

already signed your rights away!). Just as consent in healthcare can be withdrawn at any point during treatment and should periodically be re-verified, obtaining consent in the context of graduate supervision needs to be considered at two levels: formally and explicitly at the start of the relationship, and then continuously and with varying formality depending on the situation, throughout the student's program.

THINK TWICE BEFORE YOU SPEAK

As research advisors, we will gain all sorts of knowledge about students in the course of their studies. Some will be academic (e.g., delays in their academic progress), some will come from our own evaluation (e.g., a recurring weakness in a specific aspect related to writing the dissertation), others will be of a more personal nature (e.g., a break-up or a death in the family). Some information will be provided voluntarily, others will be revealed under obligation (e.g., absence due to sick leave, need to repeat a flunked course). Sometimes we will witness events that provide privileged information about a student (e.g., a student bursts into tears and reveals that the delay in completing their dissertation is due to the fact that they were assaulted a few months earlier). Moreover, it is not uncommon at various points to learn about sensitive information related to our students' physical (e.g., chronic pain, autoimmune disease, HIV status) or mental (e.g., anxiety, depression, substance abuse, ADHD) health.

The graduate supervisor is often an important and trusted figure for the student. Very often, they may hold us in high regard, whether this is deserved or not. As well as the information advisors acquire during their interactions, they are likely to receive confidences from their student. Thus, in addition to the advisor's position of authority with regard to their students, they also have the advantage with regard to information, since they generally know more about their students than the other way around. Unless you reveal the information specifically, students will not know that you once failed an accounting class, had to apply twice to graduate studies, or suffered from depression two years before defending your dissertation. These are all the kind of details you may know about your students. It's therefore important to acknowledge that, as research advisors, we have privileged access to a lot of personal and potentially sensitive information about our students, and that this knowledge mainly flows in one direction.

This imbalance raises several questions. What information should we reveal, and to whom, and why? What information is considered confidential? In what circumstances should we break this confidentiality? What information can be used to guide academic assessment? What would be relevant in a letter of reference? These are multiple questions that we might face one day or another, often under circumstances when things are not going smoothly with the student, forcing us to think long and hard about confidentiality.

In general, advisors who behave ethically will show restraint and do their best to limit the sharing of information about their students that was acquired through their privileged position of authority. Some information, however, requires action on the part of the advisor: for example, the advisor may report to the program director or department head that they are encountering difficulties with a problematic student. Also, they may want to seek advice or simply protect their own mental health by sharing with other colleagues some of the challenges they face with a student (recognizing that there is a difference between discussing sensitive issues privately with someone you trust, and venting out loud to anyone who will listen). And when students express or report psychological distress, advisors need to make a rapid and accurate assessment of the situation and act as necessary (see Box 8.2). Just as it would be inappropriate to use personal details to justify an assessment (for instance, ruling a project infeasible because the student has previously suffered from depression), it is equally unacceptable to ignore their potential functional impact (for instance, repeatedly pushing back the deadlines for a depressed student without trying to learn more about the situation). And, while it would be inappropriate to relate personal details in a letter of recommendation, it may be appropriate to comment on the student's ability to work while coping with personal difficulties.

BOX 8.2—PSYCHOLOGICAL DISTRESS: DO NOT BURY YOUR HEAD IN THE SAND

Psychological distress in university students is increasingly part of our conversations, and rightly so. A survey from the Quebec Student Union in 2019 revealed that close to 58% of university student suffered from psychological distress, and that 9% seriously thought about suicide in the last 12 months.[11] As research advisors, we often witness this distress in graduate students, whether willingly or not. Some students may react

11. Original in French: Union étudiante du Québec (2019). *Enquête « Sous ta façade ». Enquête panquébécoise sur la santé psychologique étudiante.* <https://unionetudiante.ca/Media/publicDocuments/Rapport-enquete-sous-ta-facade.pdf>

emotionally to our comments with anxiety, anger or sadness, while others will withdraw and become visibly uncomfortable when the time comes to discuss certain issues—and writing the dissertation is among the subjects that provoke the strongest reactions. We've seen students burst into tears, have panic attacks before a presentation, go AWOL for weeks at a time, etc.

Advisors can play a crucial role in identifying distress in students. Of course, not everyone can suddenly become a psychologist or counsellor. Not only is this not part of their job description, but an ill-advised intervention, even with the best of intentions, can have serious harmful consequences. During an emergency, one can provide first aid, but it doesn't follow that one becomes a doctor overnight. Having said this, ignoring all distress signals on the pretext that this isn't part of our job can also cause harm.

When a student expresses distress, whether consciously or not, the first thing to do is to pay attention. Is the student spiralling into catastrophic scenarios? Express to them that they seem anxious. If the student has tears in their eyes, tell them they look sad. If the student reveals they are experiencing difficult personal issues, express your empathy by telling them that you understand that this affects their work. No need to make a big production or dig deeper; simply validating the student's experience can make a big difference. If you want proof, think about how irritating it is to hear someone rush in immediately with advice the moment you tell them you're having difficulties, when a simple "I understand" would feel like balm to a wound.

Even if you have no notion of counselling, you can rapidly evaluate the extent of the damage. Is the distress related specifically to one topic (e.g., the student feels stuck in their writing) or is it generalized (e.g., difficulty attending class, overall lack of motivation)? Doing this often requires no more than listening and asking the student to tell us a little more about their experience. Stay vigilant for clues suggesting that the problem is serious and ongoing. Is the student just nervous in the run-up to an important evaluation like the doctoral exam, or are they often panicking? Is the student's day to day functioning affected by alcohol and drugs consumed at a seemingly endless stream of parties? If they bring up problems with attention and concentration in a self-deprecating tone, are these frequent and do they add up to something more than end-of-semester-fatigue? Does the student seem at the end of their rope?

If you're worried about a student's well-being, tell them so. Tell them about resources that are available on campus and in their community, and provide referrals to these resources. Reassure your student by telling them you do not think they are weak or losing their mind, that you think they are going through something rough and that they, like many people before them, might need specialized resources.

When someone expresses or shows signs of distress in a professional setting such as a student–advisor relationship, it's normal to feel all sorts of emotions such as discomfort, helplessness in the face of their suffering, worry about possible consequences, irritation or even anger, as we can feel that we aren't the right person to come to for such difficulties. Some advisors will react by trying to avoid the subject and any involvement in it, since they believe it isn't part of the working relationship. Some might be afraid to offend the student or come across as intrusive. However, ignoring a student's distress can have serious consequences: the distress can be so severe that the student may contemplate suicide. Second thoughts and calls for help can take many forms, including disclosing one's state of mind to one's research advisor.

All the available resources on suicide prevention emphasize the same thing: the suicidal person is ambivalent about the idea of dying. If you have serious concerns about the suicide risk of a student, don't take any chances. Gently use clear words and ask questions ("Can you tell me more about what you are going through? When you say that it might be better to end it, are you talking about ending your life?"). This might appear risky, but remember that in such a situation, a false positive (asking the question to a person who is not suicidal and dealing with their surprise and discomfort) is far less serious than a false negative (not intervening with a suicidal person). Help is available, and your action can bridge the gap between the student and that help, making all the difference. If you are worried, speak up, and don't minimize what is going on. Ask whether the student has access to resources. Does someone else close to them know about the situation? Are they consulting a mental health professional? Finally, if suicidal distress is evoked during your discussion with a student, don't hesitate to accompany them directly to appropriate resources on campus, or to the hospital.

Suicide prevention is the concern of everyone, no matter their role. Some people feel more open to discussing it, others will feel it is an overstep. But remember that graduate studies are often associated with social isolation, and it's possible that the research advisor is the only person that can perceive the student's distress. When necessary, the advisor should not hesitate to consult appropriate resources to receive guidance.[12]

12. Here are some examples in Quebec: <https://howtotalkaboutsuicide.com>; <https://talksuicide.ca/>, 1.833.456.4566.

WORDS ARE FLEETING BUT WRITING IS FOREVER... AND CAN COME BACK TO HAUNT US

As research advisors, we have to write many documents concerning our students, sometimes addressed directly to them (for instance, assessments, written comments in drafts), sometimes not (letters of recommendation). It's important that all written communication to or about the student be respectful, written in clear and non-derogatory language, and contain accurate information. In letters of recommendation sent directly to the recipient without the student seeing them first, it's important to remember that some countries (such as Canada) have laws about access to information that give the student the right to consult all documents concerning them. We even learned to our surprise that this applies to emails, when one of us was asked by a dean to provide all the communications addressed to, from, and about a specific student. Thus, it's important to be thoughtful and conscientious in all written documents concerning students, whether they are formal or not. If we need to let off steam or enumerate all the things that annoy us about a student, we'd better use our personal diary.

One common challenge in advisor–student relationships is that the advisor will almost inevitably be required to write a letter of recommendation for the student, whether during their studies (for an internship or a scholarship) or after they end (for a post-doc or a job). Writing a letter of recommendation isn't easy, and may put the advisor in a conflict of interest. On the one hand, we're asked to paint an accurate portrait of the student's skills, but it is in our own interest to over-emphasize those skills, while sweeping any weaknesses under the rug, so as to increase the chance of the student getting the job or the scholarship. Thus, a letter might be more enthusiastic than accurate; nobody's perfect. On the other hand, writing an objective, fact-based letter that balances strengths and weaknesses might hurt the student. In fact, in the current academic culture where advisors who write letters of recommendation excel at praising their protégés, a balanced letter will probably look fairly shabby next to all the accolades received by others. One might even go so far as to say that a negative letter will do less damage than a lukewarm one. The former will read more as settling old scores, and will draw opprobrium onto the advisor rather than the student.

Another question that may come up is whether the student should read the letter of recommendation or not. Whichever you decide, it is always best to write the letter after having an open and honest discussion with the student about what will be in it. An open letter will contribute to the trusting relationship between the student and the advisor, especially if it contains the exact same elements previously discussed. The advantage of writing a confidential letter is that in theory it offers more room for candour. While this might seem obviously better, remember that in many cases a student can ask to have access to the letter. If the content is surprising or even shocking to the student, the negative consequences this could have on the supervision relationship and future interactions are easy to imagine. We would like to emphasize that it isn't negative feedback we are telling you to avoid, but rather the element of surprise. We should be open about the letter's contents. If this leads to a lukewarm recommendation, the student should know about it beforehand, and have the option of choosing not to use such a letter.

Another common practice is to ask students themselves to provide their advisor with a rough draft of a recommendation letter. Often with the goal of saving time, the supervisor takes the document, changes a few words, signs and submits it as is. This does not seem to us a good practice. Writing one's own letter could be a good exercise for the student to take stock of their accomplishments and develop their skills of self-reflection. However, when we ask a student to write their own letter in its entirety, without changing it at all, then its contents will not reflect our own evaluation. Plus, having to write their own letter places the student in a very uncomfortable position. Since we've likely all been in this situation as students, let's pause a moment to recall the great discomfort that it caused, at least the first time (since the process must often be repeated). That said, there is a great range of possible approaches, including some that are quite acceptable, that fall between starting from a blank page on the one hand and asking a student to write the whole thing on the other. We can ask a student to describe their main accomplishments. We can ask them to point out areas where their skills are a good fit for the position or scholarship they're applying to. We can ask them for examples of challenges they've faced during their studies, and how they overcame them. In short, we can elicit many facts from students that we can add to our own observations and use to write the letter. This is completely different from asking them to write the letter outright.

Can we refuse to write a letter? Of course we can, but we should carefully weigh the consequences of this refusal. A letter from the research advisor is important, if not indispensable, for most scholarships or positions during or after graduate studies. In most circumstances, even a letter written with lukewarm enthusiasm will cause less damage than not providing a letter. The decision not to write a letter should not be based on the discomfort this situation raises about the having to reveal to a student that their performance doesn't meet our standards. At this point in their studies, students should know what we think about their performance.

TROUBLE IN PARADISE: IDENTIFYING AND MANAGING MULTIPLE RELATIONSHIPS

What we call a multiple relationship occurs when another type of relationship forms between the advisor and a student that is distinct from the relationship based on writing the dissertation. The other relationship can be academic (teaching a student in a course, or supervising a clinical practicum), professional (hiring a graduate student for a research or teaching assistantship), professional outside the university (hiring a student for one's business), or personal (developing a friendship with a student). The ethical issue when we add different kinds of relationships is that information and favours are being exchanged outside the advisor–student relationship (unrelated to the dissertation). It is important to distinguish good relationships that grow out of common professional interests from those than are inappropriate, like relationships based on exploitation (asking a student to work for one's business without paying them), or intimate and sexual relationships. It is also important to acknowledge that between those extremes lies a huge grey area.

Multiple relationships can develop within an excellent advisor–student relationship, with talented students who are interested pursuing an academic career like ours. Of course we would like to offer those students opportunities and contribute to augmenting their C.V.'s—and at the same time, benefit from their exceptional skills by hiring them as research or teaching assistants, or by involving them in grants and publications not directly related to their dissertation. In these cases, the extra relationships are a positive outcome of the advisor–student relationship, and remain within the academic and professional realm. This doesn't mean that multiple relationships in such contexts cannot lead to unfortunate situations. Having a favourite student can decrease opportunities for others; plus, nobody is immune from being influenced by the behaviours they observe outside the Ph.D. context (e.g., downplaying a student's lack of progress on their dissertation because we see them performing well on a project unrelated to their studies). We'll get back to these challenges in a moment.

Multiple relationships of an academic and professional nature are very different from intimate or exploitative relationships, which must be avoided. And if there are readers who somehow haven't yet made the jump to the twenty-first century, no, intimate and sexual relationships with a student are never appropriate. Yes, even if we are talking about two adults, and even if they are both consenting. There are increasingly cut and dried, but in some cases surprisingly recent, institutional policies that prohibit intimate relationships between professors and students (at Université Laval for instance, the policy to prevent sexual misconduct was implemented in 2018). In fact, even if such relationships occur between two adults, their consensual character must always be in question, because of the unequal distribution of power in these relationships. An intimate relationship has a negative impact on the assessment of the student, how the student is perceived by peers and other professors, the reputation of the professor involved in this relationship, and the reputation of the institution and the profession itself (i.e., all university professors).[13]

There is a consensus that casual sexual relationships between professors and students are harmful for all parties involved; however, opinion varies when long-lasting relationships are concerned. Even if we draw a clear line to say that such intimate relationships are a big NO-NO, there will always be situations where the people involved feel that their situation is exceptional. There are couples whose intimate relationship began during the advisor–student period and evolved into a stable and loving relationship after the thesis defense (you likely know a few, right?). In such exceptional situations where the intimate relationship cannot be terminated, it is imperative that the advisor–student relationship end (see Box 8.3).

BOX 8.3 I FOUND THE LOVE OF MY LIFE

In many situations where there is a potential for conflicts of interest, the solution is to name the potential conflict, discuss it, avoid situations that could cause problems and, finally, accept the situation with all its imperfection. This reasoning is not valid in a situation where a professor and their student are developing a romantic relationship. Remember that the student is always in a subordinate position in the research supervision relationship. They can't address the problem on an equal footing to the professor, no matter how strong the bond between them. An advisor–student relationship and a romantic relationship cannot coexist without negative consequences, and these negative consequences are not evenly

13. Did you ever notice that in TV series, movies and novels, when there is a male university professor and he is unfaithful, it's often because he starts a relationship with a female student? Also, the qualities and competency of a male professor often shine brighter thanks to the seduction or at least lustful admiration of female student (as in the case of the famous Indiana Jones). These are, of course, archetypes in the context of entertainment, but there is still something alarming in how a seduction between a professor and his adult student is trivialized in the collective imagination. It isn't surprising that we might have the first (erroneous) impression that such relationships are acceptable and harmless.

distributed: the student will undoubtedly suffer more. The professor is also at risk, for example if the situation escalates and a break-up results in an official complaint of harassment. That said, let's not demonize people who engage in such relationships in good faith; after all, "The heart has its reasons whereof reason knows nothing." Anyone who's been in love knows that this is not the best state for making rational decisions. Thus, for the sake of the love they have towards their student, a professor who wishes to pursue this relationship should at minimum end the research advisor–student relationship and make sure the student does not suffer any harm. The professor is (or should be) the person who knows most about the risks and repercussions that such a double relationship entails.

In between these extremes of the "good" and strictly professional relationships and the "bad" sexual and/or abusive relationships, there lies a sweeping grey zone of other possible relationships that aren't clearly sexual or intimate, nor exploitative, but that aren't clearly related to completing dissertation (see Figure 8.1). There is the student who offers to help you out when your babysitter cancels at the last minute; the student whose brother can help you with your income taxes; the student who happens to be in the same spinning class as you; the student you split a pizza with because it's late and the experiment hasn't finished running; the hotel room you share with a student during a scientific meeting to reduce costs; the student you start a business with; the student you supervise in their clinical work as well their dissertation; the student who's invited to your wedding; the student who invites you to their wedding; the lab dinner or party at your house; the lab party at your student's apartment; lab parties at other locations; lab parties that start at your place but finish elsewhere; lab parties that end in heavy drinking; the joint you end up smoking with a student. The list goes on, and the more situations we add, the more chance the reader will feel called out, because many such multiple relationships occur and are part of the lab or the department culture, and questioning them makes us feel attacked (see Box 8.4). We are both the first to admit that we've experienced some of those situations, and have been annoyed by the necessity of changing some of our practices because we realized afterward they did not reflect our core values.

FIGURE 8.1—Behaviours with clear and not-so-clear risks involving students

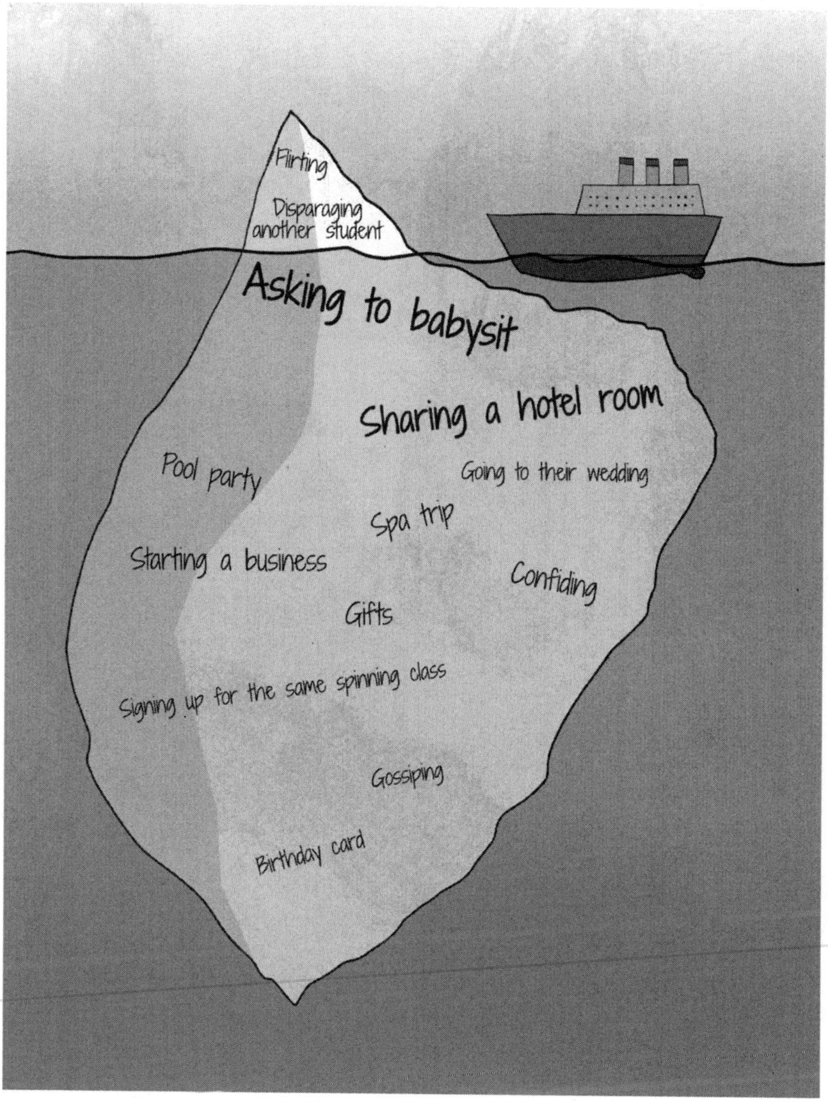

BOX 8.4—WHAT? WE CAN'T DO ANYTHING ANYMORE!

There can be many points of view regarding multiple relationships. And these points of view and attitudes are often vehemently expressed. The first question that comes up is, "What's wrong with that?" Which is often followed by irritated comments such as, "It's like we can't do anything anymore." These situations are often social occasions that lie in the underwater portion of the iceberg shown in Figure 8.1, or if they do poke above the surface it's in specific contexts that make them seem harmless. However, those of us in a position of power or belonging to a dominant group will always be the last to realize the potential consequences of inequitable situations. Remember the example of the Old Boys Clubs from the not so distance past (and sometimes present): even if women had theoretical access to jobs, decisions about promotions and career advancement were often made during after-work activities, in a bar or on a golf course, to which women had less access. Career opportunities may occur during extra-curricular activities. We can discover shared interests with students, go through positive experiences that reinforce the relationship, talk informally about projects, etc. This seems like a good thing, of course, but it's important to ask ourselves whether such opportunities are accessible to all members of the team. Would the same opportunity be offered to the student with a young child who cannot join the happy hour because she doesn't have a babysitter? To the Muslim student who prefers not to go to bars? To the student in a wheelchair who cannot enter your favourite local bar that doesn't have wheelchair access? Are you more friendly to people who have a drink with you? Has a tradition developed in your lab where people have to participate in social events to get your recognition? We said from the beginning that we would talk about ethical issues and not lecture you on the morality of a given situation, so we won't try to say what is good and what isn't. However, we think that as professors, we all have blind spots on some of those questions. Thinking and being open about them, questioning ourselves and our habits, and discussing those issues with colleagues are powerful means of avoiding delicate situations.

While we recommend caution and circumspection, we are convinced that interactions with students can go beyond the strictly supervisory relationship without necessarily having a negative impact. In the field of clinical psychology supervision, multiple relationships between trainees and supervisors are permitted under most codes of ethics because they are not necessarily harmful or inappropriate in themselves. However, engaging in multiple relationships creates boundary issues in the research advisor–student relationship. The boundaries of a professional relationship are the implicit and explicit rules and expectations that distinguish it from other types of interpersonal relationships.[14] For example, when we go to see our doctor and he asks us how we're doing, we're expected to give him details about our health, not about the latest TV series we've been watching. On the other hand, if we ask the doctor politely how they're doing, we don't expect them to give us details about their health in return. Events that deviate from the strictly professional role, without the behaviour becoming inappropriate or exploitative, are called "boundary crossings."[15] Common examples include social situations outside the academic context, sharing personal information, or exchanging gifts or favours. Boundary crossings differ from boundary violations in that, while they aren't related to the research relationship, they do not represent unethical or harmful behaviors. A boundary violation stems from an abuse of power on the part of the supervisor in which the interactions are intimate, sexual, or exploitative.

A qualitative study was carried out with clinical psychology trainees, asking them to describe positive experiences where their supervisor had crossed relationship boundaries.[16] Participants emphasized that these occasions had strengthened their relationship with their supervisor and increased their motivation towards their internship. On the other hand, many noted that these situations could lead to confusion between the roles of each party. For example, a student who sees their supervisor drunkenly participating in karaoke at a team night out may feel more comfortable from realizing that they are a human being after all, but they may find it difficult to regain professional distance and their place in the hierarchy the next day.

The biggest problem for professors in boundary-crossing situations is that, more often than not, we are ignorant, unaware, or indifferent to the ramifications of our position of authority. We can cross the boundaries of the supervision relationship with the best of intentions, for example by inviting the whole lab to our cottage for a team-building weekend, without realizing the impact on some students, who may feel they cannot decline the invitation. Thus, boundary crossings are rarely perceived as such by

---

14. Gutheil, T.G., & Gabbard, G.O. (1993). The concept of boundaries in clinical practice: Theoretical and risk-management dimensions. *The American Journal of Psychiatry, 150*(2), 188-196. <https://doi.org/10.1176/ajp.150.2.A18>
15. Gottlieb, M.C., Robinson, K., & Younggren, J.N. (2007). Multiple relations in supervision: Guidance for administrators, supervisors, and students. *Professional Psychology: Research and Practice, 38*(3), 241-247. <https://doi.org/10.1037/0735-7028.38.3.241>
16. Kozlowski, J.M., Pruitt, N.T., DeWalt, T.A., & Knox, S. (2014). Can boundary crossings in clinical supervision be beneficial? *Counselling Psychology Quarterly, 27*(2), 109-126. <https://doi.org/10.1080/09515070.2013.870123>

professors and supervisors who tend to trivialize these situations. We must also recall that different students, coming from different backgrounds, can have very different perceptions of the consequences of boundary crossings. Thus, even if the boundary crossing isn't harmful nor inappropriate in itself, the capacity of the student to consent or not to the professor's perceived or actual expectations needs to be considered. Moreover, some students may consent to some transgressions without necessarily understanding what their impact will be. And keep in mind that it should be possible to withdraw consent at any moment without repercussions.

For all these reasons, some authors are very strict and recommend simply avoiding any type of relationship outside that of research supervision in the context of graduate studies.[17] This is probably the simplest way; if we never engage in any form of contact outside of the research supervision relationship, we don't have to think about what actions are okay versus not okay. However, few advisors will choose such a rigid path, and in our opinion, it isn't necessarily an ideal goal either. The sense of security can prove false, since boundary transgressions and abuse of power can occur in formal contexts as well, while data supports that informal contacts are beneficial to the relationship and to learning. However, even in situations that seem the most innocuous, we believe that the professor must remain sensitive, empathetic to the reactions of all those involved, open to self-reflection, and cautious. After all, we have to admit to ourselves that we often don't identify the pitfalls of a boundary crossing until it's too late, after the harmful consequences have already occurred. Arguments based solely on the professor's good intentions ("I was doing this for the good of the relationship!") may be objective and truthful, but they are insufficient. The problem in such situations lies not only in what is done, but what is perceived.

The nature of boundary crossings and the context in which they occur must be taken into consideration. Some situations may seem more obviously alarming, but we believe they only form the tip of the iceberg of possible impacts that come out of multiple relationships (see Figure 8.1). The opportunity equity offered to students should also be considered. Other considerations include how many non-supervisory relationships exist, on the assumption that the greater this number, the greater the risk of the relationship becoming more personal, and the hierarchical and evaluative nature of the relationship being ignored. Also, stricter boundaries are called

17. Burian, B.K., & Slimp, A.O.C. (2000). Social dual-role relationships during internship: A decision-making model. *Professional Psychology: Research and Practice, 31*(3), 332-338. <https://doi.org/10.1037/0735-7028.31.3.332>

for when the student encounters difficulties that require closer monitoring of their activities (e.g., probation, failure), or when the professor is the one experiencing personal or professional difficulties (e.g., divorce, withdrawal of research funding, delay in promotion). At the same time, it is often only as a relationship evolves through an accumulation of individual interactions with a student that certain problems come to the surface, and by this time the boundaries may be far behind us, making it difficult to return to a more formal relationship.

Obviously, multiple relationships that fall squarely within the professional context are less problematic. Still, even in cases of strictly academic relationships which seem like they belong in the "good" relationship category, it is sometimes questionable whether the student's learning is at the heart of our concerns. It's true that offering our prize student a wide range of opportunities will enable them to develop cutting-edge expertise, and that each of their experiences is likely to enrich the content and the writing of their dissertation. On the other hand, we may be limiting the diversity of our protégé's experiences by keeping them too long in the nest. Remember, the objective is not to produce copies of ourselves (see Chapter 4). Also, if a problem occurs in one of the outside tasks (such as a teaching assistantship), the chances are good that other tasks, including writing the dissertation, might suffer. In all these shared situations that fall outside the advisor–student relationship, we should be aware of favouring or disadvantaging one student over another. We're compelled to admit that a prize student who can take charge of essential tasks, organize lab meetings and social events, train new students and contribute to multiple posters and articles can create a conflict of interest: it becomes less advantageous for us that they complete their dissertation, graduate, and leave the lab. Students, even the most eager and motivated, are not cheap labour. Sometimes we must admit that we (and the very few people in our close circle who are as intelligent/knowledgeable/expert as us) are not the only people in the world who know what's best for our favourite student. On the contrary, a diversity of viewpoints will enhance the quality and richness of their education.

When it comes to multiple relationships, there is no shortage of different opinions and reactions. The important thing is to be mindful of potentially harmful consequences for the learning and well-being of students, and not to hesitate to consult colleagues or resources when situations raise doubts. The two devoted coauthors of this book have ~~lost~~ spent many hours ~~arguing~~ discussing what is acceptable or not in different cases of boundary crossing. Even if we didn't always come to a consensus—or if the nature of that consensus is constantly in flux—the fact remains that such reflection has led us to modify some of our practices. For example, one of us used to provide alcohol to team members at lab dinners before the Christmas vacation, to thank them for their involvement. Reflecting on the issue of consent, she wondered whether all her students would feel comfortable refusing to take the drink she offered them and whether, unconsciously, she didn't naturally feel more affinity with the students who drank with her than those who abstained. Her co-author reminded her of his own experience when, witnessing some students' excessive consumption, he began to think about what his responsibility would be if, after an evening of partying, one of these students had an accident or committed an act of mischief. These thoughts led him first to reduce the number of alcoholic drinks he provided on such occasions, and then to change his practice completely (e.g., paying for the meal but not the alcohol).

In short, the more multiple relationships research advisors have with their students, the greater the risk of an ethical violation. Questionable actions become trivialized through repetition and cause the professor to lower their guard. And yet, the professor must maintain the role of evaluator in their relationships with students. In short, attending the same spinning class as your student doesn't mean you have to stop supervising their research, but it does mean that you should probably adopt a more reserved attitude than if you were participating in the class with a friend. It also means coming to terms with not being part of "the gang" anymore, perhaps not being as close to the students as you were when you were a student yourself, and yes, being a bit of an outsider and not understanding all the inside jokes that will develop between your students. Some will prefer to avoid these situations altogether, while others, on the contrary, believe that rigid restrictions will be more harmful to the mentoring relationship. That said, it's important to differentiate between multiple relationships that represent an abuse of power and student exploitation, and those that arise through the healthy growth of a professional relationship. Multiple relationships are unethical when the professor's evaluation of the student may be affected either positively (since access to such opportunities may not be equitable) or negatively, when they are intimate or sexual in nature, or when the student is at risk (apparent or real) of exploitation.

SO, WHAT ABOUT THE DISSERTATION?

"I thought I would get strategies to make my student write, and now I'm being told I can't party with them anymore!" It's true, in this chapter we've wandered far from discussing specific strategies to stimulate students' writing. Maybe we've cast doubts on some of your methods? Pause a moment before you start demanding your money back. The ethical aspects of a good supervising relationship—competency, principles of informed consent and confidentiality, conscientiousness in writing, and acknowledging and managing the potential impacts of multiple relationships—appear to be conditions that are essential, or at least highly favourable for good productivity. Not guarantees of productivity, we wouldn't go that far. However, when these conditions are not met, the problems that occur will set back the writing of the dissertation. When we think about the relationships we've seen that didn't end well, when we gossip about professors whom we call "bad" advisors, we can often spot behaviours that violated ethical principles, whether it was done intentionally or not. The professors in such cases often consciously or unconsciously disregarded how their own position of authority gave them the advantage in the relationship. Despite good intentions, a professor who fails to recognize this inequality is more likely to place students in situations that will be detrimental to their learning and their productivity.

CHAPTER 9
Is it fear or apathy? Why can't they just sit down and write?

There are probably as many different explanations and contributing factors to the blank page syndrome as there are individual students. Graduate students are good at so many things, they excel at nearly everything and amaze us on so many levels, but why, WHY, won't they write?

The gap we perceive between ourselves and our students could be related to generational differences, such as the use of new and ever more rapid modes of communication that currently seem to favour content that is short and varied rather than long and deep. But then again, this generation gap isn't a new phenomenon, but part of a cycle. We've heard about the "good old days" from our parents, who heard it from their parents, and we even end up using the phrase ourselves. Alternatively, we want to point out at least two other hypotheses that are worth exploring to explain why (according to professors) our students aren't writing enough. Both hypotheses relate to the student's mental state. The first suggests that students want to perform (they are motivated), but they become entrenched in a vicious cycle of perfectionism and procrastination. The second examines how a lack of motivation and ideas might occur if we are focused more on the task of writing than on our contribution to knowledge. Although these interpretations are presented as alternate hypotheses, they are not mutually exclusive, and in fact they're probably complementary. Taken together, they explain why it takes time to write a dissertation, and why this time is generally much longer than anticipated.

At the risk of sounding pompous, we can also acknowledge that some of us became professors because we had higher-than-average writing skills. A former advisor told one of us, when they were just starting out as a young faculty member, not to expect all their students to be as successful as they'd been as a student. At the time, they thought that the former advisor was finally paying them a compliment, but in fact the advisor was wisely pointing out the reality that many students who end up as professors do indeed start out with more writing abilities. Now that we're professors ourselves, we have to teach this skill to all kinds of students, with all kinds of skills and experiences, who face all kinds of challenges, and most of whom will not become professors like we did.

FIRST HYPOTHESIS: STUDENTS DON'T WRITE BECAUSE THEY'RE ANXIOUS

Students are anxious; they worry too much, and usually about the wrong things. Anxiety paralyzes students, and prevents them from writing. They aren't lazy, they don't lack motivation, and they aren't giving up because they're fickle. In most cases, they don't write because of perfectionism and procrastination. They are gifted but paralyzed.

At its simplest, perfectionism is the pursuit of perfection. But we can also define theoretical models of perfectionism with one, two, or more dimensions. Both of the two classical models of perfectionism are multidimensional. The model proposed by Frost and collaborators[1] is based on six dimensions: the main one is concern about mistakes, which is complemented by high personal standards, parental expectations, parental criticism, doubts about actions, and doubts about organizational abilities. The model from Hewitt and Flett[2] defines perfectionism based on the person defining the standards, and the person targeted by the standards. Thus, the three dimensions are Self-Oriented Perfectionism (standards defined by ourselves and targeting us), Other-Oriented Perfectionism (standards defined by ourselves but targeting others) and Socially Prescribed Perfectionism (standards defined by others—including our perception of their standards—and targeting us). Other dichotomous frameworks contrast adaptive versus maladaptive, positive versus negative, functional versus dysfunctional, or healthy versus detrimental aspects of perfectionism. In short, perfectionism is recognized as multidimensional with productive and unproductive elements. It should be noted that the literature also defines a clinical or pathological perfectionism, in which seeking perfection paradoxically interferes with functioning, and which is a problem associated with various mental health disorders, such as mood, anxiety

1. Frost, R. O., Marten, P., Lahart, C., & Rosenblate, R. (1990). The dimensions of perfectionism. *Cognitive Therapy and Research, 14*, 449–468. <https://doi.org/10.1007/BF01172967>
2. Hewitt, P.L., & Flett, G.L. (1991). Perfectionism in the self and social contexts: Conceptualization, assessment, and association with psychopathology. *Journal of Personality and Social Psychology, 60*, 456–470. <https://doi.org/10.1037/a0025032>

and eating disorders. Some authors recommend targeting perfectionism directly in psychotherapy.[3]

Considering that psychology experts themselves have difficulty agreeing on the nature of perfectionism, we cannot be expected, as simple dissertation advisors, to have a clear conception of it. Nevertheless, there is consensus emerging around two main dimensions of perfectionism, namely applying high standards for oneself, and worrying excessively about mistakes.[4] The latter is more clearly associated with negative consequences for well-being and mental health.

This is the aspect of perfectionism that makes our task very difficult: some students are too preoccupied by their performance and not enough by their experience. We can see this in students who focus on the products, or outputs of their work (e.g., the format of the next presentation, the number of papers needed to get a scholarship, the number of pages needed for the dissertation, the upcoming deadlines). While these aspects are important, they shouldn't take all the attention away from conversations about the ideas and actual subject matter of their research. Giroux and Girard[5] compare a performance stance with a learning stance: students who worry more about their performance are worrying less about their learning as such. Their thoughts become more rigid, they crave approval, show less confidence, focus on areas they think they can control, and are less self-reflective. They put all their energy into proving how good they are, and neglect expected tasks. For these students, mistakes are to be avoided at all costs, and a student who worries that much about making mistakes will take fewer risks and stop trying new things. They write less because they're afraid of finding out that what they've written doesn't meet their advisor's expectations. As advisors, we would like students to write and benefit from our constructive feedback, but perfectionist students fear this feedback, which they see as a negative appraisal of their abilities.

Let's not forget that these perfectionist students also often suffer from impostor syndrome: they fear, irrationally, that people will find out how

---

3. Egan, S.J., Wade, T.D., & Shafran, R. (2011). Perfectionism as a transdiagnostic process: A clinical review. *Clinical Psychology Review, 31*(2), 203–212. <https://doi.org/10.1016/j.cpr.2010.04.009>
4. Stoeber, J., & Otto, K. (2006). Positive conceptions of perfectionism: Approaches, evidence, challenges. *Personality and Social Psychology Review, 10*(4), 295–319. <https://doi.org/10.1207/s15327957pspr1004_2>
5. Giroux, M., & Girard, G. (2009). Favoriser la position d'apprentissage grâce à l'interaction superviseur-supervisé. *Pédagogie médicale, 10*(3), 193–210. <https://doi.org/10.1051/pmed/20099991>

incompetent they are, that they never should have attempted graduate studies, that their lack of ability will be unmasked, that people will realize it was a terrible mistake to admit them into a graduate program or a research team, and they will be kicked out. Some might suppose that a person who puts that much effort into hiding their incompetence must actually be incompetent. However, even relatively competent people can suffer from a lack of confidence that distorts their own assessment of their abilities, and from anxiety that prevents them from taking on the kind of new challenges (like writing a dissertation) that would help them develop such abilities. Being incompetent is very different from not having gained sufficient experience to reach a certain level of competency. The paradigm shift between undergraduate studies (when we listen and do what we're told) and graduate studies (when we make decisions and take charge of our own project) is probably more difficult for perfectionists, who like to receive positive feedback (such as good grades). By adhering to an all-or-nothing mode of thinking, in which any comment that isn't completely positive is interpreted as criticism, perfectionist students perceive each comment in a text as more proof that we think their writing is bad and that they've failed to reach our standards (but keep in mind that different ways of expressing the same comment may be more or less likely to produce a negative interpretation; see Chapter 4). These students are so afraid of failing that their efforts to hide their perceived incompetence outweigh the effort they put into learning to become more competent. The student who has yet to write a single page is the same one who volunteers to mentor new students; the student who can't clearly articulate their research question is the one who has accumulated the largest pile of articles to read; and paradoxically, despite their best efforts, a kind of self-fulfilling prophecy makes these students increasingly appear incompetent to us too.

It may be difficult to see these students as perfectionists. From the advisor's perspective, they haven't produced anything of value, so how is that perfectionism? But perfectionism is revealed through the thoughts and internal dialogue of the student, not their output. The perfectionist student sets unrealistic goals in such a way that they will never be able to achieve them. "I will write a text that will completely satisfy my advisor. After having read enough articles, I will write my theoretical background in one sitting. I know how to write a scientific article, even though I have never done it before in my life." Sometimes, we may confuse perfectionism with the fact of being very conscientious, very productive, very meticulous and successful. This might be true in the early stages of education, for instance high school, where perfectionism can be associated with high academic performance. In graduate studies, however, even if we are taught to have rigorous methods and disciplined thinking, success is determined by the ability to show initiative, to go for it and try out different things, to accept and use criticism, and to persevere even through times of difficulty or uncertainty. In order for a manuscript to receive feedback, feedback, and yet more feedback, one must write a first draft that will, by definition, be filled with imperfections. Scientific writing is the opposite of achieving a hole-in-one: excellence comes through experience, which grows out of all the detours, course-corrections, and wrong turnings that are part of learning. This is the principle that perfectionists struggle with, because they want to achieve perfection on the first shot, in a context where perfection cannot be defined. In a course, perfection is an A+ or 100%; to measure the perfect dissertation is far more challenging, if it's possible at all.

Another erroneous view is that perfectionist students are well-organized. Some theoretical models do in fact include an organizational dimension to perfectionism. But this is an aspect that might be true in other spheres, but less applicable to graduate studies, where we might actually say that a perfectionist student is *over*-organized. The perfectionist graduate student is preoccupied with principles of organization, but unable to apply them. Such students can propose many different apps to help organize their work, but they cannot make and implement a plan. They have very efficient methods of classifying articles and taking notes, but they are unable to draw connections between the findings of different studies. Much like stage magicians who are masters at re-directing our attention so we don't realize the simplicity of the trick, disorganized students deflect our attention toward the complexity of the topic, the difficulty of the statistical analyses, and many other complex interrelated elements. They are so good at it that it often takes us a long time to realize that the problem is a lack of organization, and that part of the solution lies in restricting the scope of each task and defining simple, specific and time-limited objectives (see Chapter 5). Regardless of a problem's complexity, we can only solve it one step at a time. And perfectionists hate simplicity, which their fear makes them confuse with simple-mindedness.

Perfectionists therefore find themselves in a lose-lose situation: the objectives they value most are too high to be attained, and the attainable objectives appear too small to them to be valuable. Faced with this dilemma, they spin their wheels, practice avoidance, and procrastinate. Procrastination means putting off something that can be done right now. We often joke to our students that the further we progress in graduate studies, the more we become masters in the art of procrastination. No longer do we spend afternoons procrastinating at the pub, or vegetating on the couch as we binge our favourite TV series. Doctoral-level procrastination is far more sophisticated! Students procrastinate on their writing by doing actual "work," like searching for, reading and classifying articles, actively browsing websites relevant to their topic, running and rerunning statistical analyses (theirs and those of other students!), and fine-tuning the format of their documents. This type of procrastination is very subtle as these tasks are all relevant. To complete a dissertation, one must indeed read huge quantities of articles, seek out various sources of information, explore the data through different analyses, and follow editorial guidelines carefully. However, when a student has planned to write a specific part of the dissertation and those plans change because the task seems too difficult, or because they don't feel ready, or because they don't feel like it, this becomes procrastination.

In the collective imagination, procrastination is the hallmark of lazy, haphazard, and careless people. But here we see the complete opposite. The graduate student who procrastinates is indeed busy… but doing many things other than writing. In fact, procrastination on writing can be explained in part by the anxiety related to this task. We've all postponed a task at some point because we didn't feel that we could handle it, or claimed we felt too tired at that moment. Some of these tasks were indeed completed the next day, while others still linger on our to-do lists because we never did feel up to it. Yet, how many times did we challenge our own unwillingness with a concrete demonstration that the task was truly beyond us? We bet that most of the time, our assessment wasn't quite accurate, and the task was actually achievable. However, we were worried about not being able to complete it, and this worry affected our judgement. In cognitive therapy, we call this emotional reasoning, that is, a false perception of reality that comes from basing our judgement on an emotion, a subjective impression, rather than facts. Without a doubt, writing a dissertation is scary. With all the responsibility resting solely on the student's shoulders (at least until they allow group defenses, as predicted in Chapter 6!), they may get the subjective impression that they won't make it. The issue is critical: no dissertation, no degree. Moreover, let's face it, instructions for success are often not spelled out and seem to change at the advisor's discretion (at least, from the student's point of view). What happens when we have to complete an important task for which we lack the confidence? We feel anxiety, and that's normal. Most graduate students will not take this anxiety as a predictor of their success; they will do their best to face and overcome it, and divide the writing task into parts that are small enough to handle one at the time. Others will be paralyzed by this anxiety. Instead of seeing themselves as anxious, they will believe they are incompetent. They will use emotional reasoning and rely on their feelings to assess their performance, saying, "If I don't feel competent, then I am not competent."

However, they will not always be able to recognize how anxiety is colouring their perception, and, unfortunately, neither will their advisor.

Procrastination and perfectionism thus go hand in hand. Remember that perfectionists see mistakes as personal flaws, never as an opportunity to learn. The more ambitious and difficult the writing task appears, the higher the risk of making mistakes, the greater the fear of failing, and the more anxious the student becomes at the thought of moving forward. The more anxious they get, the more they tend to try to avoid it. A student who decides to focus on something else—who procrastinates—can alleviate this anxiety in the short run. Avoiding anxiety-inducing situations leads to a short-term and temporary reduction in the anxiety. Through operant conditioning, this reduction increases the probability of repeating the avoidance behaviour in the future; the relief is so pleasant that the avoidance behaviour is rewarded. It's a bit like a person who cancels a dentist appointment at the last minute because they are too anxious. The immediate relief will be powerful, but the avoidance behavior will prevent the person from assessing the real risks of the situation and their ability to deal with it.

In fact, the longer we avoid something, the more anxiety it generates. For a student, this might sound like, "Oh my god, I didn't write my theoretical background this semester, I'm the worst, I'm so behind schedule, I'll catch up during winter break." Thus, in pragmatic terms, the initial objective of "writing the theoretical background in one semester (15 weeks)" becomes "writing the theoretical background during a holiday (2 weeks)." The objective just became much harder (doing in 2 weeks what was originally planned for 15 weeks), as well as more unpleasant (having to sacrifice a holiday), and the reasons why the objective wasn't met in the first place are not examined. The hidden objective is thus, "do the same task but in less time without changing anything about what could have caused the initial failure." The objective becomes perfectionist by virtue of being unrealistic (i.e., the expected performance is much too high). The perfectionist student does not accept failure (that they did not write their theoretical background in the planned time frame), does not learn from this experience (that they need to adjust the way they plan their work), and does not define new, more realistic objectives (I will rest a bit, then I will dedicate five mornings during the holidays to write a plan and start the section where I describe the theoretical model).

Perfectionist students never learn to proceed differently, refusing to accept failure or mistakes, or to recognize that there comes a moment during graduate studies when we humbly have to accept reality and recollect ourselves. Each time these students think about sitting down to write, the same anxious feelings of incompetence, of being stuck, overwhelm them. This overwhelming anxiety drives them towards other tasks: reading one more article, running one more analysis, making a new article search, browsing websites. Anything, in short, except writing the dissertation. It becomes the monster under the bed: the longer we go without looking, the bigger and bigger it seems, until every sound, every shadow is interpreted as another proof of the lurking danger. The moment we look under the bed, the danger disappears; we assess the situation more realistically and without catastrophic thoughts. There is no monster under the bed. There might be a cat hiding there, or a mess that reminds us we have to clean up. For some students, this monster is their dissertation. They think about it all the time but never work on it. In fact, if we could follow their train of thought, we would see a series of cycles between vague and over-ambitious objectives (too much in too little time), confusion about how to tackle the task, which is making them anxious and which they now dislike, a swerve towards easier or more specific tasks to fill the time that could have been committed to the dissertation, and a promise to themselves that they will tackle it more seriously next time, which generates another vague and over-ambitious objective (i.e., much too much, and even less time). In this case, perfectionism manifests as the inability to set small, simple, and achievable goals, thereby increasing the risk of not reaching them. Instead, they tell themselves that they will do more next time, thus increasing the difficulty of reaching the target, while their feeling of personal effectiveness has been reduced by failing to reach it. This makes the next writing session even more anxiety-inducing and, consequently more prone to procrastination. These wheels keep spinning for weeks, or entire semesters—we've met students who spent years unable to open the document containing their dissertation, despite thinking about it every day.

Students aren't paralyzed because they're lazy. If we think this way, we will involuntarily pile more onto their already overly ambitious goals, and cause them to freeze up even more. Self-reflection might be called for here because, in our desire to be rigorous, we sometimes set the bar high. During some interviews we conducted with advisors (with a biased sample that included a high number of conscientious and self-aware people of good will!), many identified strategies like dividing tasks into smaller parts, setting up schedules, and following up with students. Some, the wisest among them, also told us that they had to remind themselves that the dissertation belongs to the student, not to them, and that their own writing skills aren't being evaluated through their student's dissertation. Fostering independence isn't accomplished by writing for them, nor by leaving them to their own devices. It is done by providing sustained and helpful feedback. Sometimes the key to making them write more lies in lowering our expectations.

SECOND HYPOTHESIS: STUDENTS DON'T WRITE BECAUSE THEY DON'T KNOW WHAT TO WRITE

Behind a blank page there can also be a blank mind. This statement might be a tad provocative, but it reorients the discussion toward the contents of what will be written, as opposed to how, how often, and how fast students can write. Some students wonder why they can't seem to fill up pages of words simply by sitting at their desks, as if they expect ideas to just pop into their minds. Ideas don't always come to us when we're facing our computer or a sheet of paper, they might actually come more readily when we're running or doing the dishes. In fact, ideas often need some nourishment, and will appear once we've read a lot, tested our ideas by discussing them with others, and given the information time to settle. Writing requires time because one has to think about what one wants to write. The importance of this prelude to writing is not the same for all students; some people write (almost) as fast as they think and are good at cranking out ideas rapidly, and then spend more time sorting through the best ones. Other people will take much longer to organize their ideas before they're ready to write them down. Rare are the people who can write rapidly *and* precisely at the same time (and we hate them for it!). The romantic view of writing a paper in one sitting doesn't generally apply to writing a dissertation or sections of a dissertation. Does this mean that when we're stuck, we should pick up our books and go back to reading? Not necessarily, because some students are happy to read eternally, so much that they leave no room for thinking, much less for writing. Reading is probably the most invoked excuse for delays in submitting manuscript drafts and, as explained above, it is the paramount tool of procrastination. When people are stuck and cannot write, the problem might lie at different steps of the creative process. Sitting down with students to discuss the process might help distinguish between whether they have ideas but aren't sure how to organize or present them, or whether they haven't yet amassed enough "raw material" (knowledge) to be able to come up with their own ideas or their own interpretation.

Some research supervisors suggest always asking students to send some type of written material before each meeting. This is generally helpful for ensuring that there will be some starting point to the discussion, and it also helps to crystallize student's ideas. However, when enforced very early in the student's doctoral studies, this exercise might draw a lot of effort and attention into the production of written material at the expense of time for thinking and processing. Students could end up simply paraphrasing what they've read, or might limit their work to a single source in order to meet such demanding productivity requirements. If the writing they produce progresses based on their readings and discussions, this strategy might achieve the desired goal, but it might also be harder for a student to come up with their own ideas if they rely too much on external sources. Some supervisors will ask students for a plan very early on and tell them to fill in the sections of this plan, others will ask for a plan much later, when they have explored enough ideas to be able to generate the plan "as they go." As one colleague put it, "Whether you start with a plan or not, at some point of writing a dissertation, you'll have to make one."

Students who have a facility for generating ideas can be identified early on. They're the ones who ask questions during class or during scientific presentations (or after the presentations, if they're shy), they're the ones who are full of curiosity and respond to new information with a flood of new questions. They're the students who unearth articles you've never heard about, who attend talks that aren't directly related to their research topic, who are interested in matters that go beyond their to-do list. For these students, writing a dissertation is an extension of their scientific curiosity. This curiosity is the main source of their motivation. Such raw motivation, however, often needs to be channelled. These students need tools for imposing method and rigour to keep them on the right path. At the other end of this spectrum, students for whom method is everything, who focus on structure and output, will find themselves struggling at crucial steps like identifying the research question and hypothesis, and interpreting the findings in light of recent literature. This isn't to say that well-organized (or over-organized) people don't care about substance, but they might put too much energy into the form, and less into the contents. And as described in the previous section, over-organization can be a sign of anxiety. Diving into that deep and endless pool of knowledge can indeed be scary (fear being three short steps away from suffering, according to Master Yoda!). As we learn, we realize that there is always more to learn. Some people find this motivating, while for others it may be a source of anxiety.

Motivation for writing can come from the all-important act of reading. As Louis Pasteur said, fortune favours the prepared mind, and this is where reading has a role. One has to be ready to grab an idea as it comes by. Motivation makes everything seem easier; staying concentrated on a task and putting in extra hours comes naturally when we're motivated, and even feels worthwhile and fun! But motivation, like words in the manuscript, don't come out of thin air. It must have fuel. Through activities like exposing ourselves to different sources of information, reading articles not directly related to our dissertation topic, attending talks in varied research domains, we can relieve the pressure on the act of writing. Such activities serve to expand the mind, and unshackle us from the narrowness of the task at hand. Besides relieving pressure, they also have the advantage of providing additional opportunities to make connections between areas of research and engage in transdisciplinary and trans-sectoral research. While not everyone has the luxury of reading books about writing skills, reading itself should not be considered a frill, but rather the basis of writing.[6] It provides the many ideas that are necessary to forge our own, and offers models of how to combine words effectively, as well as counterexamples of how not to combine them. Reading is thus essential for preparing students to write. But reading can also become a snare for students; reading is the perfect excuse to postpone writing, the ultimate weapon of mass procrastination! If one wants to put off writing, there is always another article to read. Compared to writing, reading is comfortably passive; it is how we absorb ideas. However, we also need to devote time to consolidating the ideas and coming up with our own, which is done through writing. That said, reading shouldn't be seen as a task that belongs only to the earlier stages of graduate studies. We should keep reading throughout our studies (and indeed, throughout our lives). The Discussion section of a dissertation by someone who continued reading throughout the writing process will be richer than by someone who essentially stopped as soon as they began to write. Their interpretation of their findings will be attuned to the most recent developments in their field of interest, and not a banal summary, which is often what we find in the first draft of a student's General Discussion.

Expanding our minds does, however, present some risks. As we've already stated, the pool of knowledge is infinite. To grasp and assimilate the infinite is not humanly possible and the danger of too much "expansion" is to lose focus (remember the importance of setting finite objectives, Chapter 5). Another potential pitfall of this diffused focus is the danger of surfing over a shallow level of knowledge and avoiding the important step of digging down. Depth is indispensable in a dissertation, because a dissertation is a marker of the writer's expertise. Thanks to the internet, the danger of easy access to shallow information has grown. Of course, the internet has countless other advantages. However, its shallowness leads students to focus on abstracts of articles, or second and third-hand references, and

6. Pinker, S. (2014). *The Sense of Style: The Thinking Person's Guide to Writing in the 21st Century*. New York: Penguin Books.

never dig into the actual methods being described. Sometimes they even skim over the interpretation of the researchers who actually conducted the study. Increasing our breadth is undeniably important for making links between multiple domains (especially in an era of inter-, trans-, and multi-disciplinarity, not to mention multiple sectors), but it should never come at the expense of depth.[7] Adding breadth should also solidify one's arguments, not weaken them. Adding breadth should ensure that we are digging down at the right place: it improves the probability of finding those precious gems, and keeps us from getting completely stuck if we hit a very hard stone. If one changes the analogy to building instead of digging, aiming to build a pyramid, or a castle, seems like a better model for writing a dissertation than building a lonely tower.

So how do we expand *and* focus? One tip is to avoid trying to do both at the same time. The ideal is to switch modes, alternate, and stay flexible and agile in our mode of thinking. This is also how our brains are wired. As mentioned above, great ideas don't appear already consolidated and synthesized the moment we command them to, at the time we've scheduled in front of a keyboard. Ideas might come when we're in the shower, shopping for groceries, or chatting with colleagues or friends, and they might not always come as a blinding "Eureka!" They must be built, and assembled together. The stones of a castle need mortar, and mortar needs time to dry. So if writing is the focused part of the creative experience, *not* writing is the expanding counterpart. Thus, in terms of advancing the dissertation, the periods when we aren't writing are as important as the periods writing. There is indeed evidence that letting our minds wander can help consolidate strategies for solving previously encountered problems.[8] While writing a dissertation isn't only about thinking and day-dreaming, these activities fuel the creative processes and should be valued and given time (a lot of time—prompting our friends and family to comment again about how long we've been in school).

---

7. Bateman, T.S., & Hess, A.M. (2015). Different personal propensities among scientists relate to deeper vs. broader knowledge contributions. *Proceedings of the National Academy of Sciences of the United States of America, 112*(12), 3653–3658. <https://doi.org/10.1073/pnas.1421286112>

8. Baird, B., Smallwood, J., Mrazek, M.D., Kam, J.W.Y., Franklin, M.S., & Schooler, J.W. (2012). Inspired by distraction: Mind wandering facilitates creative incubation. *Psychological Science, 23*(10), 1117–1122. <https://doi.org/10.1177/0956797612446024>; Yamaoka, A., & Yukawa, S. (2020). Does mind wandering during the thought incubation period improve creativity and worsen mood? *Psychological Reports, 123*(5), 1785–1800. <https://doi.org/10.1177/0033294119896039>

At least one neurocognitive model suggests that two important brain networks work together (and possibly alternate) to support creativity.[9] One, the executive control network, is associated with the many operations necessary to engage in and perform specific tasks (the focused part of writing for instance). In contrast, the default mode network is associated with "offline" (i.e., not task-specific) activities such as introspection, imagination, and day-dreaming. Collaboration between these networks is thought to provide the underlying mechanism for a balance between the focused attention towards specific tasks and the less focused (lower pressure) operations required to explore, make associations, and generate ideas in a freer and less constrained manner.[10] The potential challenge of the latter processes is that they can take time, and the time they take cannot always be precisely estimated. How many of us would block off time in our agendas for "not writing", to protect these periods when our mind can wander? The truth is, many of us do, but they're labelled differently (cook dinner, run 5 km, walk for an hour, pick up the kids).

THE TWO INDISSOCIABLE SIDES OF A DISSERTATION

In conclusion, writing a dissertation requires both structure and ideas, and both of these come with perseverance and hard work. Our two hypotheses from the start of this chapter are in fact two complementary types of challenges, two operating modes that students need to master (and that we need to teach, see Table 9.1). Finding a balance between systematic progress and florid creativity is difficult, and the research advisor's role might be to guide the student towards this balance by encouraging both modes, rather than imposing or expecting that they excel at either of those skills. This guidance should be offered from the start of graduate studies, not when students are already suffering writers block and a year behind schedule, because balancing these skills will be essential throughout their learning. The advisor's role is also to understand that this balance might be achieved differently for different students. Some have greater skills in one mode than the other. It isn't necessary for everyone to be equally good at both, but everyone can learn to be better at each of these complementary modes of work.

---

9. Beaty, R.E., Benedek, M., Silvia, P.J., & Schacter, D.L. (2016). Creative cognition and brain network dynamics. *Trends in Cognitive Sciences, 20*(2), 87–95. <https://doi.org/10.1016/j.tics.2015.10.004>
10. *Ibid.*

TABLE 9.1—How to teach the two necessary operating modes to complete a dissertation

WRITING THE DISSERTATION (MANAGING ANXIETY AND PERFECTIONISM)	GENERATING IDEAS FOR THE DISSERTATION (INSTILLING MOTIVATION)
• Encourage students to write often. • Encourage students to set aside specific time for writing, ideally fairly short, recurrent periods. • Set specific, measurable and realistic writing goals with students. • Distinguish between the stages of writing (planning, actual writing, and editing) and offer different strategies depending on where the student is at (e.g., developing a plan through several iterations, writing down good ideas without stopping to polish, leaving yourself enough time to edit, etc.). • Be a role model. Teach your students and let them see that you set aside periods to write. • Reassure them that it's ok to set aside sections that aren't completely finished and switch to another section. It's okay to move from one part to another (as long as they don't always leave the same part unfinished). • Suggest that students quit writing when the words are still flowing, making it easier to start the next day (or "park on a downhill slope"). Help them learn not just to stop when they are out of gas, but to leave some ideas hanging to help get the next session started. • Help them face the fears that underlie procrastination, openly talk about imposter syndrome. • Identify and moderate their perfectionist high standards ("the perfect is the enemy of the good," "a good dissertation is a finished dissertation," etc.). • Remind them that excellence comes from practice. • Propose lab writing sessions (lab meetings dedicated to individual writing).	• Encourage students to write often. • Carry a notebook (or app on your phone) to write or record ideas as quickly as possible when they occur to you. • Make them talk about their ideas. Having to communicate to someone else will help those ideas crystallize. • Use drawings, conceptual maps and doodles to illustrate your ideas. • Be a role model. Let the students see you attend talks and conferences on a wide variety of topics, and engage in multi-, inter-, and transdisciplinary work. • Ask students to read and comment on each other's writing. • Talk to your students about your passion, how you like your job, and how you enjoy writing. • Encourage discussions outside the scientific focus of your lab, by discussing subjects such as critical thinking, the writing process, diversity in science, etc. • Talk about your own projects as well as theirs. It's okay to have projects which aren't those of students, as long as you don't spend all your time of these projects at the expense of taking time to provide feedback to your team. • Encourage lab exchanges and lab visits. • Attend talks and conferences.

CHAPTER 10
Embrace diversity

As mentors, professors, and lab directors, we are leaders. As the leader of the group, "our group," we are the person in authority, with ultimate responsibility for the group's good behaviour, quality of work, and adherence to good practices. We get praised for the team's good work, but we're also the ones who receive the blame if something goes wrong. As persons holding power over others, we should ask ourselves who we are and what we represent. We should pay special attention to being part of, or perceived as part of, any dominant or majority groups. As leaders, we should think beyond majority rule to balance the needs of all the people in the team (yes, that is a lot of shoulds!). It's our responsibility to learn about different cultures and practices, not necessarily to change our own methods every time we encounter someone whose expectations are different, but to reduce our blind spots and to reach out to all team members and make them feel part of the group. Moreover, if you accept the premise of this book that a student is the boss of their own dissertation, this means that writing a dissertation involves two leaders. These leaders, whatever their differences, need to work together towards the same goal. In such a context, difference shouldn't be rejected or ignored, but rather be sought out and valued. As our first case describes (Box 10.1), differences are opportunities to learn.

BOX 10.1— I TAKE, YOU TAKE, WE ALL TAKE VACATIONS

One simple example where a student's different cultural practices were the driver for change (for one of the authors, and for one student) is the concept of vacations. The average vacation time in North America is probably around two or three weeks, but in some European countries, the average (and for some, the expected minimum) is closer to five or six weeks, not including statutory holidays. Not all professors take their allotted vacation time (or indeed, take vacation at all). So, when a European post-doctoral fellow announced to their North American advisor that, having taken three weeks of vacation to go back home in August, they were going to the Bahamas with their family for three weeks at Christmas, the advisor froze and pondered for a moment. All sorts of thoughts flashed through their mind—some of which would eventually lead to constructive discussions—but on the spot, the advisor thought, "WHAT? You just came back from vacation! Three weeks??? I don't even take three weeks during the summer! When are you going to submit your first paper? In fact, when are you going to finish writing the draft of the first paper?" And so on. What some professors might see as a minor cultural difference could be a deal breaker for others. In this particular case, the cumulative effect of all the vacation days the advisor had spent working, and the ensuing discussion that ended in a good laugh, had two positive outcomes: (1) they convinced the advisor to gradually start taking full and totally unplugged vacations, and (2) the post-doctoral fellow published many papers (without taking less vacation time) and eventually got a position at a university.

THREE LETTERS, THREE WORDS, THREE PRINCIPLES!

There are numerous examples of efforts being put in place in academia to promote the principles of equity, diversity and inclusion. We hear these principles discussed, we are asked to follow short "mandatory" trainings, and slowly we see some beliefs and practices start to change. As professors, role models, leaders, and people in a position of power, we have the responsibility to play an important part in this change, and we must be aware that the supervision relationship puts us in a position where, if we ignore some inequities, we can exacerbate them. Our role also gives us opportunities to redress the numerous imbalances that still plague advisor–student interactions. We are role models, but as Chapter 4 argues, we aren't models to copy; we don't want to clone ourselves and erase all traces of individuality in our team. Ultimately, we want the student's dissertation to reflect their own perspective, and this perspective can and should reflect their own individual characteristics.

The commonly used acronym for equity, diversity and inclusion is EDI. Some people change the order to use DEI (diversity, equity and inclusion), and some also add justice, leading to the controversial acronym JEDI.[1] We prefer to spell out the words rather than use acronyms, because these tend

1. Hammond, J.W., Brownell, S.E., Kedharnath, N.A., Cheng, S.J., & Carson Byrd, W. (2021). Why the term "JEDI" is problematic for describing programs that promote justice, equity, diversity and inclusion. *Scientific American*. September 23, 2021. <https://www.scientificamerican.com/article/why-the-term-jedi-is-problematic-for-describing-programs-that-promote-justice-equity-diversity-and-inclusion/>

to lump concepts together with the result that some important differences between these principles can be lost. To offer one sad example, we remember a colleague speaking with conviction about EDI during a coffee break and making a case for how important it was, yet they were unable to recall what one of the three letters actually stood for. So let's not be that colleague, and let's learn what the words are, and what they mean.

Equity refers to the principle of fair treatment for people with different characteristics (see below for "diversity"). Some people would also say that equity refers to the just treatment of different people. The distinction between equity and justice might reside in the fact that individually we can treat people equitably, but if we want such changes to be sustainable and apply across populations, we need the system to change as well (see the definition of Justice below). Equity is fundamentally different from, and should not be confused with equality, which refers to providing the same treatment and resources to all. Spending one hour with each graduate student per month, no more and no less, would be an example of equality (see Figure 10.1). Does this mean that following the principle of equity would mean spending zero time with some students and several hours with others? Not necessarily. One could set a minimum, like spending at least one hour with each graduate student every week, every two weeks or every month, to ensure that there is some follow-up, then adjust according to the needs of each (while making sure to reserve a few hours for oneself). So, equity here refers to what we as advisors provide to students, as well as the way we interact with them. Equity involves becoming aware of the varying levels of privilege or disadvantages that our students experience, and acting to reduce the opportunity gaps created by varied backgrounds and individual characteristics. But does equity mean that the support we provide to students should be adjusted so that the outputs (the dissertations) are equal? Not necessarily. Not all students need to meet the same performance criteria. They might not all publish the same number of papers, or go to the same number of conferences, or become professors. Thus, equity consists of being aware of differences between students, not only when they join our team but also throughout their studies, up to and including their graduation.

FIGURE 10.1—Equity in practice

Inequality

Equality

"Pack your things! You're both going to this Prestigious International Conference!"

Equity

"You both can attend any prestigious international conference during your studies, whenever you're ready!"

Justice

Diversity refers to the many characteristics that can distinguish people from one another, or act as the basis on which people tend to form groups. In this and the next chapter we refer to two frameworks called PROGRESS+[2] and ADDRESSING.[3] These frameworks identify characteristics such as place of residence, race, ethnicity, culture, language, occupation, sex, gender, religion, education level, socioeconomic status, age, disability, and other factors or situations for which a person may be discriminated against or disadvantaged, whether permanently or temporarily. These characteristics can relate to people's physical and mental characteristics, but also their experiences, way of living, history, and background. Several of these characteristics are considered invisible, meaning that we cannot identify the characteristics directly from seeing or hearing someone. Thanks to social psychology, we know that people tend to associate with others that they perceive as belonging to the same group, that is, people with whom they share characteristics. While this might have played an important role in human evolution and socialization, it also has a dark side, the notion of the outgroup. When you start aggregating people in groups, you will, by definition, have people who are in and people who are out. The problem is that people tend to treat people from "outgroups" differently, with distrust and misconceptions, rather than good will and openness. When you add to this that some groups have historically held dominant roles and have enjoyed —and fought to hang onto—the advantages that come with this position, it becomes apparent that fostering diversity in itself is not necessarily enough to create an equitable environment. We have to promote diversity within the framework of inclusion.

Inclusion refers to the principle of creating environments and relationships where everyone feels accepted and is treated equitably. This implies remaining open and kind toward everyone. In order to apply this principle, one must frequently take stock of the diversity of the group and ask whether the current practices are creating obstacles for people with certain characteristics. Inclusion doesn't mean that anything and everything must be accepted. It's okay to have our own set of values that may differ from others. However, the way we behave when facing diversity can be inclusive or not.

---

2. O'Neill, J., Tabish, H., Welch, V., Petticrew, M., Pottie, K., Clarke, M., Evans, T., Pardo Pardo J., Waters, E., White, H., & Tugwell, P. (2014). Applying an equity lens to interventions: Using PROGRESS ensures consideration of socially stratifying factors to illuminate inequities in health. *Journal of Clinical Epidemiology*. 67(1), 56–64. <https://doi.org/10.1016/j.jclinepi.2013.08.005>
3. See Hays, P.A. (2022). *Addressing Cultural Complexities in Counseling and Clinical Practice: An Intersectional Approach* (4th edition). Washington DC: American Psychological Association.

"Protecting" our dominant viewpoints or our advantages is not inclusive. Trying to integrate differences, working on finding compromises, and thinking about the good of each person in the group is inclusive. Working in a diverse and inclusive environment has the advantage of increasing the number of perspectives, and thus the richness of the information available. The more ideas, the more creativity and originality. More viewpoints also equals more opportunities to confront our own ideas, question them, and perhaps change them. Some might get hung up on the difficulties of considering many positions at once, but we like to point out that the more difficult the task, the more rewarding the result.

We've mentioned a number of frameworks that also add justice as another principle that can help overcome inequities. Justice refers to a principle that emerges from the system itself in which people are acting (see last panel of Figure 10.1). In order for changes to be long-lasting, it is not enough to rely on individual changes in people. Changes to the system ensure that we have reminders embedded in our society that provide guidelines, and sometimes still stronger laws and regulations. We need to remove systemic barriers in our systems, systematically. People tend to think they can leave justice to the politicians and lawyers to worry about. But as professors in academia, where freedom of thought still remains sacred (so far), and as members of a privileged group, we have great opportunities (some will rightfully say responsibilities) to voice our displeasure with the system in place, and to implement practices that will contribute to making the academic environment free of inequities.

THE JOURNEY TOWARDS INCLUSIVE MENTORING

Applying the principles of equity, diversity and inclusion within our labs, through our mentoring of students, is not always easy, and some may find it more difficult than others. It's often more difficult for people who themselves don't belong to any underrepresented groups. These issues, which may seem to rely on common sense, do stir up emotions and can even lead to unexpected debates and conflicts. Many books describe how difficult it can be to interact with, teach, and mentor people of different backgrounds. The following paragraphs are not meant to scare you, but rather to demystify the principles of equity, diversity, and inclusion in the context of mentoring students during graduate studies. They are also meant as an encouragement towards incremental change, ranging from minimal to champion-level. Everyone can and should learn to adhere to these principles, whether these skills come instantly, or gradually over their career.

Being aware (knowing about diversity)

As mentioned above, some of the individual characteristics that contribute to diversity are visible, but many are not. When characteristics are visible, people can't pretend they don't know about them, but they may fail to realize that these characteristics could raise issues, and also fail to understand why these issues relate to inequity. Some people can knowingly fail to adopt inclusive behaviours by wilfully pretending they don't see certain characteristics, or worse, they may adopt exclusive behaviours. When characteristics are not visible, people may simply not know about them, know about them but fail to realize the issue (as in an unconscious belief, or bias), know there is an issue but fail to understand it, or know inaccurate facts about these characteristics (i.e., stereotypes). Finally, people can know about the characteristics, understand them, but still not care about the issue. This last case might still, unfortunately, exist on campus (and this is why the systems must also change), but as optimistic people, we focus on the other cases, assuming that most advisors, and especially our distinguished readers, do not have malevolent intentions.

Before learning about other people's individual characteristics, one way to start pondering such characteristics is to start thinking about our own. A simple tool to become more aware of our own characteristics is to complete a social identity map.[4] This tool was developed to help people interested in qualitative health research to identify their social identities, and reflect on how these can impact their position towards different identities, and thus their research. The same exercise can be useful in the context of research supervision. Identifying our social identities will help raise awareness about our own position with regards to different social characteristics (see Chapter 11, Box 11.6). This kind of tool can also be used at different moments in our career, since our identity can change over time, as do our views about identities. However, this tool does not provide us with information about the potential inequities associated with certain characteristics and the historical reasons that might underlie the very existence of certain underrepresented groups.

Being open (nurturing inclusion)

Reading and listening to different source materials from the perspectives of underrepresented groups can provide more information, in particular an historical perspective (i.e., learning from mistakes of the past).

4. Jacobson, D., & Mustafa, N. (2019). Social identity map: A reflexivity tool for practicing explicit positionality in critical qualitative research. *International Journal of Qualitative Methods, 18*. <https://doi.org/10.1177/1609406919870075>

While one might know about stereotypes, biases and injustices towards certain groups, learning how these emerged historically is important to understand them fully, because this will help navigate between one's own perspective and that of the underrepresented group (see Box 10.2). It should be relatively easy for scholars hungry for new knowledge to gather information, but showing interest in the history of people from different groups and trying to understand how their practices differ from ours does take time. Obviously, a person cannot read and know everything about every group, their different histories, viewpoints, behaviours, and all the potential intersections (meaning some people have characteristics associated with more than one minority group). There may even be some danger in consuming a large amount of superficial information, without taking the time to reflect on it. Modern means of communication, including the ever-growing role of social media, favour the rapid exchange and access to of all types of information, but these come with less quality control. They can therefore actually increase biases and perpetuate stereotypes. Simply gathering more information without an open mind and some critical thinking may actually work against inclusion. Yes, it's easier now to learn about people from all over the world; however, this sudden increase in opportunities to communicate and interact with people who may be "like us" or "different from us" has also contributed to polarizing group differences.[5] Nurturing inclusion implies actively seeking out what is good about diversity, highlighting it and trying to disseminate it. As with any learning exercise, firsthand experience through social interaction is the ultimate way to expose ourselves to diversity, and interacting with diverse people will provide a deeper understanding than reading about them. Finally, let's not forget that promoting inclusion is not only beneficial for us individually, but also for all of our team, including both students and personnel (see Box 10.3).

Another great source of information comes from listening to champions and people who specialize in equity, diversity and inclusion. Most faculties or departments have designated resource people who know more about these issues than others. Talking to these people and asking questions may require some humility, but it also represents a good learning opportunity. To the less knowledgeable among us, these people can be intimidating, or may even appear self-righteous (see Box 10.4). However, if we have the humility to accept the fact that we have many blind spots, these people provide a wealth of valuable information and can inspire us to change.

5. Keum, B.T.H., & Cano, M.Á. (2021). Online racism, psychological distress, and alcohol use among racial minority women and men: A multi-group mediation analysis. *American Journal of Orthopsychiatry, 91*(4), 524–530. <https://doi.org/10.1037/ort0000553>

BOX 10.2—GUIDED BY EMPATHY

Contemporary models inspired by work in social psychology and neuroscience conceptualize empathy as a multi-dimensional process involving at least two main components. One component relates to emotions and our varying degrees of sensitivity to the emotional signals sent by others (called affective resonance). The other component relies on controlled and effortful cognitive processes that allow us to mentally enter into the perspective of someone else and understand their point of view and their mental state (called perspective taking). The ability to balance these two components of empathy differs between individuals, as well as depending on the context and the person with whom we empathize.[6] When diversity is lacking, these components can create unfavourable impressions upon sudden exposure to difference, because it's easier to empathize with people who have similar experiences to our own. However, with conscious perspective taking, we can increase our level of empathy towards people who are different from us. Thus, developing empathy in the context of diversity becomes a path towards inclusiveness. In the end, aiming to optimize one's empathy should mean developing a more equitable empathy, i.e., by learning to respond to other people's suffering and help the person in need regardless of what group or groups they belong to.

BOX 10.3—TEAM SPIRIT

For one of our colleagues, the first international graduate student they supervised made them realize how people from different backgrounds, and who have studied in different environments, can not only bring challenges but also new light and positive vibes to the group. This professor was roaming the poster area of a scientific conference, pushing a stroller (this was before conference organizers started to offer childcare services!) when they saw the student running energetically down an aisle of posters towards them, sweating, and brandishing the conference program, while yelling, "We won, we won, we won!" When the student reached the professor and caught their breath, they explained that one of the students in the lab had won a poster presentation prize. The professor was obviously pleased by the performance of the student who had won, but they also realized that the international student took just as much pride in the win and was as happy, if not happier, than the winning student. This

6. Coll, M.P., Grégoire, M., Latimer, M., Eugène, F., & Jackson, P.L. (2011). Perception of pain in others: Implication for caregivers. *Pain Management, 1*(3), 257–265. <https://doi.org/10.2217/pmt.11.21>

shared joy can happen in multi-authored work, probably more so when the work has multiple first authors (see Chapter 6), but this international student hadn't participated in the research at all and was in fact newly admitted to the program. Whereas most students may be pleased about a teammate's success, or even sometimes a bit envious, this student was simply and genuinely very happy. Not happy in the sense of taking credit for the win (he was shouting "*we* won"), but happy that the lab had won a prize, and, feeling a full member of this lab, they felt this happiness for the success of another member as much as if it were theirs. At that moment, the professor realized that the sense of community must be much more developed where the student studied previously, and that the competitive attitude that takes hold in most students often comes at the cost of team spirit.

BOX 10.4—THERE IS ALWAYS A BIGGER EDI FISH

One of our colleagues was leading a grant proposal at a time when equity, diversity and inclusion principles were starting to be systematically introduced by grant agencies. The agency had recently changed the application forms and had added one criterion that could be addressed in up to four (out of thirty) pages, describing the team in terms of the principles of equity, diversity and inclusion. These new pages took almost as much time to write as the other 26 pages together, because they required the grant applicant to think differently. Not only must they learn about these principles, but they must apply them to their research team and program, and outline specific actions they would take. At that time, very few of the co-investigators had gone through a similar process, and none had been required to address this issue in such depth. Today, most agencies not only ask researchers to write a section on equity, diversity and inclusion, they also ask them to attend online seminars or training, sometimes before submitting their application, sometimes before getting access to the funds. The process of writing those four pages was hard, not only because it was new, but because they weren't well prepared for this exercise.

They tried seeking help by asking people who'd been appointed as "EDI experts" on their campus, but they soon realized that they would have to go through the work themselves to be able to truly address the issues related to their specific proposal. Just when they thought this was hard enough, the process became even harder when they showed drafts of this section to researchers who were well-versed in the principles of equity, diversity and inclusion through their own work. Some of these people seemed to know so much more than them about these concepts that it made them feel like an ignoramus. Even if they were well-intentioned and approached this topic with humility, they felt totally incompetent. Note that the tone and brusqueness of some champions might have contributed to this feeling. In fact, they were feeling the major gap that existed at that time between the average researcher and experts in equity, diversity and inclusion. Some of these experts knew and felt the urgency to change practices with regards to underrepresented groups. This urgency sometimes translated into extreme positions and direct and somewhat condescending feedback (e.g., correcting the word "grantsmanship" by clearly pointing out how inconsistent the authors were with regards to sex and gender equity). To people from privileged groups, the experts' positions seemed extreme. These experts were uncompromising in some regards, rightfully arguing that such urgent injustices needed to be rectified yesterday, while the process of compromise, letting everyone learn at their own pace and go through different steps, would take too long to resolve. Moreover, time itself is not always sufficient to make significant changes. The bottom-up approach, in which all people voluntarily learn and apply principles of equity, diversity, and inclusion, doesn't always work, and some solutions need to emerge from the system itself (a top-down approach; see the previous discussion of the term Justice). People who have unearned privileges will have to relinquish some of them, not hang on as if they'd worked hard to earn them. Being forced to go through the process of writing those mandatory pages, to understand the process, and to think of measures to be put in place and why, is a revealing experience that paves the way along the humble road of inclusion.

Being open or learning to become open does not guarantee that we will know everything about all the characteristics of people from our team; however, acknowledging with humility that people do not have the same trajectory nor the same opportunities, while being aware of who we are, will lay the groundwork for an inclusive lab. Being humble also means that we're prepared to let go of some of the unearned privileges that have been arbitrarily granted to us. To achieve equity, people from underrepresented groups need to receive more, but people who are in positions of power because of numerous unearned privileges must also accept that they will receive (or claim, or take) less (e.g., fewer free cocktails at a conference to pay for on-site childcare; see Figure 10.1).

Being proactive (making changes towards equity)

Kindness, good will, and empathy could be sufficient drivers for adopting principles of equity, diversity and inclusion, but relying on these favourable conditions would induce changes sloooowly. So, what can we do to accelerate this process? As described in the next section, we can have a plan and identify specific actions or best practices that we could adopt. Before proposing some best practices, we want to express three aspects that require greater awareness once we start taking proactive steps to promote equity, diversity and inclusion. The first is the risk of highlighting elements of diversity either awkwardly, naïvely, or for the wrong reasons. We all have to tolerate a certain discomfort when we start adopting new practices, when we first interact with people who have been historically made invisible and excluded from certain academic circles. Drawing attention to differences in a casual or superficial way in a very homogeneous group, especially from a position of dominance, carries a risk of sliding into exoticism (see Box 10.5), which some even characterize, in certain cases, as racism (or sexism, or homophobia, etc.). Feeling a passing intrigue about someone's different characteristics is different from showing genuine interest and treating them as a whole person. Being interested in diversity isn't about entertainment and curiosity, but should be driven by intentions of reciprocity and sharing different ideas and viewpoints with others.

A second aspect that should make us careful is the way we introduce new or different practices. Forcing or imposing different practices, even with noble intentions, can trigger people's discomfort and resistance (see Box 10.6). It's important to explain the reasoning behind these changes, as well as evaluate their impacts.

BOX 10.5—DIVERSITY VERSUS EXOTICISM

Making positive comments that highlight differences between people can paradoxically perpetuate certain bad practices. Pointing out differences as "cool" can give the impression that we value the person for this "rare and exotic" feature. One of the authors recalls several occasions of brief discomfort when people would reply "that's cool!" or "no problem!" when she had to correct them that she had a girlfriend instead of a boyfriend. Another incident in one of our colleagues' lab also provides a good illustration of this issue. A group of undergraduate students were presenting their project to the team as a practice run for their final seminar. After the presentation, there were many interesting theoretical and methodological questions. Once most people had exhausted their questions, a grad student asked one of the undergrads, "Where are you from? Your accent is super cute!" This was asked in a context where a large majority of the students in the lab came from the same region. The "accent" of the undergraduate student was clearly from another region (and easily identifiable for people who have heard people speak from this region). The question came from genuine interest and was well-intentioned, but the way it was expressed, in front of the whole group during a seminar practice, may have been perceived as condescending by the undergrad student, who was well aware that they sounded different than most students. So, putting the undergrad student on the spot, even with a compliment, may have been unpleasant for them (by insisting on their difference). The fact that the comment about the "foreign accent" was made by a person speaking the same language but with a "dominant accent," and in front of a group, might have added to the discomfort of the situation. The professor, perceiving this discomfort (i.e., an awkward silence, the student blushing), and not knowing exactly what to do, simply interjected that everyone has an accent, it's only a matter of perspective (as their Dad, who was also an immigrant, used to say). This attempt to point out the discomfort, without knowing how to open the discussion, unintentionally resulted in a still more awkward silence. In retrospect, realizing that the initial comment might have been a microaggression, and that the professor's own response might have (1) added to the discomfort of the undergrad student, and (2) created additional discomfort in the student who made the comment, since the professor's intervention could have been perceived as "calling out" the microaggression (see Chapter 11, Box 11.2), the professor now thinks they might act differently. They could, for instance, choose to speak after the meeting to the student who was targeted by the comment, and ask whether they actually felt some discomfort, and if so "call in" the student who made the comment to explain how the situation might have been uncomfortable for the undergraduate student. The over-protectiveness that the professor showed towards the undergraduate student might have actually been perceived to be as awkward as the initial comment.

BOX 10.6 *LET'S TALK ABOUT SEX*

Sometimes, we decide to take the initiative and put our good ideas into practice... sometimes with a little too much enthusiasm. During a supervision session, one of our colleagues asked a group of students to do a take-home exercise that consisted of writing an identity map that provided details about their socio-cultural background. After waiting for several weeks, one of the students still hadn't handed in the homework. The professor privately asked the student if they were experiencing any difficulty with the exercise, and the student responded that they were uncomfortable with the idea of having to discuss sexuality with other students (one of the questions was about sexual orientation). At this point, the professor realized that the exercise, which they believed represented a normal level of sharing within a small group of upper-level psychology students, might come across as more intrusive for some than others. Additionally, they hadn't been sufficiently clear about the purpose of the exercise (to reflect on, but not necessarily reveal, personal details). Perhaps they'd also failed to clarify that the emphasis was on belonging to culturally specific groups (e.g., 2SLGBTQI+) rather than the characteristic itself (e.g., gender of their sexual partners). For the professor, sharing the contents of this exercise shouldn't have been difficult, and in some ways might have seemed a necessary part of the training (i.e., knowing yourself in order to become a "good" psychologist). However, as professors we sometimes forget that we belong to a dominant group in relation to the students. Would the student have been more comfortable sharing the exercise only with other students? Perhaps. Perhaps not. But this conversation was sufficient for the professor to adjust the way they introduced this exercise in their supervision practice, by moving it later in the training and giving it more context. The exercise had been intended as a means of fostering self-reflection, for the students to think about who they were, rather than to reveal themselves to others. It is fine and normal not to be willing to share everything with fellow students and with supervisors. Knowing and pushing against our boundaries is important, but that isn't the same as having to pretend we don't have any.

A third and perhaps more tricky aspect that requires vigilance is that wanting to know more about people can also raise challenges with regards to boundaries (see Chapter 7). As we learn more about a person's characteristics, we may have access to their personal lives that reaches beyond what is usually considered work-related information. This is another reason why people, and particularly advisors, should be careful about why and how they plan to use knowledge about personal characteristics. The person involved may also consider such knowledge confidential, raising questions about how to take this information into account without compromising its confidentiality. A good example, and one that is not uncommon in the context of graduate studies, is the presence of mental health issues. Knowing that someone has temporary or permanent limitations can help determine what expectations and level of support are appropriate, but the person might not want to share this fact with other members of the group.

IDENTIFYING AND APPLYING BEST PRACTICES

In the following paragraphs we provide examples of best practices at various levels, whether interpersonal, research group, program, or university, which we've either put into practice or plan to, in order to foster the principles of equity, diversity and inclusion. These don't claim to be guidelines or even the "best" best practices, as their effectiveness depends on a number of factors including each person's history and background, their context, and their knowledge about the principles of equity, diversity and inclusion.

Interpersonal best practices

Provide information / discuss expectations: This should be easy, since we already covered it in Chapter 3! It's essential to take time to talk with new students about the city they'll be working in, the campus, administrative procedures, scientific expectations, lab attendance, and anything else that should be included and discussed in the collaborative agreement. Don't assume that people know everything about lab interactions, graduate supervision, where to get coffee on campus, etc. Professors know how the system works and can help, either by providing the information or by guiding students to relevant resources.

Put yourself in the student's shoes: Showing empathy is a noble goal, but it's easier said than done. Beyond making yourself available, listening to students, and being aware of their emotional state, you may sometimes need to make an effort to understand what they're going through (see Box 10.2). This requires dedication and time, but also a foundation of trust. Perspective taking requires us to know about the student's context. The professor is responsible for creating an environment where such information can be shared safely.

Speak up to friends or colleagues: We can and should speak up when we hear people use expressions that may not be inclusive towards some groups (e.g., mankind versus humankind, and, yes, grantsmanship versus grant-writing skills), or may even be offensive (e.g., using names of Indigenous groups given by colonizers). Speaking up to a person we know should allow a certain degree of flexibility as to how and when to address the issue without risking jeopardizing the relationship (remember Box 10.4). Calling out a perfect stranger can be unproductive or perceived as offensive, especially if done in front of other people.

Research group best practices

Talk about equity, diversity and inclusion: Talking openly about different issues relating to equity, diversity and inclusion will show lab members that it's okay to address these subjects. These discussions shouldn't identify people directly, unless someone offers to discuss their specific situation, but should be more general. Applications for grants and scholarships now often ask candidates to address equity, diversity and inclusion issues, so this may represent a good starting point for discussions.

Track turn-taking: One very simple action that all advisors can do during group meetings is to keep track of who speaks and at what frequency.

While it can be intimidating to be asked to speak on the spot, without preparation or time to think, keeping alert for people who speak less and providing them with opportunities to jump into the discussion is an inclusive gesture (see Chapter 11, Box 11.2). Similarly, keeping track of which people are provided with roles and opportunities (leading the journal club, going to conferences, etc.) can help us identify whether we are perpetuating stereotypes (e.g., giving leadership roles only to more experienced students, assuming that artistic tasks will be handled better by women and technological challenges by men, etc.).

Recruit inclusively: A survey of the characteristics of the people of our lab could reveal that we tend to recruit people with similar characteristics, and might prompt us to take deliberate action to diversify the group. For instance, if we notice that we tend to accept students coming from a given program or university, we can decide to review more requests from potential graduate students outside of these groups.

Vary the hours and days of events: Lab meetings and social events are important for sharing information and building a sense of belonging. Choosing the same hours and format for these meetings might work to gather together the majority of students, but it might systematically exclude others. A lab meeting every Monday at 8:30 might exclude people who need to travel during the weekend, or people who have class. Social gatherings on a Sunday night might interfere with family and other responsibilities for some groups of students.

Adopt a gender-neutral vocabulary for communication: This method can be more difficult to apply in some languages other than English, but it's one way to start pushing back against a male-dominated practice which is often perpetuated on the pretext of simplicity.

Beyond the lab, the university

Reduce intellectual "inbreeding": Perhaps inspired by a biological principle that warns against the disadvantages of limiting a species' genetic pool, many university programs have an explicit or implicit rule not to recruit students from their own undergraduate programs. This has the advantage of bringing in a diversity of training and ideas that can be shared during graduate studies. Recruiting students from other countries increases diversity even more, but does come with additional challenges related to visa status, financial considerations (higher tuition fees), etc. Many universities have an International Students Office that provides a number of services (legal and financial advice, language courses, etc.) to reduce the barriers that students from other countries can face.

Use positive discrimination and quotas: Some programs identify minority groups and reserve spots for them in their programs, either as a percentage or a fixed number. The percentage may be relative to all accepted candidates, or to the number of proposals received from members of this group. Note that the latter practice may help maintain proportions of people from different groups (e.g., men and women), but would not allow greater representations of some groups (e.g., gender-diverse people) if members of these minority groups do not reach the step of applying to programs in the same proportion, or in some cases, at all.

Change the definition of excellence: There is evidence of hidden correlations and, more alarmingly, bias, in admission criteria that maintain systemic discrimination against members of certain minorities (e.g., racial bias against Black, Indigenous and People of Colour applicants[7]). Adopting a broad definition of excellence that takes into account factors other than marks, traditional achievements (talks, paper), and prizes can increase diversity. The choice of new criteria is not always easy, and could introduce other factors that contribute to inequities. For instance, if a program values volunteering and starts considering this as a desirable criterion, people might start counting volunteering hours as a marker of excellence. While a student might be interested in volunteering, the capacity to dedicate many hours to this activity during the course of an undergraduate program may be easier, for instance, for people who don't have to work to pay for their tuition, or for students who don't have kids.

BEING CONSCIENTIOUS (OBSERVING AND MEASURING THE IMPACTS OF OUR ACTIONS)

In conclusion, keeping an open mind and a humble attitude is necessary for us to make progress in the context of equity, diversity and inclusion. Is it sufficient though? Not likely. Just as the social identity map is a first meta-cognitive effort to learn about ourselves in relation to other groups, we also need to take a few steps back to assess the practices we put into place around us, and see whether these are having the desired impact. We must integrate principles of equity, diversity and inclusion rather than simply learning what these words mean. We also need to be challenged by and consult with others, to keep us on our toes and continue monitoring

7. Sarr, F., Knight, S., Strauss, D., Ouimet, A.J., Cénat, J.M., Williams, M.T., & Shaughnessy, K. (2022). Increasing the representation of Black, Indigenous, and People of Colour as students in psychology doctoral programmes. *Canadian Psychology / Psychologie canadienne, 63*(4), 479–499. <https://doi.org/10.1037/cap0000339>

for potential long-standing or new blind spots (see Box 10.6). Adhering to principles of equity, diversity and inclusion is difficult. Writing this chapter was difficult, and led to several respectful-yet-heated discussions between the co-authors, but throughout this process we continued to do what we do best: we learned. Then we jumped into the most difficult and humbling task of all, and put our money where our mouth is (as you'll see in the next chapter!).

CHAPTER 11
Mirror, mirror, help me see my blind spots

Now it's our turn to dive in. After having described multiple issues related to diversity that can affect the supervision relationship, we turn up the lights and put ourselves in front of a mirror to scrutinize our own practices and potential blind spots. We'll start by considering one central aspect of equity, diversity and inclusion, namely gender. We would like to ponder how our experiences have been influenced by our gender. By exploring the triple intersection between our gender, our life and academic experiences, and our careers, we can use this lens to examine our supervision practices. We take advantage of the fact that, in addition to being two authors, professors, and former students, we also have two distinct identities as male and female, in order to compare our very personal experiences and shine some light on our attitudes towards students that we think are related to gender. However, this process expanded rapidly to encompass other dimensions of diversity, as we discovered that the differences along our paths were not only a function of our genders. Through this exploration, which took us some unexpected places, we discovered intersections with other aspects of diversity that contribute to how we supervise students today.

As this exploration is based on personal experiences, the chapter is divided in two separate stories, first Philip's then Geneviève's.

PHILIP

Let me start first, humbly, from my masculine perspective. Who we are affects how we interact with students. One of the most obvious personal characteristics that most people are aware of (even those who say they are blind to it) is our gender. Gender, by definition, is constructed through years of socialization. It can be related to, but is different from sex, which is biologically determined (yet not unchangeable). Many of us are assigned a gender even before we are born, and the behaviours of our parents and of others towards us contribute to shape our perception of our own gender. Who we are is a function of who we think we are and who other people think we are.

As a sad example of the many gender-based social injustices throughout humanity's evolution as well as recent history, we can point out that women in North America have only recently obtained the right to vote (Canada, 1918, except for Québec in 1940; USA, 1920; Mexico, 1953). Also, to this day women are still paid less than men for similar jobs and are more represented in jobs that pay less overall. Even in instances where salaries are determined by a collective agreement, like professors in our university, meaning that all professors with the same experience should theoretically receive the same salary, women may be expected to contribute more (e.g., to mundane administrative tasks, teaching, etc.), and fewer women have access to salary bonuses (e.g., retention bonuses, senior management bonuses). Men are a privileged group and have acted, in the past and to this day, as the dominant group. This dominance differs from that of other groups described in Chapter 10, in that men do not form a majority. There are roughly as many women as men on earth (49.7%[1]) but a number of factors affect this ratio across countries, such as age, socio-economic conditions, and so forth.[2] Thus, the dominance of males over females does not come from a sheer majority: other factors, including the distribution of roles, probably contribute to perpetuating it. A set of underlying sex-based differences, physical and related to reproduction, has expanded to all sorts of roles and behaviours, and has been generalized to gender. Even today, there are still more men than women in positions of authority on university campuses,

1. Population, female (% of total population). *World Bank Group.* <https://data.worldbank.org/indicator/SP.POP.TOTL.FE.ZS>
2. Ritchie, H., & Roser, M. (2019). Gender ratio. *Our World in Data,* June. <https://ourworldindata.org/gender-ratio>

including directors, deans, and presidents. Thus, as a male heterosexual professor, it is important to recognize that, whether I want to or not, I carry an extra authoritarian aura that I've inherited from history and the recent past, regardless of whether I contributed to it or not. With great additional power comes great additional responsibility. Pretending that the male–female distinction doesn't exist is not the solution. If we want to interact equitably with all students, we need to be aware and stay aware that our gender can and will interact with the gender of students, either implicitly or explicitly. Recognizing the difference between genders is important, not to compare them and pit them against each other, but to ensure that we don't systematically favour or penalize one, and to put measures in place to reduce and even counteract the effect of male dominance in academia. Note that thus far we've addressed the topic of gender as a dichotomy or at most a continuum along a scale that ranges from femininity to masculinity. But as we acquire more knowledge, more and more people recognize the non-binary aspect of gender. Thus, the perception of gender and the definition of gender itself is another source of diversity that can vary from person to person, and this should be considered in an inclusive and culturally sensitive mentoring approach. As professors, we need to keep an open mind and avoid stereotypes, and we need to stay informed about social and cultural changes that are transforming the community of students we work with and mentor.

As a White heterosexual man, who was raised in a privileged neighbourhood in Quebec City by a French-Canadian (Québécoise) mother and a British father, I have been privileged. My mom was raised as a Catholic, my dad as a Protestant, but they chose to withdraw me from of religious classes in grade school and high school. Whether that was a privilege is debatable, as I was one of just four kids in my school (my sister being another) not taking the religious program. Both of my parents pursued careers in education, which no doubt influenced my path. As a high school teacher, my dad taught French in an English school, while my mom was a university lecturer teaching French to non-francophone students (yet I wrote part of this book in English!). My dad liked boats and my mom flowers, but neither were much at cooking. I like cars, my wife likes gardening, neither of us are good cooks, and we're both university professors. My mom and dad both had professional careers when I was young, which was the first model I saw of deconstructing traditional gender roles. While the apple never falls far from the tree, there is more to this story, since I would be exposed to several other examples as I grew up.

Another model of non-traditional roles came during my bachelor's degree, from a relationship with a woman who had strong feminist views.

I say strong now, but I used to think very, very strong. She opened my eyes to all kinds of inequities, from the job market to politics, and even related to the use of certain words. I joined her at protests and rallies and added a few books like *The Beauty Myth* to my small library, which already contained *The Lord of the Rings* and five different editions of *The Hobbit*. She got into heated arguments with my friends pointing out their sexist comments and sexist views on relationships. I would usually take her side, despite conflicted loyalties, since her views, however harshly stated, aligned better with mine than my friends' did. Some of these discussions with my friends were still ongoing years after my relationship with this woman ended, confirming that she had an impact on my views, and that part of me was already, perhaps implicitly, questioning traditional roles. Needless to say, those years accelerated my learning curve on issues of equity, diversity and inclusion!

Graduate studies were also a period where I interacted with women in positions of authority: the co-supervisor of my dissertation was female, the director of the research centre where I conducted my studies was female, and so were most students in my Ph.D. program. And although my main supervisor was a man, his own supervisor (thus my academic grandmother) was a very successful female researcher and pioneer in her field. Throughout my clinical training, out of the ten clinicians I worked with more directly, only two were men. Skipping ahead a few years, I dated and married a woman who is now also Professor of Psychology, and who followed a research-oriented career path similar to mine (research scholarships, research salary awards, sabbatical abroad while I took care of the kids, program director, etc.). Overall, I can say that there were many women in my life who directly or indirectly challenged the traditional view of gender-roles, and this has no doubt influenced my views about gender.

My career as a professor almost started in 2004. I'd applied for a professor position during my first year of a post-doc fellowship and was invited to a job talk that I aced (according to a few, perhaps biased, sources), followed by an interview that also went well. This was my second opportunity to get a position after another attempt at another university where a different candidate (a woman) with much more experience was unsurprisingly offered the position. But this second opportunity was not resolved the same way. Several weeks after the process, I received a letter stating that I didn't get the position. The reason invoked was that the position had been offered to the other candidate, a woman, because the university where I'd applied had a policy of hiring women over men when two candidates had an equal level of competence (to balance the fact that there were more men than women in the department). Thus, I'd been rejected on the basis of a positive discrimination policy. At the time, I was obviously disappointed not to get the position (I can now admit with shame that I was actually furious and outraged), and I couldn't understand why the hiring committee couldn't come up with another justification. After all, I thought I had more research experience while the other candidate had more clinical experience. And during the interview process, they'd made it clear that they expected the new professor to be highly involved in clinical training. They could have simply said that they were putting more emphasis on clinical experience, and that would have been understandable. But it may be that this department weighted research and clinical experiences equally, and by doing so showed more inclusivity. The result was that we had equivalent, albeit different, profiles. Had the department favoured a candidate with a stronger publication list, for instance, they might have fallen into the male publication bias. Such biases had possibly led to the department having many more male professors in the first place, prompting them to adopt an affirmative action policy. The department's decision was right and fair. I fully understand that now. I know more about the past, and sometimes prevailing, discrimination that led to these much-needed affirmative action policies that were and sometimes still are in place with respect to gender. Incidentally, more than twenty years later, when my university launched a campaign to recruit new Canada Research Chair holders and specified that the competition would only be open to women and candidates from other underrepresented groups, I was surprised that this caused some commotion on campus and even in local media. People still failed to understand, twenty years after I encountered affirmative action, the rationale behind this policy, i.e., that at the time only 30% of Canada Research Chair holders on campus were women, and only 10% came from self-identified minority groups. Through principles of affirmatives action, I was de facto excluded from this competition. But did I feel like a victim of discrimination? No. I've had my share (and mostly likely more than my share) of opportunities.

Now, considering my background and previous experiences as a person with privileges, could we say that this affects my role as a research advisor? Undoubtedly. But though everyone can have blind spots, it is always possible to learn, one experience at a time. The student–advisor relationship is built on trust and openness, and can lead to different levels of closeness (some, such as sexual or romantic closeness, to be avoided, as addressed in Chapters 7 and 8). For some, this level of closeness can become something like friendship. But as the examples below will illustrate, becoming friends with students can be detrimental to the relationship, firstly because the relationship is not between equal members of a group, since one person is in a position of authority, and secondly because being friends with some students but not with others can lead to inequities in the team. As an example, gender can contribute to these inequities if an advisor becomes friends, or friendlier, with members of only one gender.

Consider the hypothetical situation where a male professor, me for example, finishes working late and sees a person leaving their lab at the same time. Let's pretend I didn't have parental duties that evening and that I wasn't expected home until later that night. In a friendly relationship with a co-worker, I might spontaneously invite the person to come have a drink or to grab something to eat. But what if the person is a student? Should my behaviour be different if the student is a man or a woman, if they are single, dating someone, or married? (Most of you are probably thinking, "No, don't do it, don't go out with the single student!") Does this matter? Should my behaviour be the same if I'm not married? What if the student is new in town and doesn't know anyone else yet? Now, what if two students are leaving the lab at the same time as me? Would that make a difference in my behaviour? Would it depend on the gender of the two students? While many of these situations appear to be inconsequential and may even seem like a good idea in some cases, the simple act of sharing a drink or a meal with a student or students creates opportunities for closeness, even if the meal is shared in a professional environment like the noisy and brightly lit campus cafeteria. This added closeness might not necessarily lead to personal closeness, but it could provide professional advantages to the student or students, and thus create inequities. We don't need to go as far as sharing a meal with candles, wine and music to cross the line between what is acceptable and what isn't.[3] An extra meeting under social circumstances between a professor and a student could be the moment when, for instance, the professor talks about their international collaborations and the student learns that an internship position is available in one of those labs and is offered this position. Such information, that the professor's collaborator has an open internship position, should be communicated to all eligible students, and not only those who share a late-night drink with the professor. In short, opportunities should not be offered to a selected few, because this selection can reflect some bias, including gender bias. Some professors will only engage in such social activities with people of one gender, fearing what other people might think.

3. Katz, S. (2000). Sexual relations between students and faculty. *University Affairs*. December 1st. <https://www.universityaffairs.ca/opinion/in-my-opinion/sexual-relations-students-faculty/>

Let me illustrate this in another context, not at all hypothetical this time, and emphasize how gender might have played a role in the sequence of events. At some point in our career, we may be lucky to have enough funds to pay for all of our students to travel to an international conference. At other times, we may be able to pay for a few, sometimes just one, sometimes none. Sometimes it may be that only one student has any new data to present (if this is the criterion for sending a student to a conference). This happened to me two years in a row when only one student, a different student each year, attended a conference with me. During conferences, there can be many opportunities to discuss science in a less formal way than usual, and to socialize. People organize dinners for one or multiple lab groups, students from different teams meet and go out. At both successive conferences, I introduced my students to other researchers, invited them to discussions and meals with other teams, and I even had a few drinks on a bar terrace. Actually, when I look back, I had drinks with only one of them. This difference might be explained by a series of factors. Perhaps one of the students had met people from another lab and spent a lot of time with them, so was less available, or perhaps that opportunity to have a drink on the terrace came up spontaneously after an afternoon talk, while the same opportunity did not occur with the other student? Perhaps I had more meetings with researchers, or I was busier at one conference compared to the other? Or perhaps, more simply, one student was a man and the other was a woman, and my behaviour only differed according to their gender. Now, if this characteristic, gender, was the reason behind the difference in social activities during a conference, then it may illustrate inequitable treatment on the basis of gender, regardless of what direction it actually took (i.e., whether I only had the drink with the man or only with the woman), which resulted in me providing additional mentorship to one of them. As described earlier, I'm a heterosexual married man. Does this change anything? Should my decision to have or not have a drink with some students be different if I were a homosexual man ? Or a homosexual married man? Is it really my identity that matters, or more simply my position of authority (see Box 11.1)?

Another possible blind spot that I've had for years is the potential interaction between gender and success. I've been privileged, plus I've worked hard and pursued excellence, at least since I started my studies in Psychology—don't tell anyone, but I did flunk an accounting class. Some of the excellence might have stemmed from privilege, some from hard work. It's difficult to know the proportion, but at least I am now more aware of how these interact. For many years, I've praised excellence, encouraging my students to apply for every possible prize and scholarship, to present at conferences, to participate in committees, and to engage in debates during lab meetings. Many students have adhered to this model, but I don't know the extent to which each student was comfortable with it. I know that some did not adhere fully and that at least one person didn't like it at all. She had stopped coming to lab meetings, and when I asked why she replied that the experience was intimidating. I learned that what I was perceiving as scientific discussions and debates, was perceived by her as comparison, judgment, and unhealthy competition. She did not feel valued in the group. In retrospect, I realize that I didn't react with openness to her comments. I now think that I could have shown more effort to be inclusive and solicit opinions from people who weren't voicing theirs as strongly as others. I could have been more attentive to whether everyone had opportunities to contribute to the discussion. One element that makes me realize today that what this student felt was partly related to gender issues, is that I learned later that she and other students felt intimidated by male students who were more involved in discussions and who never hesitated to challenge others. Some female students in the lab were also very good at discussing and debating scientific issues, but they did so differently, perhaps by showing more respect for the opinions of others. I tried to address the issue, which later affected at least one other female student, by trying to change the tone of the discussion and making lab meetings less formal and more inclusive, but I hadn't picked up on the fact that it was male dominance behaviors that contributed to the divisive atmosphere.

BOX 11.1—OFFICE DOORS, TO CLOSE OR NOT CLOSE?

When meeting students, why do we choose to close the office door? Maybe it's to avoid disturbing other people nearby, but more likely it's for privacy. Whose privacy are we protecting, the advisor's, the student's, or both? Often, questions of privacy are implicitly or explicitly related to gender issues. Why? Perhaps because of some abuses that have been perpetrated mostly by male professors towards female students, and in very rare cases, female students accusing male professors (and male professors' fear of the low probability of a false accusation). The decision whether or not to close the door shouldn't be related to gender, but to the fact that the professor is in a position of authority and a closed door could feel threatening to the student. A closed door could exacerbate this power imbalance, which intersects with gender, but it is the position of authority and the potential abuse of this authority that people are trying to hide by closing the door, or expose (or prevent) by opening it.

Geneviève used to close the door for all meetings with students, and never hesitated to do so. She's now ashamed to admit that she actually used to suggest to male colleagues that they don't close their doors when meeting female students, advice she no longer gives now that she understands the negative bias against women that this advice is based on. I have also often heard, and was specifically told by former mentors, that male professors should not close their office doors, especially when meeting a female student. Over the years, I was able to detach myself from that sexist model, whose underlying assumption is not that men are predators, but that women will use their "power of seduction" to put men and their careers in serious jeopardy. Today, both Geneviève and I let the students decide what to do with the door. It is not up to me to impose either a closed or open door. Some students will spontaneously close the door behind them, from which I infer that they might want to address some sensitive issue that they don't want to share with other people on the same floor. Some students will come in and ask if they should close the door or not. When the choice is theirs, I say, "It's up to you." However, when the professor knows they have to discuss a sensitive issue and they know that the discussion might generate tension, they should warn the student in advance and explain why the door should be closed. So, closing the door or not isn't the most relevant part of the question. Beyond the stereotypes and unjustified fears, one needs to consider the numerous potential factors that can accentuate the difference in authority, and the potential of abuse of power, behind a closed door.

Writing this chapter fueled many engaging and fascinating discussions between the two authors. Geneviève wanted to highlight positive aspects of masculinity. By brainstorming about examples, however, it turned out that many of the "qualities" associated with masculinity were those characteristics that were encouraged specifically in men and led to male domination (e.g., being confident, taking action, demonstrating strength and leadership). Perhaps we don't need to look for specific reasons to value one group over the other; we need to remain open to differences and to understand that diversity is not about only one dimension. People should be valued for all of their characteristics and their individuality. It is my belief that we should not have to pump up men to compensate for the feminism movement that was (and still is) necessary to put an end to millennia of male dominance. All men have characteristics worth appreciating other than being a man. Men shouldn't be systematically depreciated of course, and we can even value masculinity at times, but as long as inequities persist this shouldn't be our emphasis. Positive discrimination is necessary to reverse entrenched imbalances. The fact that some competitions (e.g., for Research Chairs) are only open to women does not devalue male researchers. Male researchers should recognize that they have held advantages over women for most of their careers, and if they're at the beginning of their careers, they should recognize that they have held advantages in society in general since birth that contributed to obtaining their current position. They need to remain humble and aware that they have been privileged and will remain so until sex and gender bias are significantly reduced. People in power must recognize their privilege, and learn to let go of some of their power.

GENEVIÈVE

It's my turn to explore my female perspective on the interaction between supervision relationships and gender (as well as many other factors…). I think Philip did a good job of uncovering the gender inequalities that remain today. For my part, I grew up in a context where we believed that sex-related inequalities, or male–female differences as we referred to them, were a thing of the past. As a girl, I could do whatever I wanted, and everything was attainable. This was true up to a point. Certainly, I had more opportunities than my mother or my grandmothers had, in terms of education and work, but also more generally in terms of recognition and respect. However, it seemed like behind each open door, there was room for only one of us. One Smurfette per village, one Gwen Stefani per garage band, one Princess Leia per galaxy. The message for girls was supposed to be, "You can do whatever you want," but the truth was more like, "You can do whatever you want, but you are more likely to succeed in male-dominated spaces where the men find you competent enough to make room for you." Thus, as a university student, I unconsciously selected activities supervised and endorsed by men, because it increased the value given to my work. Cutting-edge fields that I wanted to join were mostly led by men, but men also appeared to be more competitive, more influential, and surrounded by more success. I wasn't aware at the time that I'd bought into to this sexist view, but it sure felt important to gain experience with people with prestige, and these people were men: objectively, there were more men with prestigious jobs, but subjectively I attributed more prestige to jobs that were held by men. At my thesis defense, I was proud that the jury included only male professors, because my work was being recognized by what I thought were the greatest experts in my field. I stood out in a group of men: it was as if I'd survived the toughest level in a video game. It's hard to criticize a sexist system when we've bought into it… I'd become a Smurfette *par excellence*!

As a professor today, I have the opportunity to work in a department that has as many women as men, and the climate is favourable to my development as a professor. This doesn't mean that this environment is exempt from sexism. For instance, there are as many women as there are men, but they aren't in the positions of power. At the time of writing these lines, there has yet to be a woman at the head of the department (with the exception of an interim department head, who is helping out during the permanent department head's absence). It's important to underline this especially because in Psychology, the vast majority of students are women, but the more advanced and the more specialized the program in terms of research, the smaller the proportion of women gets. Thus, the more advanced and closer to positions of power, the more men there are. And positions of power imply many privileges.

It is difficult to discuss gender and privileges without talking about missteps and abuse. In supervision relationships, there can be rapport, sharing, and mutual appreciation. The positive emotional connection with students is a central component of a good working alliance. We've already spoken about the importance of not confusing this closeness with intimacy, and that the supervision relationship is incompatible with one of friendship, love or sex. Intimate relationships between professors and students can have serious consequences for both students (often women) and professors (often men). We have discussed this already when referring to professional distance in Chapter 7, and multiple relationships in Chapter 8. Yet, this kind of misconduct, which is unfortunately heavily gendered, also has indirect consequences for professors as a whole and for the work environment in academia. When we hear about inappropriate actions or professors making comments of a sexual nature, it undermines everyone's sense of safety, regardless of gender. For male colleagues, it triggers fear that innocent gestures in the supervision relationship can be misinterpreted (see Box 11.1). Because some people haven't respected the boundaries of the supervision relationship, others worry that elements of building rapport or expressing appreciation will be interpreted as romantic or sexual advances. This generates uneasiness in the supervision relationship between male professors and female students, which makes these relationships less relaxed, less easy-going than those between a male professor and a male student, and results in inequities. We can look at the example given by Philip, who (it was implied, but we can readily guess) didn't hesitate to have a drink alone with a male student but not with a female student during a conference.

As a woman, my first reaction when I hear about misconduct from a male colleague (something that, unfortunately, has happened too many times) is to doubt the integrity of all other male colleagues. If one person could do this without me knowing about it, who knows what this other person could have done. My main fear isn't about being the target of such misconduct, even though I know that no one is immune to this, but that my trust in colleagues I work with and appreciate might one day be shattered by learning that they behaved inappropriately. I ask myself if I'm right to trust them, if I should be more wary. I wonder who is guilty, what I might not know. My feeling of trust and security is thus affected by doubt.

It becomes even more difficult when such doubts and insecurities are misunderstood, trivialized or invalidated by male colleagues. Leadership, a quality that is frequently glorified in the C.V.'s of top researchers, is often the result of dominance behaviour over other people (see how *I* get more funds, *I* publish more, *I* work harder). Many very successful colleagues do not seem to want to explore the effect they can have on others. They don't want to hear that there is even a slight possibility that their behaviour could have had a negative impact, or that they have contributed even indirectly to an unfavourable climate for women and people of other genders. When men vigorously defend their points of view without realizing the privileges that have benefited them, they are making an additional show of force that increases this feeling of insecurity. What's reassuring is when members of a dominant group, men for instance, react with humility rather than anger, toward members of the disadvantaged group who reveal their concerns.

This isn't true only for men, but for anyone in a position of power. We have likely all made mistakes, been oblivious to other people's plight, or taken advantage of situations in our favour. As a White person who was taught to treat everyone equally and not "see" differences of skin colour, I have failed to see discrimination issues based on ethnocultural origins for a long time. Movements such as Black Lives Matters, awareness-raising activities like National Indigenous Peoples Day, or representatives of Asian communities speaking out to denounce racism, all made me realize the extent of my ignorance, and that some of my behaviours were contributing to keeping these groups excluded. Realizing that I was privileged because of my skin colour and, most of all, realizing that I was acting in ways that may have offended people and contributed to maintain inequities, is not pleasant.[4] It can make us feel attacked and want to justify ourselves

4. Peggy McIntosh has written a series of articles that are very effective and have been used in different contexts. They were a revelation to me. They helped me realize that I was seeing people like me (White) every day on TV. That people in authority (police, government) looked like me. That I was entrusting my kids to people that looked like me in kindergarten or at school. I had never realized the extent of my privileges

(see Box 11.2), when what needs to be done is repair relationships and make room for people who were excluded. This learning experience is continuous, and will be filled with mistakes.

BOX 11.2—THE PROBLEM OF MICROAGGRESSIONS

Microaggressions are behaviours or comments from people from a dominant group that seem trivial but are offensive to people from a minority or underrepresented group. The problem with microaggressions is that, despite being an important topic, it tends to make everyone feel attacked: people who are targeted by them, and people who are told they use them. In fact, this topic generates fear in both majority and minority groups, but for different reasons. As a non-expert on the topic, I would like to propose a simplistic analogy, which I hope is not threatening. It's meant to illustrate my perspective of microaggressions as a person who belongs to both underrepresented and privileged groups.

Imagine you are at a festival or in a packed subway station. When you're moving in a crowd, it's hard not to bump into anyone. Even if you're careful, you still might step on someone's toes. Some people will say "ouch!", while others won't react, either because it didn't hurt that much and they want to remain polite, or because they didn't even feel it. Still others will react very strongly because the pain is very intense. These people might be suffering from a recent or long-past broken toe. Some of these people in pain might even accuse you of having stepped on their toe on purpose, because they've heard of similar things happening often in their community, or have experienced this themselves.

In an inclusive and welcoming environment like a university, there are more people who inadvertently step on other people's toes than idiots who shove thoughtlessly through the crowd (such people exist, but we

---

before reading this. McIntosh, Peggy. (1989). White privilege: Unpacking the invisible knapsack. *Peace and Freedom Magazine*, July/August, pp. 10-12. <https://med.umn.edu/sites/med.umn.edu/files/2022-12/White-Privilege_McIntosh-1989.pdf>; McIntosh, Peggy. (2014). Inviting a better understanding of privilege and disadvantage. In R.A. Bean, S.D. Davis & M.P. Davey (eds.), *Clinical Supervision Activities for Increasing Competence and Self-Awareness* (pp. 173–181). New York: John Wiley & Sons Inc.; McIntosh, Peggy. (2019). White privilege and male privilege: A personal account of coming to see correspondences through work in women's studies. In *On Privilege, Fraudulence, and Teaching as Learning* (pp. 17–28). London: Routledge. For male gender privileges, there are several examples of articles, but one that left an impression on me is this: Johnson, M.Z. (2016). 160+ examples of male privilege in all areas of life. *Everyday Feminism*. February 26. <https://everydayfeminism.com/2016/02/160-examples-of-male-privilege/>

doubt they will have read this far in the book, so we won't address such cases). There are probably (hopefully) more microaggressions than overt cases of sexism, racism, homophobia, etc. And the worst problem is often not the microaggression itself, but the different reactions when people say "ouch."

Let's first put ourselves in the perspective of the person who stepped on the other person's foot and provoked the "ouch." Some people react by becoming immediately defensive and respond vehemently, "Why can't you move over," "Get out of the way!", "That probably didn't even hurt," etc. Others will feel that they are the ones being bullied, that that they can no longer walk normally in a crowd for fear of bumping into someone and provoking an "ouch" reaction. In this way, the wound becomes twofold for the owner of the said toes: they get stepped on *and* they're punished for reacting about it (i.e., "You're just making a fuss," "You're bullying me"). This may explain why some people from underrepresented groups may choose not to draw attention to the interaction that hurt them. And this may also explain why, when they decide to react, people from dominant groups are surprised and think these events as isolated cases. In fact, scientific data and testimonials from people of underrepresented groups show that microaggressions are frequent.

What if the solution was simpler? What do we normally do when we step on someone's toes? Most of us will simply apologize. We don't blame the person for their reaction. We don't accuse them of being too sensitive. We don't run back home crying and saying that we can't go for a walk the way we'd like to anymore. No, we apologize, and we continue on our way, while trying to avoid stepping on other people's toes. People must be allowed to say "ouch" freely when we step on their toes, without us feeling attacked.

Does the person who says "ouch" have a role to play in how the interaction unfolds? Of course. If the person who stepped on their toes apologizes sincerely, there is no need to keep blaming them. Similarly, shouting out loud, "Oh my God, this person just stepped on my toes" in order to attract other people's attention and ultimately ostracize the offender is probably not the best solution. When an offensive remark is made in a meeting, Pamela Hays[5] reminds us of the "call in" strategy, that is, taking the person aside at an appropriate moment to explain calmly how the comment was hurtful, which is less confrontational and probably more effective for changing mentalities than the "call out" strategy, in which we denounce

5. Hays, P.A. (2022). *Addressing Cultural Complexities in Counseling and Clinical Practice: An Intersectional Approach* (4th edition). Washington DC: American Psychological Association.

the offender in front of everyone (often while emotions are running high). Conversely, when someone has waited for a meeting to end, chosen an appropriate moment and the right words to put themselves in a vulnerable position to share their reaction to a comment we've made, the least we can do is accept their words without becoming defensive. People from underrepresented groups are the ones who can teach us about microaggressions, not people from dominant groups. In the end, it doesn't matter whether or not the action in question corresponds to the exact definition of a microaggression: if we have hurt someone, regardless of our intention, our reflex should be to apologize.

In my experience, small tangible gestures of inclusion and reparation happen in subtle ways. No need for long speeches about social justice, in fact just the opposite. For instance, in a meeting where male colleagues were more numerous and dominating the conversation, one of them said that he would be interested to hear what I had to say and gave me the chance to speak. In a social gathering where one person seemed to take for granted that I was living with the "father" of my children, another colleague asked me how my girlfriend was doing. These gestures are subtle, but they offer a healing balm of reparation. Of course, I would prefer that people not step on my toes, but when they do, at least unintentionally, a simple apology, a simple gesture of inclusion or reparation, makes all the difference in the world.

It can also be useful to remind ourselves regularly that we only know a small portion of other people's reality. Sometimes while debating the nature of a microaggression ("Shut up! NO, I did not attack you!" spoken while slamming one's fist on the table), we might force the person from the underrepresented group to reveal personal aspects that they might not want to reveal. Let me offer an example from my own life. I'm a woman who has been in a relationship with another woman for over twenty years, and we have two beautiful children. On a few occasions since their birth, I've been asked in a social context—but not by someone close, with whom such personal conversation might arise naturally—"How did you manage to have kids?" People don't ask me if I have kids, they ask me how I got them. This has happened during casual interactions at the daycare center, during a department happy hour (yes, by a colleague, unfortunately), at the hairdressing salon. The only reason people ask me this is because I live with a woman. I don't know of any heterosexual woman who has been asked this same personal and invasive question spontaneously during a casual conversation. This is a microaggression. It is my sexual orientation that emboldens people, heterosexual and operating from a majority stance, to ask such a personal question at the grocery store or after a work meeting. I'm fortunate to have many female friends who are also in same-sex relationships. Most of them have wanted children. Some have had kids easily, some less easily, and some not at all. Some have had to go to fertility clinics, others made alternative arrangements. Some have lost their child. Some have yet to have kids. So, like many of them, if I allowed myself to be totally honest I would answer your question, "How did you manage to have kids?" with the response that this is none of your business. I don't say this, however, afraid of hurting your feelings in return. But if you're genuinely interested in my family and you want me to talk about my kids the way we might talk about the weather, you will ask me, just as you would anybody else, how old they are, what their favourite subject is in school, or how we're surviving the flu season (which lasts from September to June in Quebec, with occasional peaks in July or August).

I have been an open member of the 2SLGBTQI+ community since my graduate studies. This had a big influence on my academic path at the beginning of my university studies, and my experiences of coming out are linked to my young adult years. My own experience was that academia is generally an open environment, and a place where I can be myself. There was a 2SLGBTQI+ student association (at the time called "*le groupe gai de l'Université Laval*"). This is where I met not only my partner, but also the godfather and godmother of my children, as well as some of my closest friends. I can say that I was never personally targeted by homophobic remarks (note that I steer clear of social media!), but hearing such attacks towards other people in conversation or in the media does indirectly hurt me. Moreover, although I was never attacked, I did have the feeling that some supervisors were less interested or less at ease discussing my personal situation because I did not fit the same mold as other students. This gave me the impression that I wasn't as close to my supervisors as, for instance, students who talked openly about their personal relationships or their wedding plans. This may seem hard to understand today, perhaps even blown out of proportion (some will say that our supervisors avoided all personal conversations equally, with everyone!), but let's remember that marriage between same sex partners was only legalized in Canada in 2005, at the end of my graduate studies. This subtle form of exclusion, which I don't attribute to malice on anyone's part, quickly made me aware of the impact of not following the norm. I know how it feels to be accepted by the group, yet at the same time different from its other members.

Speaking of feeling different, I was also a first-generation university student. This means that I was the first to reach university level studies, not only in my close family but also in the part of my extended family that I grew up with, including my aunts, uncles, and cousins. I was the first to complete a bachelor's degree, a Master's, a Ph.D., a post-doctoral fellowship, a second post-doctoral fellowship, and, as you might have guessed, the first to become a university professor. This list is not trivial: each level represents a degree of separation between the people I grew up with, and the people with whom I now work.

Difference in socio-economic status, often associated with being a first-generation university student, is another important diversity factor. Yet, this kind of discrimination is the one that is least recognized in academia. Derogatory comments about people from a socio-economic status different from the one most prevalent on campus are still commonplace, and are treated less seriously than, for example, sexist and homophobic comments. This explains why I found this aspect the most difficult one to explore here.

Briefly, I lived for many years in a socio-economically disadvantaged environment. Money was a source of stress, conflict, and dissatisfaction: we didn't have enough, we blamed each other for not being frugal enough, we felt the constant threat of running out of money, and so on. Even today, the idea of being in debt generates an instinctive aversion, which explains why I got a credit card and bought a car and house much later than most of my peers, even though, objectively, I had the means to acquire them. In this disadvantaged context, belonging to a group that felt daily frustrations about meeting basic needs, it was acceptable to legitimize our existence or to vent some of the financial stress by blaming "the rich." Being "rich" was obviously an abstract concept, and we gave this label to anyone who possessed something we didn't: a luxury car, a pool, a trip to Disney World, a Vuarnet t-shirt, etc. It was okay to mock rich people: they had warped values, were selfish, made our lives miserable, etc. All our frustrations regarding unmet needs were channelled towards the rich. These expressions of scorn were frequent in my family and my circle of friends, who mostly lived in the same neighbourhood and shared a similar socio-economic status. Even in high school, where the cruelest comments were about situations related to such status, I was still surrounded by people who were experiencing a similar context to mine.

The more I progressed in my studies, the fewer allies I found among my peers. It became suddenly obvious that judging someone on the basis of them owning a BMW put me at risk of being rejected myself, by exposing my difference, the part of my identity which was neither an advantage nor the norm. It was thus necessary to modify my speech and attitudes to fit in with this new group of academics. Slowly, I was becoming more similar to highly educated people, but also, incidentally, to more socio-economically advantaged people. I also developed meaningful relationships with people from very privileged groups, which helped get rid of my prejudices about the "rich" (as did the fact that they would offer me lifts home in their BMWs).

However, in this advantaged group, it is just as common to despise people from the other group, "the poor" and people with low levels of education (see Box 11.3). Through my studies, I'd become different from my group of origin, and by socializing with people from more and more advantaged backgrounds, I gradually realized that some traits were considered undesirable because they betrayed a person's association with poverty.

BOX 11.3.—DISCRIMINATION AGAINST POOR PEOPLE?

Some examples might be necessary here. If I say that we often hear harsh judgements and mockery about the way economically underprivileged people dress, eat, and entertain themselves, you might react as Philip did by saying, "Do you really hear jokes about people on welfare in the campus hallways?" The conversation that followed this incredulous question made us realize that there are several examples of common expressions that reflect discriminatory attitudes towards people from a low socio-economic status. To draw a parallel with other underprivileged groups, it's increasingly acknowledged that sexist and racist attitudes aren't always explicit. It might not be a sexist joke about women drivers; instead, it might look like discrediting the words of a female leader by calling her emotional. Discrimination based on social class—classism—is based on economic criteria, which include indirect factors (e.g., living in a certain neighbourhood, owning certain possessions, socializing with specific groups, etc.). Signs of classism can be just as subtle as signs of sexism, racism or homophobia. In fact, we don't (usually) hear jokes against poor people on campus. However, in casual conversations, we hear caricatures based on offensive stereotypes: going to Old Orchard Beach on vacation is a bit dumb, wearing clothes from Walmart implies not being well-dressed, eating baloney sandwiches shows a lack of sophistication. We don't always realize it, but there are many characteristics we associate with inferiority (intelligence, behaviour, personality) that are in fact related to socio-economic status. The more advantaged your background, the less likely you are to notice this in conversations, while those from less privileged backgrounds can detect them easily: lack of money is too often associated with lack of intelligence. When I hear such stereotypes, I feel a conflict of loyalty because, while I appreciate and admire the colleague who is speaking, I feel that my uncle, my mother, or my past teenage self are being indirectly mocked.

In academia, success and excellence are highly valued, but this can become a double-edged sword because it also tends to create an elitist environment. The system is a meritocracy in which success is supposed to come from our own efforts. Similar reasoning is often applied to social success, such as having a house, a car, or a certain standard of living: if we succeeded, it must be the result of our own great efforts. Yet, as university professors we belong to a privileged social class. Some of us have benefited from those privileges for a longer time than others.

My career as a professor (and the generous paycheque that comes with it) has allowed me to cross over to a privileged socio-economic status; I am no longer in the disadvantaged group. But I still don't know how to fit into this new privileged environment. There are still certain moments during daily situations where my background takes over and which, in some instances, make me feel inferior and excluded from the new group, even when no one has said anything to make me feel that way. It often feels like I'm missing part of the software that would make my "computer" run the same way as my colleagues. For instance, I'm missing the piano lessons that would help me take part in discussions about classical music, English immersion camps that would help me become bilingual, ski trips that make people familiar with the names of different mountains in the area, backpacking through Europe which gives a sense of geography, etc. These instances are always subtle, but they are frequent. One colleague who shares my modest background once told me a story that illustrates the feeling we both have. She was having lunch with colleagues and the main conversation was about how the schools their kids attended all had restrictions about lunchboxes. All her colleagues were frustrated by how staff at the school were monitoring their kids' lunchboxes (for inappropriate content such as candies), which they considered very paternalistic. My colleague, who'd experienced going to school with an almost empty lunchbox, told me how she was upset and spoke sharply to her colleagues. "I wish I had people monitoring the contents of my lunchbox when I was in school! These procedures at school are not there for you, they are there to protect underprivileged kids!" She still remembers today how her comment created an uncomfortable silence, and how the topic of conversation was swiftly changed. Her colleagues had not only failed to understand the situation she was speaking about, but also the emotion this situation had stirred up in her.

This is an additional challenge for first-generation students who come from socio-economically underprivileged backgrounds: their exposure to the academic milieu gradually distances them from their backgrounds, even as they never become fully comfortable with the new advantaged group. By becoming a professor, I have joined the dark side. From our families' perspective, the disappointment and feeling of powerlessness that stems from seeing someone they love change into something different from themselves, even if it is for the better, can be expressed different ways, some of them good, others less so (see Box 11.4). My success is bittersweet because I no longer belong to the same socio-economic group as members of my family. Socio-economic status also interacts with gender, which may create even higher obstacles for first-generation students.

BOX 11.4—THE DISSERTATION THAT TORE A STUDENT AWAY FROM HER FAMILY

A colleague once told me this anecdote. During one specific thesis defense, he was proud of his student, who'd done a remarkable job, and while he was offering his congratulations, he said something along the lines of her being well on-track to becoming a professor. He knew she was ambivalent about the next step in her career, and he thought she was torn between a clinical job or continuing to a post-doc and a more "standard" academic path, but he himself was convinced that she had what it takes to be a professor. He understood her doubts and, to be fair, he knew she was also doubting whether she wanted to pursue this job given how many (too many) professors make sacrifices and keep insane schedules to stay at the top (acknowledging that he himself had given her this model). Yet, he sensed that something else was holding her back. This feeling crystallized at the happy hour following the defense where he met her parents. He is not sure to this day whether it was something he saw or something he heard, but it was clear that at least one of the parents was not demonstrating any pride, but was rather looking at the daughter with what seemed like contempt. The professor was incredulous. In fact, he disclosed to me that he had a very negative gut reaction towards these parents, who didn't seem to acknowledge his student's excellence. However, the student was a first-generation academic: my colleague's observations, and the student's ambivalence towards an academic career, were perhaps linked to this double glass ceiling.

How do all these experiences, coloured by many privileges and a few disadvantages, influence the way I supervise students? This line of thought is by no means complete, and will undoubtedly continue to evolve after writing these lines and after you have read them. One thing is clear, as a queer first-generation student, I think I benefited from an extraordinary faculty for ignoring background noise and persevering. It might be because I ignored comments from others that I kept going in academia, even though I didn't have any model to guide me. All these remarks, direct and indirect, saying that, on the one hand, I didn't have the sophistication it took, or on the other, that my head would get swollen—I had to ignore them all (an example of equity!). It's unsurprising that the message I often convey to students is something like, "Use what you have, and go for it." This is the attitude that worked for me. Blocking out the background noise and focusing on one's projects (article, dissertation, etc.) involves ignoring the comments that say that nothing you do can be excellent, whether these come from the outside (manuscript reviewers, dissertation committee members), or inside yourself (back off, impostor syndrome!). Ignoring comments is what I had to do throughout my journey to get my own professor's office. Even today, I still have a limited capacity to welcome comments, and I ignore many, much to the dismay of co-researchers with whom I write grant proposals. I supervise students, especially the most insecure ones, with this philosophy in mind. Of course, I often doubt myself, especially when I'm confronted with different perspectives, or in situations where it's important to focus on every small comment, to be more rigorous, more scientifically credible, and demonstrate higher "excellence." In the end, I think there are students who need to learn how to receive and benefit from comments, and others who, on the contrary, need to learn to ignore them and forge on regardless. I suspect that male students are more prevalent in the first group, while female students and those from other genders (and from minority groups in general) are more prevalent in the second. I don't know if an outside observer would perceive that I supervise students from these groups differently, but there are definitely some things I pay more attention to when supervising female students. It saddens me when female students abandon their dreams, for instance if they intended to pursue a research career but gave up and followed the clinical track because they considered research too tough and stressful. This makes me think that I have failed to provide a positive role model: I might have let too much of my own challenges bleed through, and not enough of the joys of a research career. I am sensitive to female students who have wavering confidence. In those students, I tend to see lack of confidence as a warning sign, a cue that I need to intervene as a mentor, while I perceive the same level of doubt as being well-founded and appropriate in male students. To female students, I want to say, "Go for it," as I was once clearly told (see Box 11.5). To male students, I want to say, "Go for it, but don't push, and be careful not to step on anyone's toes!"

BOX 11.5—THE WORDS THAT GALVANIZED ME TOWARDS AN ACADEMIC CAREER

Towards the end of my Ph.D., I hadn't seen many signals that I should pursue an academic career, at least not that I recognized at the time. The manuscript that I'd written for my master's degree was rejected after the first submission and, unfamiliar with the usual publication process, I hadn't dared to resubmit it somewhere else. I had two manuscripts in my Ph.D. dissertation, but they weren't ready to submit. I'd made a few presentations at conferences and contributed to a narrative review paper and a book chapter, but I didn't consider myself as being in the game. I'd taught half an undergrad course and I received evaluations from students that were ~~traumatizing~~ disappointing. So, while I did have a few achievements, I didn't think they were sufficient, quantitatively and qualitatively speaking, to justify taking my place in academia, an environment dedicated to excellence. I was proud of what I'd accomplished, make no mistake, I wasn't suffering from poor self-esteem. I simply thought I had reached the ceiling on my potential.

One day, I had a conversation with the head of the department, a professor I admired for his work, his teaching (including his super tough exams), and his outspokenness. He asked me what I wanted to do after my Ph.D., and I told him that I was weighing my options, and that I thought a university career was out of my reach. To my utmost surprise, he started to laugh and told me, "You young ladies question yourselves too much. No guy ever thinks about whether a career as a professor is in his reach: they go to the interview and they get the position or not."

Those words had the effect of an electric shock. What if my doubts had nothing to do with my accomplishments, but more about my self-confidence, related to my gender? What if confidence was the key? This revelation changed my way of thinking completely, drastically, and all at once. And so I started going to interviews.

On the darker side of things—because we have to expose the shadowed areas as well—what I realized through the exercise of writing these lines is that my personal experience of being disadvantaged paradoxically contributes to making me adhere more to the meritocratic model. "Put in the effort, follow your path, and you will succeed no matter your background." This worked for me. I tend to attribute a lot of my success to my efforts, but in fact I benefited from major privileges related to the colour of my skin, an ethnocultural identity that is related to the dominant one, the lack of significant disabilities, and an aptitude to perform well in school. However, my belonging to nondominant groups in terms of gender, sexual orientation, and socio-economic status makes me both more sensitive, and more critical of students' situations. I am understanding towards people from minority groups, but I'm uncompromising towards students in whom I perceive (rightfully or not) a lack of effort. I only recently realized that, because of adhering to a meritocratic philosophy, when I'm faced with a path that differs from the norm (read: that deviates from excellence), my first, reflexive reaction is to attribute it to a lack of effort. This is my blind spot. This means that I must beware of spontaneous reactions and reach beyond my biases and mental shortcuts to ponder more about the context and the reasons, other than effort, which can explain the different situations of students.

2025: A DIVERSITY ODYSSEY

What to conclude from our two paths? First and foremost, neither of us possesses the ultimate "truth"! The way we think about supervision (and the contents of this book) is coloured by who we are and our background. Completing one's social map is an enriching exercise of self-exploration (which we propose you try out in Box 11.6), and helps bring to light the privileges we might benefit from by belonging to certain groups. Assuming that one completes it honestly and with humility, this exercise sheds light, little by little, on some of our blind spots. It can highlight how criteria for excellence that we cherish in academia often stem from privileges. What we consider signs of excellence, i.e., number of presentations or articles, professional mobility, diversity of research experiences, and even GPA, undervalue certain groups.[6] At the larger scale of academic programs and universities, many people have started to take action to increase the representation of certain groups, for example by reserving program spots for First Nations, Inuit or Metis people. On a personal level, we can decide to build a more diversified team, both to improve the science that will come out of our lab, but also to provide a richer experience to students. This commitment requires us to expand our definition of excellence and to value different strengths and types of experiences. We must explicitly devote efforts towards achieving diversity and building groups that are less representative of Western spheres of knowledge and power. The aim is not to have all groups systematically represented in all labs, but to work towards avoiding a situation in which our group is built around a single norm. Obviously, this venture into the unknown does generate discomfort. We must create a welcoming environment free from discrimination (and microaggressions). When we belong to dominant groups, we might, without noticing it, contribute to maintaining an environment that is not comfortable for people who don't adhere to our model of excellence.

---

6. Sarr, F., Knight, S., Strauss, D., Ouimet, A.J., Cénat, J. M., Williams, M.T., & Shaughnessy, K. (2022). Increasing the representation of Black, Indigenous, and People of Colour as students in psychology doctoral programmes. *Canadian Psychology / Psychologie canadienne, 63*(4), 479–499. <https://doi.org/10.1037/cap0000339>

The need to redefine our criteria for excellence, make space for diversity, and not recruit only people with similar profiles to us, are all actions that may leave us feeling as if we're going backwards. Some might feel they need to be on their guard, that they cannot establish the same level of rapport with people who are different from them: some men definitely felt something like this when women "invaded" traditional Boys Clubs. Effortless rapport might be lost, but at the same time we are no longer perpetuating systematic discrimination. We will have to find new ways of building rapport (other than around a beer pitcher at the local pub). Remember that this feeling of loss is felt only on the part of those belonging to the majority, to the dominant group who have received the most privileges. We might get the impression that we are moving backwards, but in fact, we are taking a step sideways in order to move forward together.

BOX 11.6—TRY IT!

Build your own social identity map by identifying the individual characteristics that represent you and the people in your different circles (for instance, friends, family, colleagues). The general idea is that for each element, there is a majority group, overrepresented and sometimes dominant, that benefits from privileges linked to the fact of belonging to that group, at the expense of people from minority or underrepresented groups. While completing this exercise, keep in mind that belonging to a majority group often means having blind spots related to our own attitudes towards minorities.

This list of cultural influences is inspired by Pamela Hays's conceptual framework ADDRESSING,[7] with some additions taken from the PROGRESS+ framework.[8] This list is not exhaustive, and is bound to expand as our knowledge and recognition of differences evolves.

Warning: this activity may lead to an addiction to social justice and intolerance of exclusion.

---

7. Hays, P.A. (2022). *Addressing Cultural Complexities in Counseling and Clinical Practice: An Intersectional Approach* (4th edition). Washington DC: American Psychological Association.
8. O'Neill, J., Tabish, H., Welch, V., Petticrew, M., Pottie, K., Clarke, M., Evans, T., Pardo Pardo, J., Waters, E., White, H., & Tugwell, P. (2014). Applying an equity lens to interventions: Using PROGRESS ensures consideration of socially stratifying factors to illuminate inequities in health. *Journal of Clinical Epidemiology*. *67*(1), 56–64. <https://doi.org/10.1016/j.jclinepi.2013.08.005>.

A = Age and generational influences: political, social and family-related

DD = Developmental (or acquired) disability

R = Religion and spiritual beliefs

E = Ethnicity and race

S = Socio-economic status

S = Sexual orientation

I = Indigenous heritage

N = National origin

G = Gender identity

CHAPTER 12
I have feelings too!

"Sometimes at work I feel like I'm in the middle of a long game of Tetris. Blocks appear and I only have a very limited amount of time to figure out how to make them fit. The more experience I gain, the faster the blocks appear. No matter what I do, the mismatched blocks pile up, and blocks continue to appear. I have to place blocks by instinct, but I start making mistakes and there's no time to reflect on my bad decisions. I feel like I'm forced to decide rapidly at the expense of the big picture. At one point, the music accelerates as a reminder that I'm careening towards failure. My breath speeds up, my chest feels tight. What a stupid game! Pushing ourselves to the limit at every possible opportunity is simply inhumane. The whole time, I snatch glances at my colleagues who seem to reach much higher levels than I do and with more skill and less effort. What's wrong with me? Back to the game, and dammit, I just lost another life."

Many chapters of this book discuss how to develop methods, organizing principles, or guidelines for mentoring graduate students and supporting their writing. Articulating clear expectations and getting them attuned with the expectations of the students should improve the quality of this facet of the professor's job, and make it more pleasant. After all, 97% of professors report being satisfied or very satisfied of their interactions with graduate students.[1] We enjoy working with graduate students, and this is one of the things that attracted us to this job, right? So if some relationships with graduate students turn sour, there must be other aspects outside of the student–professor interaction to consider. Could it be that some elements in the specific context of the university contribute to writing difficulties and related conflicts? We've already addressed anxiety, perfectionism, and procrastination, problems that, combined with the multiple opportunities for all sorts of non-dissertation activities, can all seriously hinder a student's

1. Leclerc, C. (2016). Synthèse de quatre enquêtes quantitatives. Enjeux de la recherche: santé psychologique des chercheurs. *ACFAS Magazine.* <https://www.acfas.ca/publications/magazine/2016/05/synthese-quatre-enquetes-quantitatives>.

progress. We've also suggested that these problems of anxiety, perfectionism, and procrastination can affect the advisor's role and their recommendations to students. These problems are not necessarily a sign of the advisor's weaknesses. We will not rehash the difficult context in which university professors have to work, as we've already gone over this at length previously, but let's remind ourselves what we are faced with: overwork, explicit and implicit pressure, role conflicts, a competitive climate, low administrative support, isolation, etc.[2]

There is a great paradox in the act of proposing individual coping strategies when the environment is fundamentally maladapted and potentially harmful. We are not totally comfortable writing this section (see Box 12.1), which can be interpreted as if we are telling professors to relax when the environment is irremediably stressful, or telling you to work fewer hours when you might still be struggling to get a tenure-track position. But let's be honest, we are operating in an environment that glorifies maintaining a busy and intense work schedule at the expense of healthy life habits. The standards we've adopted are impossibly high. There are real external sources of pressure, but there is also an intrinsic component to which, in some ways, we ourselves contribute, for instance when we venerate people who respond to emails at any time of the day or night, who sacrifice sleep to finish a grant proposal, or who have lunch (and breakfast, second breakfast, elevenses, afternoon tea, dinner, and supper) in front of their computer. Do people who leave the office every day at 4 p.m. receive as much praise and admiration? The adaptive strategies we propose here are not new and will not turn you into rockstars. All of us have heard of them, and we usually agree that they are good ideas. What we should and will discuss is why we fail to apply these strategies, and what the cost of not applying them might be.

---

2. Leclerc, C., & Bourassa, B.. (2016). Santé psychologique des chercheurs. *ACFAS Magazine*. <https://www.acfas.ca/publications/magazine/enjeux-recherche/sante-psychologique-chercheurs>

BOX 12.1—THESE WORDS WERE WRITTEN BY A HYPOCRITE

While planning this chapter, I listed several positive adaptation strategies that I was ready to endorse with great enthusiasm and conviction. As I was developing this plan, however, it felt tainted with phoniness. Why this sudden hesitation? One very recent experience in the academic world might have something to do with it. Here's what happened. It was the deadline to hand in all the necessary documents to apply for my next promotion as professor. I'm usually well organized, but just 20 minutes before the Human Resources office closed I was still adding lines of information to the report. This moment that should have been the triumphant culmination of all these years of achievement was rather a frazzled race against the clock. The report was finally handed in, probably full of typos and missing appendices, yet I was not celebrating, I was exhausted, my mind still racing down multiple other tracks, including three up-coming deadlines, the courses I had to teach, my daughter who had a fever, and my son who was anxious about an upcoming oral presentation but whom I couldn't help as much as I'd hoped, and whom I'd told (like an excellent role model!) not to worry about it. I got home that day feeling exhausted and angry. I felt somewhat as if I'd gone to my wedding without having had time to shower, knowing that the ceremony would still happen and that I would still hear the expected "I do," but feeling that things didn't go at all the way I'd been planning them for years. It wasn't as if I was worried about getting the promotion (the success rate at our university is very high), but I felt utterly frustrated at handing in a report about my professional achievements that was less polished than I'd hoped. Isn't this one of the signs of burnout? Feeling obligated to complete tasks at a standard well below our own because of excessive workload?

These feelings clearly signalled the need for adaptive strategies, which also reconciles me to this feeling of hypocrisy in writing. Let's be honest, our work environment is sometimes—most of the time—far too demanding. Adaptive strategies are meant to steer us out of the trap of taking things too personally. While the ultimate solution likely lies in fundamental organizational changes, until these take place we still need to equip ourselves to tackle day to day challenges.

TACKLING THE PROBLEM

When a situation makes us uncomfortable, it may be time to adopt active problem-solving strategies. This starts by defining and operationalizing the problem: what prevents me from ending my workday at the ideal time for me? Why can't I mobilize the energy to start this task? What is wrong with this student? Only when the problem is defined can we expect to come up with specific solutions. It might be a good idea to generate many different solutions, even if some seem irrelevant or wacky at first glance. Who knows, a wacky solution could be useful to generate another one that is more down-to-earth and applicable. Once we're done generating potential solutions, we select one, or many, and we apply them! By that we mean that we take action. This might sound trivial, but applying solutions can become the most difficult part of problem-solving when we tend to worry and second guess everything even before trying. The last step, which may soothe our worried selves, is the debriefing, through which we assess the impact of the applied solution and decide whether to keep it or try another one.

Unfortunately, we often end up choosing passive solutions, which seem easier to apply on the spur of the moment. Strategies of avoidance ("I won't go to the meeting"), withdrawal ("I'll go to the meeting but I won't say anything"), and acquiescence ("Is this worth fighting for? I'll agree so we can move on") are tempting as they provide some form of instant relief. This also holds for our graduate students who encounter difficulties during the writing process: avoidance ("I won't meet them or respond to their emails"), withdrawal ("Sure, whatever you want"), or acquiescence ("I don't find your plan realistic, but it will be simpler if I don't say anything") seem to be good solutions when we can't come up with something better or when we fail to take the time to think about alternate solutions. The more problems we have and the more difficult to solve they seem, the stronger the temptation to sweep them under the rug. In conclusion, we see the problems and know we must try to solve them. But (there is always a *but*)...

LETTING GO

... applying active strategies might not work when there are no solutions, when we do not have any control over a situation, or when we do not have access to the required resources. When diligent attempts to apply active strategies fail, insisting on trying to solve everything amounts to stubbornness. Some battles are a lost cause, e.g., conversations with an obnoxious colleague, interactions with a student who sabotages all our attempts to help, battling the university's ever-growing bureaucracy, obtaining ever scarcer research funds, trying to reason with the hopelessly strict first grade teacher of one of our kids (sorry, getting carried away!).

Sometimes, all we can do is let go and embrace the chaos. We can use mindfulness to observe our own emotions: enjoy the positive ones, accept the more difficult, focus on the present moment and thus move away from brooding about the past and worrying about the future. Or, on the contrary, we can project ourselves far into the future, and see ourselves old and wise, sitting on a rocking chair looking at the sunset. Will today's issues still bother us then? Or look the other away, far into the past, and recall how young, green and naïve (and sometimes arrogant) we used to be. Are those precious ideals reflected in what we do today? Daniel Boucher, a Québécois singer-songwriter, sang “Deviens-tu ce que t'as voulu?” (Are you becoming what you wanted?). In order to answer this important question, or at least start coming up with some kind of answer, we need to master the next strategy.

MAKING SENSE

To have fun playing Tetris, each different piece needs to make sense and carry some kind of value. Out of the possible choices presented to us, we must ask ourselves which ones correspond best to our values and what we are trying to accomplish. Our mentors and role models taught us to seize opportunities and make choices that will pay off, taking us from one springboard to the next, and so forth (see Figure 12.1). But how often do we actually ask ourselves, at the outset, whether we feel like doing something or not? We are grateful here for the wisdom of the daughter of one of the authors who, when she was four years old, based her decisions to accept or refuse a directive only on two options: I feel like it, or I don't feel like it. As professors, we've matured past this Freaking Four period,[3] or most of us should have, but it still does us good to remember this period of time when everything we did was solely based on a very self-centred impression of what we felt like at that moment.

3. The Freaking Four, more commonly known as the F***ing Four, is a stage of development familiar to all parents, turning their little angels into unrecognizable monsters and making them long for the happy days of the Terrible Two.

FIGURE 12.1—Ever higher?

Making sense also applies to how we use our schedule. The freedom that comes with a professor's position is a double-edged sword: we have the autonomy and flexibility to create more or less whatever schedule we want. But having no external constraints also implies that if we fail to apply any for ourselves, work will infiltrate all aspects of our lives (see Box 12.2). For some people, this steady creep of work may be in line with their values and life goals, at least for a period of time. However, for most people, having to work harder all the time doesn't feel like a choice but rather an obligation always to do more. The problem is that we choose, consciously or not, to follow one single model of excellence that dictates always pushing harder and further. Following this model isn't the only option; there are other models out there (see Chapter 2, Box 2.2).

BOX 12.2—DIARY OF A 9 TO 5 MIDNIGHT PROF

I used to fulfill my duties as a professor by trying to avoid the regularity of a factory schedule: I arrived around 9:00 a.m. (still yawning) and left at 5:30 p.m. (or whatever time daycare or school closed), I actively engaged in family life until everyone fell asleep, and I then started working some more until midnight, Monday to Friday. On weekends, I did everything in my power to work only one day (I was so reasonable...). I used to bring student drafts to the ice-skating rink, I learned how to read while driving (or rather, while being driven), and, most importantly, I could empty my inbox on a ski lift, in the bathroom, anywhere except at the dinner table (see, I was reasonable). With only rare exceptions, I used to work every night and every weekend. This was until about halfway through out writing this book.

I had known I wanted to become a professor from my first registration as an undergraduate student in Psychology. I had a few alternate plans brewing, but these didn't prove necessary and were in fact quickly forgotten in the frenzy of my career getting off to a flying start. Such a flying start that I never took the time to define any limits: Why should I limit my passion for work? It was where I got my fix. And these habits were only reinforced by seeing colleagues getting out late from the research center like me, or seeing that the department chair was at work on the weekends as well. What can be more validating than to repeatedly meet with the same people who are as intensely involved in their work as ourselves? I chose this intense work schedule, I dove in without asking any questions, I loved it, I was proud of it. Proud to obtain ever more funding, to supervise an ever-growing team, to publish more, and to become better at getting more work. Bring on the 60-hour plus weeks. I had become a proud workaholic. Predictably, this recipe led me straight to my limit. In this blind race towards supreme excellence, I went too far and lost perspective on my career, my family, my friends and myself (all the while somehow projecting a well-balanced image to my students). I lost my way and one day, much like Forrest Gump, I stopped running, tired. Inspired by colleagues such as Geneviève, a champion for a more balanced way of life, as well as my readings related to writing this book, and a pandemic that forced a hard reset on our schedules, I started to build my new identity as a professor. But how? I could talk about my decision to jump back in the classroom, to reduce the number of grant proposals that I would take part in, to take more time to talk to people at work, be they colleagues, staff or students, to be choosier in selecting new opportunities (and to decline many), to buy a snowmobile and reconnect with hobbies... but more simply, the plan can be summed up like this: I arrive at 9 a.m., and at 5 p.m. I shut down my computer, then I leave. I repeat the same thing the next day. I skip weekends. That's it.

SEEING THE POSITIVE SIDE

Compared to the many unsolved problems running on an endless loop through our heads, the issues which we handle with utmost competence, and which end well seem to take up much less mental space. Worse, we tend to undervalue and even discount most of our successes on the spot. Completing a Ph.D., no problem. A post-doctoral fellowship, piece of cake. A pilot grant, nothing to it. But the grant proposal that follows, the one that robs you of precious hours of sleep, that makes you skip the annual family trip to the sugar shack, that one is tough, and deserves all of these sacrifices and more. Or so you think, until you get the grant and dive right into the next one. Whatever we achieve, no matter how difficult, tends to become the norm, to the point that we almost trivialize it. It's like in a game of Tetris, where a line simply disappears as soon as it's completed. We get so involved in planning the next steps that we forget to celebrate what we achieve.

Appreciating our success does not imply putting on rose-tinted glasses or resting on our laurels. When life goes by fast, taking some time to appreciate our achievements, and acknowledge how much effort we actually dedicated to reaching those achievements, does take deliberate effort. But it also begs the question, why do we tend to devalue our work? Are we afraid to become less competitive, or to fall in a shameful pit of incompetence as soon as we slacken the pace? Keeping one eye on our accomplishments as well as on current challenges will not make us less efficient—on the contrary. And perhaps if we start doing this ourselves we can instill the same behaviour in our students, who also need to see a balance between positive and constructive feedback. This is essential for them to learn and to remain motivated. Increasing students' productivity by treating ourselves with compassion, what a crazy idea!

BEING NICE TO OTHERS

We work in an environment where we are in constant competition with our peers. Even if we're probably the only person in the world with our very specific expertise, our work is constantly being evaluated both quantitatively and qualitatively. We're all fighting for the same resources. We're all playing the same game of musical chairs. When the music stops, if you're not running a multimillion dollar project you get an extra class to teach, or better yet, you get to be program director. Sometimes we're tempted to stick our leg out just a bit and trip someone to be the one to reach that last available chair; we're tempted to draw attention to our colleagues' incompetence in hopes that people won't scrutinize our own performance, which we never feel is quite enough; we keep quiet when we benefit from any kind of perk, afraid that it will be taken away or that we'll be accused of freeloading. Sometimes, we're simply fed up with the trivial complaints of colleagues and students, while we ourselves stoically endure real problems without whining.

Despite the constant pressure, let's not resort to nastiness. On the contrary, good relationships with our colleagues are worth fighting for. A supportive community is the best antidote to the insidious poison of daily stress. We need our colleagues, and they need us. We should take the time to ask others about their interests outside of work, and celebrate their achievements, which need not be perceived as a threat to our own. Let's share tips and strategies for solving common problems. Let's set aside quality time for non-urgent and not important tasks like having coffee with a colleague (see Box 12.3), participating in social activities, writing a card to a colleague who is retiring or one who is going on parental leave. When a colleague has a good idea, let's take the time to acknowledge it. Don't get the wrong idea about this message; being nice to others doesn't mean pretending to love everyone and making ourselves socialize with people with whom we share no affinity. It's normal not to get along with everyone, and differences of opinion, which imply that we don't share the same ideas as everyone, are one of the most wonderful features of academia. Instead of complaining that people are incompetent, let's use our creativity to find their strengths. Not all colleagues need to become our friends, but we should always find ways to respect them.

BOX 12.3—WEAVING A SAFETY NET

This text is adapted from an article which the Union of Professors of Université Laval invited Geneviève to write for a special newsletter on the theme of social isolation.[4]

There is no need to go into the details of a professor's job to describe the difficulties we're presently facing: heavy workload, rapid ballooning of administrative tasks, lack of recognition, psychological distress... We love the incredible autonomy and the exhilarating sense of accomplishment we get from of our jobs. However, these come with many corrosive elements that affect our health.

Without minimizing the impact of these factors on our mental health, this invitation from our union to discuss "social isolation" made this author want to talk about our ability to resist and withstand these daily frustrations without depleting our health reserves. In the field of post-traumatic stress disorder, we know that the vast majority of people will be exposed to all kinds of traumatic events in their life. However, only a minority will develop serious mental health consequences. The most important protective factor? Social support.

By social support, I'm referring to the connections we make with those around us that make us feel that we belong to a network, and that help is available. The most important aspect of support isn't so much the quantity of actual help a person receives, but rather the *perception* that adequate support is available when needed. The perception of support is thus built, little by little, through the repetition of positive interactions with valued people. Being asked how we feel, laughing together, confiding in others and receiving their confidences in turn, venting, developing positive bonds, friendship, positive rapport, mutual help, etc. These interactions make up the small links of the net that provides a sense of security, a feeling that we are protected against hard times.

Unfortunately, our job as professors seems designed to fray whatever net we manage to weave. We get less and less opportunity in terms of time or space to exchange gestures of support at work. We often find ourselves absorbing each frustrating disappointment alone in front of our computer.

4. The original text is available in *SPUL-Lien: le bulletin socio-professionnel du Syndicat des professeurs et professeures de l'Université Laval,* Volume 16, number 1, May 2020.

Esprit de corps

We could think that social support is developed mostly outside of the work environment, and prefer to keep our professional relationships with colleagues distant and utilitarian. By doing so, we underestimate the power of the Force—er, that is, the benefits of the support of our peers, who are living through the same experiences. In fact, we need both the support of friends and family, who give us an external perspective, and of colleagues who understand our challenges. Let's look at the example of military personnel and veterans. These people who have been exposed to severe traumatic events need social support to recover and maintain good mental health. We now know that this social support can come from their families, but also from other military personnel, something we call esprit de corps. This kind of support has unique benefits that can sometimes be more important than support from other sources. As university professors, we may not be deployed in armed conflicts, but we know the difference between confiding in a colleague versus confiding in people who think research is just about playing around with chemistry kits, or running around with kites during thunderstorms as we plan our four-month summer vacation. The support of colleagues who understand our work and its challenges has a unique value.

We need to start putting more value on developing peer support. This won't be achieved through new training seminars, nor from learning new skills or filling out new forms, or even taking a new meditation class. Our schedules are already full. Professor Gilles Dupuis, a leader in quality of life and yoga enthusiast, confided at one of his talks that when industries ask him to organize yoga classes during lunch hour to reduce their employees' stress level, he is sometimes tempted to tell them to simply reduce their workloads instead of adding something else to their schedule. We spend all day solving problems, searching for and applying solutions. We thus spend all our energy on the offensive, neglecting our equally important defenses, the slow knitting together of our safety net. What if part of the solution was to reclaim some time and space just for ourselves, time and space that need not be assigned to anything in particular?

The coffee machine in the broom closet

I was hired as a professor at Université Laval in 2009. In the early years, I suffered from loneliness at work. My department had no specific areas dedicated to socializing. I learned to have lunch in my office, to treat breaks as an abstract concept. I arrived, I did my work, then I left, sometimes without having spoken to anyone. But now, thanks to removing the coffee machine from my office, this happens less and less often.

There was a locked door right in front of my office that for years I never saw anyone use. Eventually I learned that this room, barely 20 square feet, was dedicated to housekeeping. Though obviously intended as a large broom closet, it seemed long since abandoned. I went through endless requests and procedures, and was finally given the go-ahead to make use of this space for myself. I decided to install my coffee machine in this cozy space. I should say tiny rather than cozy, because it could barely fit two people at once, and was far from the cleanest part of the building (don't tell building maintenance!). Still, now that I've taken the coffee machine out of my office and put it in an accessible area, I get to see people, real people, in person! Sometimes they just grab a cup and leave, sometimes they have their coffee right there with me. Yes, I admit it's happened once or twice that I spent (lost) half a day absorbed in conversations. But now we greet each other, we ask how everything's going, we laugh a bit, we plan to get lunch, we share a moment together, we live and remind ourselves that we exist. Subtly, we weave our net.

What's sad is that in our mental balance sheets, we tend to think of this as wasted time. This time doesn't add to any performance index in our C.V.'s or in the eyes of our employers. But these moments are worth gold! Work-related psychological distress happens in academia, the numbers are there to prove it. The moments that push us closer to the precipice are many and recurring. I have often reflected upon the fact that excess work might lead me straight towards a medical leave. Fortunately, I can call to mind many supportive remarks that showed me other points of view and reminded me that there is a safety net between me and that chasm. These helpful words were all spoken without agenda, not within a formal meeting, but standing around my coffee machine.

BEING NICE TO OURSELVES

We have known for a long time that to encourage changes in behaviour, positive reinforcement of the desired behaviour, or related ones if the target is very hard to reach, is more effective than punishing undesirable behaviour. This applies to all the self-recrimination that comes from constantly judging our own actions. Encouraging ourselves, praising our strengths and smart decisions, is certainly more effective than self-blame. Pats on the back are more effective than beating ourselves up (and more enjoyable—just try it!). It's worth reminding ourselves of this from time to time, and might also be good advice to some of our students. While kindness and caring aren't necessarily prized in competitive environments—we're still waiting for an h-index or impact factor that will let us quantify these qualities and put them on our C.V.'s—they are powerful vectors of mental health and, probably, productivity.

MOVING. EATING. SLEEPING.

No need here to preach on the benefits of physical activity. An active lifestyle has positive impacts in warding off all kinds of disorders. Especially for us scholars, who are always stressed out and shackled in front of our computers, physical activity is a powerful remedy for stress, an instant anti-depressant with euphoric effects, a cognitive stimulant, and a powerful yet non-addictive sleeping pill. Yet, the most common excuse for all of us not to exercise is our busy schedule. No time left for that super beneficial work-out! This quickly becomes a vicious circle; the less time we have to exercise, the more stressed we get; the more stressed, the less productive. Being less productive leads to us getting overwhelmed and having less time to exercise. Or is that *taking* less time? How do we get out of this trap? Maybe we think exercising is a luxury that we can't afford right now. But what if we were to include exercise in our schedule as part of work, such as thinking about how to solve a problem during a run or bicycle ride (as advocated in Chapter 9)? We can also conceptualize exercise as an investment that will allow us to be more efficient at work, for example seeing a work-out during lunch hour as a pause that will allow us to reset our brains and come back afterwards with a clear head. Exercise can also be the way we actually commute to work. Isn't it when we have the least time to exercise that we need it the most? In terms of productivity, cutting into our work time to increase our exercise is more beneficial in the short and long run than doing the opposite.

The same goes for eating and sleeping.

We don't develop healthy habits because we have to, or because some data says it's good for us, we do it for ourselves. We do it because it makes us more efficient and happy, and even live longer. Maintaining healthy habits will help us realize that we have the best job in the world, that we belong to a group of extremely privileged people who get to be university professors. We want to offer our students a human role model, not just a model C.V.

BEING AWAY

We have already mentioned the importance of being available. This is one of the most valued qualities in a professor according to students, and probably contributes directly to their productivity. Having said this, as important as it is to be generally available, it's also okay to be away and unavailable at times. When it's Sunday, it's Sunday for us too.

It will be easier for students to follow the advisor's wishes (and for the advisor to correct those who don't) when the advisor has clearly established when and how they should be contacted. Once this is made clear, students can adapt. This works better than trying to accommodate the schedules and communication preferences of all our students. For example, as nice as we are, we don't want to get phone calls any time of the day or night. Emails are okay, but there should be reasonable expectations around response times. Surprise visits to our offices are risky, unless there is a nuclear disaster, or you've brought chocolate. Someone who takes the time to visit us in person rather than through a video call, with the time agreed on in advance, will definitely get bonus points. Expect a minimal period of ~~two~~ ~~three~~ four weeks before receiving feedback on a draft. If you're swamped and running behind, thank you for not expecting us to compensate by working faster and putting off other responsibilities for the benefit of your priorities.

Some of us will choose to warn our students in advance about prolonged absences, to help them manage their expectations. This can lead to a sudden flood of paper drafts and urgent problems a few days (or hours!) before leaving. If you would rather not receive a to-do list just before leaving on vacation, tell your students that. Sometimes we need to remind our students that we too are looking forward to our winter break, that we're also tired at the end of a semester and trying to get everything finished, including last minute shopping, and that we can't wait to spend one full day in our pajamas binge-watching the latest TV series. When a student arrives on December 23 with a final draft of their paper, thinking they've met their goal of finishing it before Christmas, it's okay to say, good for you, great job, but please re-send this to me early next year, and enjoy your winter break!

We have, or should have, the right not to answer emails. We have the right to use an automatic out-of-office message, and we don't have to hide behind flimsy excuses like "I will have limited access to internet." And do we think we're convincing anyone when we say we'll "respond to emails in order of priority"? These are tricks to make your colleagues feel guilty about disturbing you, or worse, make them think that if you ever take too much time to respond, they are at the bottom of your priority list. We can simply say that we're on vacation. We can say that we won't be checking our emails (see Box 12.4). We can tell the truth and say that we'll probably check our emails but still won't respond. We can even put no message whatsoever *and* not respond. Where does it say that we need to answer all emails immediately? Our schedule is our business.

BOX 12.4—CREATIVE OUT-OF-OFFICE MESSAGES

I am currently on vacation, and I usually only respond to emails to procrastinate from work...

Patience, my friend. I'll be back on July 24th.

***

I'm on vacation, enjoying the illusion that this inbox no longer exists.

Back on August 28th.

***

It's that time of the year when I'm drinking hot chocolate, eating a strict diet of cookies, and memorizing each line of Love Actually wearing old sweatpants.

Please do not bring me back to reality before January 8th.

***

Error 404: Geneviève not found

Did you try:

- Restarting your computer?
- Sending the email again?
- Waiting for her return from vacation on July 23rd?

***

I am out of the office, jet-lagged, and busy finding my way around a foreign transit system (possibly hindered by my investigations into Belgian beers). There may be a longer than usual delay before I respond to your message.

Back on October 29th.

***

Charging batteries...

This operation may take a few minutes.

(Until January 7th in fact)

***

afk[5]

***

Looming brain beset.

Seeking respite and reset.

Sun, beach, books, all set.

Back on August 15th

***

I'm on vacation and I'll be back on January 6th. I have incredibly easy access to the Internet, but I assure you that I will not be using it for work purposes.

Happy holidays to you too.

***

I need vacation so badly that I am not able to compose an out-of-office message.

Back on July 15th.

***

5. This message might be understood only by gamers and no one else, but so what?

> Oops, I've already left for the holidays.
>
> To pass the time until my return on January 6th, test your knowledge of classic movies to watch during the vacation.
>
> What's the name of the Grinch's dog?
>
> On which street did the miracle occur?
>
> What song makes the British Prime Minister dance after standing up to the President of the United States?
>
> Where were Kevin McAllister's parents going when they forgot him the first time?
>
> Is *Die Hard* a Christmas movie?

Beware of the return from vacation. In the middle of a Tetris game, if we pause the game when pieces are falling very quickly and several lines are incomplete, we will inevitably lose as soon as we un-pause the game. We cannot come back to work at full speed. Some choose to continue working during vacations to keep everything (especially emails) under control, some will come back to work a few days early so the transition isn't so abrupt. These solutions sometimes seem unavoidable. However, the more we let work interfere with our vacations, the less effective they are for recharging our batteries. Have you ever thought of doing exactly the opposite, i.e., indicating a return-to-work date later than the day we will actually get back? Coming back to work while leaving the out-of-office message on for a few extra days while you have no meetings planned? Or better yet, plan such a "ghost" week before leaving for your vacations, which lets you be somewhat present but mostly gives you the opportunity to finish some tasks and leave more relaxed. After all, our schedules are often flexible enough to allow such smooth and progressive transitions between work and vacations. Another strategy consists of taking vacation very early in the quiet season (i.e., summer) and leaving first, risking the annoyance of your colleagues who are still at work. This way, when you come back to work, many of your students and colleagues are still on vacation or about to leave, giving you more flexibility for a gradual return (and quietly finishing chapters for this book!) while enjoying fond memories and a relaxed brain.

SAYING NO

We say yes to everything, to everyone. Sometimes we say yes because we feel we have no choice, but our reasons for saying yes are often legitimate: it's a great opportunity, we owe our colleague a favour, we think we have plenty of time to add this to our to-do list. But sometimes we might say yes because we do not know how to say no. Because we imagine catastrophes happening if we refuse. In short, we say yes because we lack practice at saying no.

Sometimes we overdo the "being nice to others" and we neglect the "being nice to ourselves." Being nice to others doesn't mean having to say yes to everything. We can be nice and still say no (see Table 12.1). Caught off-guard by a colleague who asks you something on the spur of the moment? Smile, breathe, and say that you will think about it. Wait a few hours and think how to politely, yet clearly, decline.

The more we say yes, the more we will fill up our schedule and to-do list, the more we become overburdened until the accumulation of pressure may make us crumble or worse, explode. We gradually lose any sense of being in control and get more and more swamped. During a typical brainstorming session about the content of this book—venting our problems, imagining what the perfect university environment would look like—we tried to understand and illustrate why we constantly find ourselves swamped and close to a burnout. We are sharing this story on the condition that you forgive us for having engaged in an emotional and quite raw outburst. We affectionately named this graph the F***-Off Graph (see Figure 12.2). We have even started using this vulgar reference in our daily conversations. It has stuck with us... and we believe you might be able to understand why. It is thus with a combination of pride, shame, and silliness that we present this graph. It illustrates how, as we keep saying yes, we will end up reaching a point of saturation, by which time it will be too late to manage that accumulated pressure. This graph is a warning to help us avoid reaching the breaking point of exhaustion where we lose control, slide into burnout, lose our minds and start yelling F***-Off out loud, at our students, our colleagues and even ourselves.

TABLE 12.1—How to say no and remain a nice person

RECOMMENDATIONS	EXAMPLES	COUNTER-EXAMPLES
Being direct	**Direct**	**Not direct**
	Thank you for the offer but I must decline.	*I thought about it and it's not that I wouldn't like to maybe take part, or not, in the brainstorming processes that might or might not lead to the development of this project, and I'm still hesitating. In fact, I'm still confused writing these lines.*
Being clear	**Clear**	**Not clear**
	I am sorry, I have to decline this offer.	*I don't know. Maybe. I don't think so. It depends.*
Being within our rights	**Legitimate**	**Too much information (we are all swamped!)**
	I am presently not in a position to accept this assignment.	*I already have five meetings, six commitments, seven activities, eight committees, and nine other very important things. I don't have time.*
Being polite	**Polite**	**Not so polite**
	This project is very interesting, but I will not be able to contribute to it.	*Are you out of your mind?*
Being sweet	**Sweet**	**Not so sweet**
	I'm very pleased that you thought about me, but I will have to decline this time.	*No.*
Being rational	**Rational**	**Emotional (very close to the edge—see Figure 12.1)**
	Thank you for thinking of me, but I cannot at this time.	*I apologize, I'm worn out. I'm sorry. This really makes me sad. It's my fault, I'm not good enough. OMG, I'm such a terrible person, I'm sorry for existing.*

FIGURE 12.2—The effect of accumulation a.k.a *The F***-Off Graph*

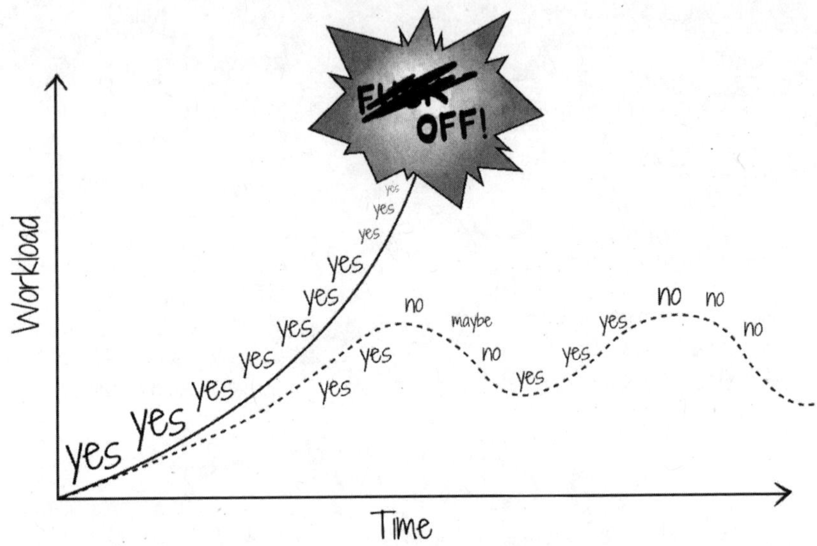

It is difficult to say a calm "no" after we've reached this breaking point. It is difficult to calmly and rationally analyze a new request when we're already being pulled in all directions. When we reach this point where we have nothing left to give, the reflex when people attempt to add anything to our workload can be harsh and defensive. Each new request is seen as an unreasonable demand and makes us feel that we're being taken advantage of, and that our true value isn't being recognized. At the moment of reading this book (we picture you with a glass of wine, on your flight back from an international conference), it surely makes a lot of sense that the clear, direct, legitimate, polite and rational way of saying no to new tasks is the way to go. But it takes a lot of practice to be able to apply these skills in the heat of the action, when we're swamped and harried. Once you've tried it, though, saying no (politely, rationally, calmly) can be a major source of satisfaction.

WORKING HARD WITHOUT TAKING OURSELVES TOO SERIOUSLY

In a previous chapter, we have already proposed that not being perfectionist does not mean being lazy and disorganized. Valuing enjoyment in work is not in contradiction with aiming for excellence. When all the fun has been sucked away, when the sense of accomplishment disappears from work, it's time to raise the alarm. It's time to make significant changes somewhere, be it in our schedule, our workload, the types of projects or activities we take on, or simply in the amount of time we dedicate to different types of tasks. Let's continue to aim for excellence, let's be passionate about our work, let's have fun. There are no research questions or academic achievements that are worth sacrificing our physical and mental health. We are professors, we should be smarter than that.

> *"Sometimes my work feels like a game of Tetris. But I like this game. What I don't like is losing, when the music goes faster and I lose control. But when I do complete those lines—four lines at a time using one vertically placed straight red block—the reward is such that I am compelled to continue. I'm good at this game and I choose to play it. I admit that the satisfaction I get from finishing a level is balanced by the stress I felt completing it. I want more challenges. I would be bored to death if I had to repeat the same level over and over again. I just need to remind myself occasionally that I can pause the game, that completing the next level is not worth jeopardizing my family, my friends, and my health."*

CHAPTER 13
One down, many to go

Congratulations, you did it!

This is not addressed to you for reading this book, but is what we say to our students after their thesis defense. Mind you, some of us have spoken this same phrase to a colleague after one of their students finally graduated. We might have said it in a humorous tone, but the truth is, this congratulations is usually well-deserved, because advising, supervising and mentoring graduate students is quite a task. A fun task for many, a difficult task at times, and full of surprises, especially given that we have not been taught specifically how to teach others. Still, it's a task that definitely comes with many rewards.

Even though, as we have repeated many times throughout this book, the dissertation belongs to the student, not to us, it's okay to appreciate and partake in their success. Empathy is not exclusively reserved for negative states, where we feel our students' pain. We can also share their joy. Some might even indulge themselves with a little pride. Sure, it's the student's dissertation, but we have accompanied them throughout, and if we did our job correctly, we have been there for them when they needed it. We were there, not to compile or analyze their data, nor to write for them, but to guide them through their thought process, sometimes to cheer them on, sometimes to act as a sounding board, sometimes to challenge them. The simplest response to the question raised by the title of this book about how we can make them write, is just to be there for them. As professors, we have this privilege. We tend to forget it when we get swamped by work and by challenges related to supervising students, but our job is the greatest in the world. Say this aloud three times, and repeat if necessary.

"Congratulations, you did it!" is also a phrase that we could have said to each other as co-authors of this book. The time has come to fill in the second eye of the Daruma doll, as our wish to finish this book has finally been granted. The end of this book has been a long time coming, and we should definitely have included a specific year of publication in our original wish! We wrote this book in the spaces between our busy schedules and amid many challenges. Starting many, many years ago with that first proposal by Geneviève on the train ride back from that scientific conference, we have navigated many responsibilities as graduate program directors, co-leaders of scientific groups, and parents of four children who have spent more time than was planned home from school or at the emergency room, plus additional complications from a global pandemic, and a professors' strike. We have learned that the price of taking so many years to write a book is to increase the probability of facing unforeseen events. Yet, the adventure was worth every minute. We argued a little, we had fun a lot, we've quoted Star Wars way too often, but most of all we learned a great deal through this process. Writing sessions over Zoom were nice at first, but like Zoom happy hours, they tended to lose their spark and spirit. Working together was part of the magic of writing this book. We initially each had designated chapters to write, which could have made it easier to assign the responsibility to one person (don't blame me, I didn't write it!) but in the end, we both wrote them all. Why? Because much of this book didn't come directly out of individual writing sessions, but from spontaneous interactions and insights during extended breaks around the coffee machine.

Speaking of long breaks, the 2023 Université Laval professors' strike was one of the most challenging events, yet one that gave us new insights into what we appreciated most about our jobs. Every event and picket line gave us more opportunities than ever to meet our colleagues and discuss the nature of our work. We heard passionate speeches at rallies. We were forced—but with an ironclad excuse—to miss deadlines and cancel important meetings. We entered into very, very slow professor mode. Slowing down gave us perspective. It reminded us that some aspects of our jobs are more important than others, that one aspect of our jobs is central: students! During the strike, we lacked interactions, discussions, and courses with our students; and we realized how much we missed them. You know, these people that the universities increasingly tend to see as clients, but who are the reason we actually stay in this job? So, while we wrote this book with professors in mind, in the hopes that professors would get some good out of it, our secret hope is that their students will also benefit from them reading this book. We have graduated 20 students during the years it took to write this book, and we have many more to go if we count the number of people currently in our labs. We are thus extremely grateful for all these students who gave us opportunities to become better mentors.

Now that the book's finished, what's next? At the speed at which new knowledge develops, will the contents of the book soon become an outdated relic? This would give us an opportunity to write a new edition, sure, but mostly this would mean that some aspects of this central challenge in a professor's job, making their students write, have evolved so much that writing about them is not as necessary as it is now. However, the few workshops that we've given during this writing period suggest that this subject remains close to the hearts of professors, seasoned and new alike. The issues seem to be timeless. On the other hand, if, as we hope, discussions on the subject continue to multiply, we are bound to recognize the extent of the issues we have left unaddressed. Thus, to write the next edition of this book, we might wish to visit colleagues around the world to compare notes and discuss the many cultural differences that are no doubt contributing to some of the blind spots in our perspectives. Before we plan this world tour, though, we still have a few students' manuscripts to read and ~~fix~~ comment on.

The relationship with our students is at the heart of our work as professors. Long before formal teaching institutions such as universities existed, there were students (apprentices) and professors (masters). School, up to and including undergraduate studies, provides learning opportunities to many students at once, but graduate studies mostly remain a realm where not only teaching but advising is individualized. Labs can hold group meetings, and teach methods and discuss papers in groups, but the process of writing of a dissertation is largely individual and personalized, adapted to each student. This takes time. Regardless of how well-organized a professor is, the interactive aspect of the relationship with a graduate student implies that information is exchanged back and forth on a regular basis, a model which differs from the large-scale teaching at the undergraduate level, where the student writes a term paper that receives one final mark from the professor.

Dedicating time to students is necessary not only to facilitate them gaining specific knowledge, but also to stimulate their critical thinking. They, like us, need to go beyond learning facts and learn to produce, disseminate, and share new knowledge. The innovations that make their way through the rigorous review process to finally reach publication become the knowledge that will be taught in years to come. Graduate studies offer opportunities to interact with other people around similar topics, defend ideas, learn new knowledge and, throughout this process, learn about the student–professor relationship. Students begin implicitly to learn what it takes to be a professor, just as we learn to be better professors through the experience of supervising many students. We may have successfully extracted one dissertation without making (too much of) a mess, but hopefully we have learned something along the way that will make extracting the next ones an even more organized, competently-executed, boundary-sensitive, inclusive, caring and (insert the adjective from your favourite chapter) process.

Not all graduate students choose the academic road and wish to undertake the long years of post-doctoral studies that are often necessary after graduate school to become a professor. We have told you that we shouldn't aim to clone ourselves. Our lab is the heart of our career, but for students, it is only the springboard from which their own careers will start. We send them off on their next adventure, better prepared. Thus, the abilities and values we pass along in the student–professor relationship are crucial to various types of careers. Collegiality, curiosity, empathy, equity, and kindness are all values that that we can share that will be essential to many jobs. What students learn during graduate studies goes beyond the actual topic of research, or how to become a professor: it is about becoming a better thinker, and perhaps a better person. So, along with the many privileges of being professors, we also carry the responsibilities that come with forging the mind of another person. We all remember the mentors who left their mark on the people we are today. Reminding ourselves that the privileges and responsibilities of mentoring students go hand in hand, and that one does not come without the other, is the key to the second part of the title of this book, to mentor without making a mess.

MARQUIS

Québec, Canada

MIXTE
Papier | Pour une gestion forestière responsable
FSC® C103567

PCF

BIO GAZ
ÉNERGIE

PERMANENT

Ce livre est imprimé sur des matériaux issus de forêts bien gérées certifiées FSC® et de matériaux recyclés.